W9-ASE-143

STEWART STREET
TORONTO, ONTARIO, CANADA
M4Y 2R5

WITHDRAWN

Regis College Library
15 ST. MARY STREET
TORONTO, ONTARIO, CANADA
M4Y 2R5

Studies in
OLD TESTAMENT
THEOLOGY

Studies in
OLD TESTAMENT
THEOLOGY

Editors

ROBERT L. HUBBARD, JR., ROBERT K. JOHNSTON
ROBERT P. MEYE

BS
1192
.5
O43

Regis College Library
15 ST. MARY STREET
TORONTO, ONTARIO, CANADA
M4Y 2R5

WORD PUBLISHING
Dallas · London · Vancouver · Melbourne

99185

STUDIES IN OLD TESTAMENT THEOLOGY

Copyright © 1992 by Word, Inc. All rights reserved. No portion of this book may be reproduced in any form without the written permission of the publisher, except for brief excerpts quoted in critical reviews.

Scripture quotations in the text marked RSV are from the Revised Standard Version of the Bible, copyright 1946 (renewed 1973), 1956, © 1971, 1973, by the Division of Christian Education of the National Council of the Churches of Christ in the USA and are used by permission.
Those marked NRSV are from the New Revised Standard Version of the Bible, copyright © 1989, by the Division of Christian Education of the National Council of the Churches of Christ USA.
Those marked NIV are from the New International Version of the Bible, Copyright © 1973 by the New York Bible Society International.

Library of Congress Cataloging-in-Publication Data

Hubbard, Robert L.
Studies in Old Testament Theology: Historical and Contemporary Images of God and God's People / edited by Robert L. Hubbard, Robert K. Johnston, Robert P. Meye.
     p. cm.
   ISBN 0-8499-0865-5
   1. Bible. O.T.—Theology. I. Hubbard, Robert L. II. Johnston, Robert K., 1945- . III. Meye, Robert P.
   BS1192.5.043 1992
230—dc20   92-33070
                                                    CIP

Printed in the United States of America

23459 LB 987654321

CONTENTS

Introduction

Personal Tributes To David A. Hubbard

I. Methodology

II. The Old Testament

The Torah

The Prophets

III.   The Old Testament and the World

PREFACE

It has long been a tradition in academia for colleagues and friends to honor a highly esteemed peer by publishing a collection of essays in his or her subject specialty. This volume is such a book, that unique literary genre known in scholarly guilds as a *Festschrift* (German for "celebration book").

In this case, it honors the lifetime of Christian leadership and scholarship given by David Allan Hubbard. Its academic nature notwithstanding, in a real sense it is a "labor of love"—a humble attempt by David Hubbard's many friends to express their gratitude for all that he means to them. Accordingly, the contributors are all colleagues, former students, or friends of David Hubbard (some even qualify in all three categories!). Besides relationship with him, each also shares a scholarly expertise and a ministry concern. Each was personally invited to contribute an essay on an assigned topic.

Special thanks are due several without whose help this book would have never seen the light of day. The Word Processing Centers of Denver and Fuller Seminaries have borne the brunt of manuscript production and reproduction and, hence, have earned our deep appreciation. In Denver, Rebecca Barnes deserves special mention for serving as the secretarial clearinghouse and final typist. Her unfailing cheerfulness, efficiency, and enthusiasm for the project merit a personal word of thanks. Her co-workers, Jeanette Freitag and Maggie Cummings, also ably assisted the editors. We owe a great debt to Denver Seminary Reference/Catalog Librarian Robin Ottoson (M.A., Fuller, 1981) for compiling the select bibliography on the honoree. Finally, we thank Mr. David Pigg of Word Books, Incorporated, the book's publisher, for overseeing the book's publication.

Some introductory remarks about the book may help the reader better benefit from its contents. From the beginning, we decided that the honoree would best be recognized by a book that closely reflected the breadth and quality of his own ministry. And what incredible breadth and quality it has! The bulk of the book, of course, is about his field of study, the Old Testament, and its organization follows the three-part structure of the Hebrew canon. But we have also included an essay on preaching from the Old Testament ("From Exegesis to Proclamation") to address one of David Hubbard's concerns—that ministers preach regularly from the Old Testament.

Further, since David Hubbard is a theologian and Old Testament scholar, the book focuses on Old Testament theology—more specifically, the theology of God and the people of God in each canonical section. Our main goal, however, is to have this book do what David Hubbard himself does so well—first, to skillfully interpret the Old Testament, then to apply it to the life of faith today.

Hence, besides exposition of Old Testament theological topics, this volume has three unique features. First, whatever his or her topic, each contributor seeks to draw implications for contemporary life from each essay's discussion. Second, each canonical section has an essay that specifically targets the integration of that section's theology with religious life today. Third, the book's concluding part offers essays that draw on biblical theology to address contemporary ethical or ecclesiastical issues.

Now, while assigning specific topics, we allowed each scholar the freedom to pursue the assignment as he or she saw fit. Hence, the finished collection reflects the wide variety of opinion on methodology and interpretation to be found among scholars. In our view that variety properly honors David Hubbard, whose professional and personal friendships and breadth of interests transcend the denominational, theological, and geographical boundaries that typically divide God's people.

On the other hand, our hope is that this book will find a special home in contemporary colleges and seminaries as a textbook on Old Testament theology. We believe it offers the beginning theological student both an overview of Old Testament theological content and insight into its relevance for today. If it does, indeed, find such an academic home, the book will realize our fondest wish—that its continued use serve as an ongoing tribute to the life and ministry of David Allan Hubbard.

Robert L. Hubbard, Jr.
Robert K. Johnston
Robert P. Meye

Editors

ABBREVIATIONS

AB	Anchor Bible
ABRL	Anchor Bible Reference Library
BCE	Before the Common Era
BET	Beiträge zur evangelische Theologie
BETL	Bibliotheca ephemeridum theologicarum lovaniensium
BKAT	Biblischer Kommentar: Altes Testament
BLS	Bible and Literature Series
BTB	Biblical Theology Bulletin
BZAW	Beihefte zur Zeitschrift für die alttestamentliche Wissenschaft
ConBOT	Coniectanea biblica, Old Testament
CBQ	Catholic Biblical Quarterly
DBSup	Dictionnaire de la Bible, Supplément
EncJud	Encyclopaedia judaica
EvQ	Evangelical Quarterly
ExpTim	Expository Times
FOTL	The Forms of Old Testament Literature
GKC	Gesenius' Hebrew Grammar, ed. E. Kautzsch, tr. A. E. Cowley
HBC	Harper's Bible Commentary
HBT	Horizons in Biblical Theology
Heb.	Hebrew text
IDB	Interpreter's Dictionary of the Bible, ed. G. A. Buttrick
IDBSup	Interpreter's Dictionary of the Bible, Supplementary Volume
Int	Interpretation
ISBE	International Standard Bible Encyclopedia, rev., ed. G. W. Bromiley
ITC	International Theological Commentary
JAOS	Journal of the American Oriental Society
JETS	Journal of the Evangelical Theological Society
JSOT	Journal for the Study of the Old Testament
JSOTSup	Journal for the Study of the Old Testament, Supplement Series

JTS	Journal of Theological Studies
LXX	Septuagint
NCB	New Century Bible
NEchtB	Die Neue Echter Bibel
NICOT	New International Commentary on the Old Testament
NIV	New International Version
NJB	New Jerusalem Bible
NJBC	The New Jerome Biblical Commentary
NRSV	New Revised Standard Version
NT	New Testament
OBT	Overtures to Biblical Theology
OT	Old Testament
OTG	Old Testament Guides
OTL	Old Testament Library
REB	Revised English Bible
RSV	Revised Standard Version
SBLMS	Society of Biblical Literature Monograph Series
SBT	Studies in Biblical Theology
SJT	Scottish Journal of Theology
TDOT	Theological Dictionary of the Old Testament, ed. G. J. Botterweck and H. Ringgren
THAT	Theologisches Handwörterbuch zum Alten Testament, ed. E. Jenni and C. Westermann
TOTC	Tyndale Old Testament Commentaries
TynBul	Tyndale Bulletin
TZ	Theologische Zeitschrift
VT	Vetus Testamentum
WBC	Word Biblical Commentary
WTJ	Westminster Theological Journal
ZAW	Zeitschrift für die alttestamentliche Wissenschaft

INTRODUCTION

Personal Tributes to David A. Hubbard

SERVANT-LEADER-MENTOR

You became our leader at a tender age, perhaps taking comfort from the first part of Paul's admonition to Timothy: "Don't let anyone look down on you because you are young" (1 Tim 4:12a, NIV).

After following your lead for thirty years, we honor your constancy and consistency and your commitment to the whole church of God.

You have been both servant and giant among us. In your wisdom you have been our mentor; in your humility you have allowed us to be among your teachers.

You have discovered our gifts and helped us to polish them. You have enabled us and, in so doing, have laid the groundwork for a legacy—always encouraging enduring fidelity and values.

You have always spoken out for solidarity and harmony, for civility and truth and sincerity, for peace, not violence.

You have eschewed self-interest and quick and shallow satisfaction, both personally and institutionally, always insisting on the legitimacy of our vision. You have demonstrated to us that the leader often stands alone, always takes the heat, bears the pain, and tells the truth.

You have prepared us in myriad ways for the future; trusting in God we are ready to move on.

From you we have received the gifts of scholarship and vision, openness and accountability, wisdom and justice, opportunity and equity, love and devotion.

This is a description, though incomplete, of you as our leader.

You have, to finish Paul's advice to Timothy, "set an example for the believers in speech, in life, in love, in faith, and in purity" (1 Tim 4:12b, NIV). We give thanks in all these for your faithfulness.

We love you as one of God's great gifts to us.

Max DePree

EVANGELICAL STATESMAN

As an Old Testament scholar, David Hubbard realizes, no doubt far more keenly than most of us, that human beings are relatively insignificant. A text like Isaiah 40:15 reminds all earthlings that nations collectively are in the eyes of the eternal God like dust on the scales. Yet Dr. Hubbard realizes, too, that every person on our planet is of absolute significance to the loving Creator who not only calls the stars by name but, as the psalmist writes, "heals the brokenhearted and binds up their wounds." We are relatively insignificant yet absolutely significant because each of us is Jehovah's image-bearer, and He who names each star has likewise named each of our names. In other words, our individuality has been willed and affirmed by God from the beginningless eternity that is the existence-span of deity.

A contemporary younger than myself by fourteen years, David Hubbard would be the first to see the truth in those hackneyed lines by Henry Wadsworth Longfellow:

> Lives of great men all remind us
> We can make our own sublime,
> And in passing leave behind us
> Footprints on the sands of time.

Our influence, Longfellow points out, is at best like ephemeral footprints made in the sand. However pervasive and profound it may be, it is destined with the passing of the years to undergo gradual erasure. Nevertheless, as an extraordinarily knowledgeable biblicist, Dr. Hubbard would also insist that like Israel's King David we are called upon to serve our own generation by the will of God (Acts 13:36), trusting Him to raise up new leaders for the oncoming generations. By impacting our own generation, however, we may decisively help to prepare the way for the emergence of that future leadership. And throughout his career, Dr. Hubbard has been doing precisely that for the world-wide Christian community.

If I remember aright, his name first came to my attention when I was working in the mid-1950s on my doctoral dissertation researching Freud's concept of love. The Collected Works of that pioneer of modern psychotherapy was then being published in the British Isles. I wrote to Dr. Hubbard, a total stranger to me, who was engaged in his own doctoral program at St. Andrews University, requesting that he arrange to have each forthcoming volume mailed to me from a Scottish bookstore. (This would represent a considerable saving!) Graciously, he consented to do so. Now whenever I glance at that shelf of Freud's writings in my library, I recall the kindness David Hubbard showed to a presumptuous brother.

I came to know him personally when I visited the campus of Westmont College in the early 1960s while my daughter was a student there. I heard enthusiastic comments regarding a brilliant professor—David Hubbard, of course—who in his classes made the Old Testament come alive. In my casual contacts with him I was impressed by his affability, his friendliness, his open spirit, and his acuity. It was no surprise, therefore, when the Presidential Search Committee of Fuller Seminary asked me my appraisal of Dr. Hubbard. Yes, he was indeed rather young—only thirty-four—but he possessed remarkable abilities that would enable him to serve worthily as a successor to Edward John Carnell. And in 1963 Dr. Hubbard was providentially chosen to become the head of that increasingly influential seminary.

Occupying that strategic position down to the present time, he has made a powerful impact, not only on American evangelicalism, but on the Christian community globally. As a visionary educator and courageous administrator, he has guided Fuller Seminary's development into a prestigious institution recognized appreciatively by religious and secular people alike. Outstanding scholars have been attracted to this increasingly dynamic center of evangelicalism. While the School of Theology has emphasized and very ably taught the traditional theological disciplines, various schools have come into being, giving Fuller a university-like stature: the School of World Mission, and the School of Psychology. More and more international students have enrolled, and as Fuller alumni, they have made their own impact on the twentieth-century scene far beyond the United States. Dr. Hubbard would insist, characteristically, that his colleagues on the board of trustees and his fellow professors on the faculty deserve the credit for the growth of the seminary. They, to be sure, have contributed greatly, yet the creative vision and administrative skill of David Hubbard have been primarily responsible for Fuller's steady progress.

As a scholar in his own right, Dr. Hubbard has likewise made a significant impact. Author of thirty-six books and scores of articles on a wide range of issues as well as editor of an important commentary series, he has served as professor of Old Testament at Fuller Seminary. Somehow, despite his onerous duties as president and his involvement in all sorts of educational and civic activities, he has managed to stay on the cutting edge of theological thought and even contributed to its advancement.

In addition to all this, as a communicator of the Christian faith he has made a vital impact. From 1969 to 1980 he was heard regularly on the popular radio program, "The Joyful Sound." Constantly he has been in demand as a preacher crossing all denominational lines. At the same time, he has given single lectures and series of lectures in our own country and overseas. Articulate, insightful, relevant, with an engaging style of public address, Dr. Hubbard has been a most persuasive spokesperson for biblical convictions and values.

One final mode of his impact merits mention. David Hubbard has been, to use the only appropriate term, an evangelical statesman. Participating repeatedly in organizations, conferences, and symposia, he has been recognized as a wise, discerning, irenic leader whose counsel and perspective are invaluable. On different occasions and various situations I have listened profitably to his comments and analyses, grateful that the Christian community has been blessed with so able and winsome an advocate.

Vernon C. Grounds

A GOOD STEWARD
AND VISIONARY OF
THEOLOGICAL EDUCATION

In the *Many Lives of Academic Presidents,* Clark Kerr and Marian Gade contend that some institutions survive, some fail, and some improve or decline marginally because of their presidents. But occasionally an institution moves ahead clearly and rarely some segment of higher education is advanced because of the contributions of presidents. David Hubbard is among those very few whose presidency can be measured by the vast distance his institution has traveled in search of its fuller mission and by the extent to which theological education for our generation has been crafted in his image.

The institutional legacy of his leadership is a seminary that by all standards has become a flagship for evangelical theological education throughout the world. The history of the Hubbard years is a story of unprecedented institutional growth and change. For almost three decades, he charted the course of Fuller Theological Seminary with clear vision of its shaping purposes and with steadfast implementation of them. In the process, the school increased its student numbers tenfold, tripled the faculty, and invented a new type of theological school as its institutional format was repeatedly recast in the endeavor to embrace ever more effectively its more inclusive callings. Throughout these changes, there has endured a constancy of institutional identity borne not of mere fidelity to the past but of a stewardship that remained steadfastly responsive to the Great Commission (Mark 16:15) as an institutional imperative and guiding rationale.

The more significant product of David Hubbard's leadership is to be seen not primarily in Fuller's institutional growth but in its role within the world of theological education. During the past several decades, theological schools have been engaged in transforming themselves from instruments devoted almost exclusively to the education of clergy to institutions serving educational and formational needs of the household of faith. This transformation constitutes the most important change that has occurred in theological education during the past century, and it has permanently altered the landscape of seminaries. Fuller has been at the forefront of this movement. No account of David Hubbard's presidency would be complete without taking into account the extent to which the seminary, under his leadership, participated in this revolutionary development and influenced, in ways yet to be discerned, the course of the entire profession.

It can be argued that leaders are made great by virtue of high offices to which they are called. More convincing is the claim that great minds and spirits enhance even the highest offices and are the more decisive sources of leadership. But greater than contention with roles and individual gifts is the measure of important purposes and causes. David Hubbard's presidency has been a vocation of such commitment. By virtue of his steadfast devotion to the church's ministry, to his calling as a biblical scholar, to the one institution that claimed him through years of service, to associates and colleagues whose lives and work he honored, and to the future of a profession he viewed in terms of its high callings, he has been a significant force in our times and a leader without peer. The love of heart, mind, and soul has conspired throughout a long and remarkable career to render him a faithful steward and prophetic visionary to the benefit of Fuller Theological Seminary and of all who labor in the wider vineyard of theological education.

Leon Pacala

HIS LIFE AND MINISTRY

When David Allan Hubbard retires in June, 1993, after thirty years as president of Fuller Theological Seminary, he will relinquish his title as the longest sitting seminary president in America today. At a time when C.E.O.s in the marketplace come and go with blinding speed, being the head of *anything* for three decades is bound to get attention. Even the leaders in theological education find it difficult to stay put for long. According to Robert W. Lynn, a recent study by the Association of Theological Schools revealed that in North American seminaries "the turnover rate for chief executive officers now hovers between 15 and 20 percent each year."[1]

As impressive as survivability is in higher education, by itself a lengthy term in office is not proof of great deeds done. Some people stay long but accomplish little. Put bluntly, not all retiring seminary presidents rate books in their honor simply because they endured to the end; only those who have something significant to show for their years of service merit recognition. In this case, David Hubbard deserves kudos for what he did, not just for how long he lasted.

The story of David Hubbard's life and ministry is closely tied to the story of twentieth-century American evangelicalism, the movement into which he was born and which he so significantly helped to shape. Both man and movement came of age and made their mark during the same time.

In fact, into the Hubbard family flowed a variety of evangelical traditions. David's father, John Hubbard, was a Methodist from Clear Lake, Iowa. After graduating from the University of Southern California in 1906 and serving a number of Methodist congregations around Los Angeles, John went to Puerto Rico as a Methodist missionary. There he found a wife and fathered a son, Paul. When his young wife died of a tropical disease, John returned to the States with his infant son, enrolled at Drew Theological Seminary in New Jersey, and resumed Methodist parish ministry. In 1914 John married Helena White of Gouverneur, New York, a friend of his first wife and a devout Baptist who had already studied at New York Bible Institute and had developed into an effective Bible teacher.

Soon after their marriage, the Hubbards returned to Puerto Rico, where John resumed his work as an evangelist and church planter. Helena carried on her own ministry of Bible teaching while being a stepmother to Paul and, in short order, a mother to John, Laura, and Robert. In the early 1920s John began teaching at a newly organized interdenominational seminary in Puerto Rico, which required him to finish his theological degree at Drew. But the Hubbard family's plans to remain on the mission field were changed when Helena became seriously ill. Not wanting to lose a second wife to the tropics, John moved his family to northern California, where he was assigned to a Methodist church in Yreka.

Shortly after locating in California, the Hubbards became pentecostals, thanks in large part to the influence of Aimee Semple McPherson, who had electrified Los Angeles with her dynamic preaching, healing, and institution. From that time on, the ministry of John and Helena Hubbard emphasized the gifts of the Spirit, divine healing, casting out demons, and fervent prayer, all of which were characteristic of the pentecostal revival that was still in its early stages. After serving pentecostal congregations in Yreka and the Stockton area (Escalon), the Hubbards moved to Oakland, where David was born in 1928, the last of the Hubbard children.

David Hubbard has frequently commented on the influence of his parents, both of whom were ordained ministers, during his childhood. He watched his parents live out their callings, preparing sermons and Bible lessons, holding services at the church three days a week, providing pastoral care, praying for the sick, and sometimes struggling when their prayers went unanswered. The message the Hubbards preached was "full gospel" and fundamentalist, which means that they affirmed the necessity of personal conversion, the power of the Spirit, the need for correct doctrine and righteous living, and the truth of dispensational premillennialism. "Mother Hubbard," as nearly everyone called Helena, was a consummate Bible teacher who studied hard and taught often. In 1984 David looked back: "My earliest childhood memories include sitting at her feet in various study groups as she quarried the books of Ezekiel, Daniel, and Revelation for their wealth of insights about the future which God had in store for Israel and the church."[2]

Outsiders might wonder how anyone could survive growing up in a family where Wesleyan, Baptist, pentecostal, dispensational, and fundamentalist influences jostled. But the Hubbards evidently put them together with grace and flexibility.[3] At fourteen David felt a call to the ministry.

After graduating from high school, he attended Lutheran College in Oakland for two years, then transferred to Westmont College in Santa Barbara, from which he earned his B.A. in 1949. David then entered Fuller Theological Seminary in Pasadena. He graduated with a B.D. in 1952 and was ordained a Conservative Baptist minister.[4] He stayed at Fuller as a teaching assistant to Dr. William LaSor and earned a Th.M. in 1954. He then moved on to St. Andrews University in Scotland, where he received the Ph.D. in Old Testament and Semitics in 1957.

After finishing in Scotland, Hubbard returned to Westmont College as assistant professor of biblical studies. In early 1960, during his third year of teaching in Santa Barbara, he was approached by Charles E. Fuller about the possibility of becoming Fuller Seminary's third president. Hubbard was only thirty-two years old at the time and claimed "the suggestion came as a bolt from the blue."[5] As it turned out, Hubbard had plenty of time to get used to the idea. It took the seminary nearly three years to decide on David Hubbard, mainly because its faculty and trustees were locked in an intense debate over what kind of school Fuller should be.

Fuller Theological Seminary had been founded in 1947 as part of a new movement to reform fundamentalism. Taking shape around World War I, fundamentalism was a loose confederation of committed Protestant conservatives who decided to do battle for the Lord against theological liberals, higher critics, evolutionists, and other kinds of "modernists" who, as the fundamentalists believed, undercut or denied the essentials of historic Christianity.[6] In the 1920s and 1930s, fundamentalists tried and failed to drive liberalism from the mainline denominations and Darwinism from the schools. As a result, many of the more militant fundamentalists withdrew from their churches and created a vibrant, new separatist subculture. By the 1940s, however, many more moderate fundamentalists were convinced that their movement had become needlessly marginalized. They longed for the days when evangelical religion really mattered in American culture and decided to rid fundamentalism of its excesses and negative image and create a "new evangelicalism."

Among the most articulate of these reforming fundamentalists was Harold John Ockenga, the pastor of the prestigious Park Street Church in Boston, who joined forces with Charles Fuller, a pioneer in religious radio, to establish a new seminary where the new evangelicalism could take root. Ockenga dreamed of a revitalized fundamentalism, stripped of its anti-intellectual and culture-denying elements. He believed that a more moderate evangelical movement could engage modern thought and recapture the culture for Christ. In short, the co-founders of Fuller wanted a school where evangelical piety, commitment to evangelism, and solid scholarship worked together. What they got, however, was an institution in which the lines separating fundamentalism and the new evangelicalism were sometimes hard to distinguish and where different visions for a renewed fundamentalism often threatened to tear the new seminary apart.

It did not take long for the cleavages to become obvious. "Progressives" argued with "conservatives" over how far to follow the trajectory of fundamentalist reform. Some faculty wanted to keep the ties to historic fundamentalism intact, while others preferred to pursue a more classical and scholarly Reformed approach in which typical fundamentalist concerns like premillennialism and even biblical inerrancy were less significant. Some Fuller faculty continued to "contend for the faith" against its perceived enemies on the theological left, while others worked hard to develop an evangelical theology that could get along with other perspectives and show civility toward those with whom it disagreed. Thus, Fuller conservatives and progressives had differences of both style and substance.

These deep-seated philosophical debates that occasionally pushed the Fuller community to the breaking point were exacerbated by chronic problems over presidential leadership. For the first seven years of Fuller's history, Ockenga served as president *in absentia* from Boston. When this arrangement finally proved to be unworkable, in 1954 Edward John Carnell, the seminary's best-known theologian and apologist, became president. But Carnell resigned after only five years, finally worn down by bouts of depression and his uncanny ability to alienate Fuller's still sizable fundamentalist constituency by criticizing its separatism and calling important aspects of their movement "cultic."[7]

By the time the seminary started searching for Carnell's replacement, both conservative and progressive factions on the faculty and the board clearly understood that the next president would tip the ideological balance in one direction or the other. At first, the progressive party was not particularly enthusiastic about a Hubbard candidacy: his dispensationalism and firm belief in biblical inerrancy made him appear too much in the conservative camp. But over the months, then years, of the presidential search, progressives both on and off the search committee were persuaded that Hubbard's commitment to solid evangelical scholarship and his ecumenical spirit would serve their cause well. After intense political maneuvering, the search committee finally came back around to David Hubbard. In January 1963, he was elected president, and nothing has ever been the same at Fuller Seminary.

Under Hubbard's leadership, the course of Fuller Seminary was firmly set. The early days of his presidency were extremely difficult. One after the other, faculty members who had fought to preserve the school's fundamentalist ethos either retired or left for other institutions. A series of public relations nightmares threatened the seminary's financial base and survival. But Hubbard found ways to rise to each new challenge.

Possibly his greatest demonstration of leadership occurred during the furor following the publication of Harold Lindsell's *The Battle for the Bible* in 1976.[8] Because the seminary dropped inerrancy from its statement of faith in 1972, Fuller's former vice president charged it with departing from evangelical orthodoxy and declared that the seminary was on the slippery slope to religious apostasy. Hubbard handled the crisis with finesse and courage. In the ensuing controversy, which George Marsden called the school's "last battle with fundamentalism,"[9] he deftly defended Fuller's standing as an orthodox and evangelical institution by positively stating the seminary's case and never apologizing for the course that the seminary had set for itself.[10] To be sure, the seminary suffered losses over its dropping of inerrancy; but in the long run, the controversy forced Fuller to develop a new constituency and become a stronger and larger institution.

Early on, Hubbard realized that as a nondenominational seminary, Fuller needed to develop a loyal, self-conscious base of support. Therefore, he worked hard to make Fuller a movement as well as a school. Over the years, he assembled a new, more-or-less progressive evangelical coalition that eagerly identified with Fuller and its programs. He reached out to evangelicals in the Protestant mainline denominations and let it be known that pentecostals and charismatics were also welcome on the Pasadena campus. As a result, changes in the student body clearly showed the demographics of the seminary's new constituency. When Hubbard assumed the presidency in 1963, most of Fuller's students came from denominations that were clearly part of the fundamentalist-evangelical religious subculture. Thirty years later, the largest number comes from mainline Presbyterianism and the second largest from pentecostal/charismatic churches. Ironically, the seminary's most significant growth came *after* the inerrancy controversy. By the eighties, Fuller was the largest nondenominational seminary in the world. Proclaiming its identity as a progressive evangelical seminary left Fuller with little competition.

Of course, Hubbard does not take all the credit for Fuller's success. He surrounded himself with the best faculty he could find and hired a core of creative, entrepreneurial administrators who were encouraged to come up with new ideas and programs. Under Hubbard's leadership, new schools of psychology and world mission were added in the 1960s; and during the 1970s special programs for black, Hispanic, and Asian pastors were established. Fuller's doors were opened wide to women, minority students, and international students. An aggressive extension program expanded the seminary's outreach like never before, which helped to create a clientele that looked to Fuller before it looked to its own denominational agencies. During Hubbard's second decade of leadership, then, Fuller became famous for its innovation and readiness to take educational risks. Even the evangelical seminaries that publicly criticized Fuller's open and progressive stance often copied its curriculum and envied its resources during those years.

How did David Hubbard pull it off? He divided his time and energy into thirds: scholarship and teaching, administration, and developing the seminary's vision. There is a discernible Hubbard style. One would be hard pressed to find a better public representative for an institution than David Hubbard. Faculty might not always agree with his policies, but they never worried that he might embarrass them or the seminary: Hubbard was always prepared and in good form. A gifted preacher and teacher, Hubbard made friends for the seminary wherever he went. His leadership in the Association of Theological Schools during the seventies brought Fuller prestige and evangelical theological education in general more recognition. His membership on numerous boards and agencies provided a kind of map for the institutional limits of the new evangelical coalition. His own continuing commitment to biblical scholarship and his steady production of popular and technical publications over the years set him apart from most other seminary presidents and served as a strong reminder to the faculty that at Fuller scholarship was a priority.

What kind of a leader has David Hubbard been? He does not practice "management by walking around" or demonstrate a sleeves-rolled-up and feet-on-the-desk leadership style. He has always kept in close touch with his vice presidents and has been widely recognized in educational and management circles for the way he develops and works with the board of trustees.[11] On occasion, he seeks out different faculty members for consultation on particular issues. But in general, faculty do not expect to see him walking the halls or knocking on their office doors in search of fellowship or advice. Despite his warm public persona, Hubbard is an intensely private man who keeps pretty much to himself. In fact, it is not unusual for a Fuller faculty person to go for months or years without an in-depth, personal conversation with the president.

To be sure, being president of Fuller Seminary has not always been easy. Hubbard has noted how much personal freedom he has had to give up to be president and how hard his work has been on his wife Ruth, who has had health problems during most of his presidency. Sometimes attacks by the religious right on the seminary have included personal attacks on him, which undoubtedly left their mark. As any successful leader will admit, there are always limits on what one can do and how fast one can go. Hubbard has said that one of the most frustrating parts of the president's job is being "in the position of saying no to the vision and ideas of very good people." Over three decades, Hubbard has learned that presidents "have more power to make things *not* happen. Our power to block is much stronger than our power to effect."[12]

There have been disappointments, often brought on by things over which presidents have no control: for example, the untimely deaths of Fuller's first two provosts, Glenn Barker and Lawrence DenBesten, which forced Hubbard to take up again administrative responsibilities that he had already relinquished. And sometimes Hubbard has been criticized for taking unnecessary risks or not acting early or decisively enough when matters seemed to be moving out of control. When the controversial course on "Signs, Wonders, and Church Growth" began making headlines because of the exorcisms and fervent prayers for divine healing going on in class, Hubbard refused to follow the advice of those who wanted it stopped. He preferred to affirm evangelical diversity and adopted a wait-and-see attitude. When most of the faculty eventually objected to the course, Hubbard put together a faculty task force to study the situation.[13] Though many people believed that he procrastinated in bringing the matter to a conclusion, his approach was Hubbardesque: stay cool, be willing to take risks, and go through channels no matter how long it takes. As Hubbard learned early on, at Fuller Seminary there is so much diversity and there are so many different agendas that it is impossible to please everyone. What appears to some people to be administrative confusion and even disarray is seen by others as the way that Hubbard and Fuller get things done.

It is too early to speak of Hubbard's legacy to Fuller Theological Seminary, let alone his contribution to the broad evangelical movement and the church catholic. It is safe to say that his coming to Pasadena in 1963 set the seminary on a new course and enabled it to pull away from the rest of the evangelical theological pack. His leadership both inside and outside Fuller gave shape to a new kind of evangelicalism that is open, progressive, and ecumenical, and in its own way as ready as ever to do battle for the Lord.

Timothy P. Weber

NOTES

1. R. W. Lynn, "Presidents: Endangered Species," *In Trust* (Easter, 1991) 16. See also his *Good Stewardship: A Handbook for Trustees* (Washington, DC: Association of Governing Boards, 1991).

2. D. A. Hubbard, *The Second Coming: What Will Happen When Jesus Returns?* (Downers Grove, IL: InterVarsity Press, 1984) 8.

3. It is worth noting that, of the five Hubbard children, one remained a Methodist, one a pentecostal, while two became Baptists and one a Baptist-turned-charismatic.

4. In 1984 Hubbard transferred his ordination to the American Baptist Churches of the USA.

5. G. Marsden, *Reforming Fundamentalism: Fuller Seminary and the New Evangelicalism* (Grand Rapids: Eerdmans, 1987) 198.

6. G. Marsden, *Fundamentalism and American Culture* (New York: Oxford University Press, 1980).

7. E. J. Carnell, *The Case for Orthodox Theology* (Philadelphia: Westminster, 1959).

8. H. Lindsell, *The Battle for the Bible* (Grand Rapids: Zondervan, 1976).

9. Marsden, *Reforming Fundamentalism*, 277–98.

10. See "The Authority of Scripture at Fuller," *Theology, News and Notes, Special Issue* (1976); "Reflections on Fuller's Theological Position and Role in the Church," cassette tape of a seminary convocation, April 8, 1979; D. A. Hubbard, *What We Evangelicals Believe* (Pasadena: Fuller Theological Seminary, 1979).

11. See "An Effective Board: Interview with Dr. David Hubbard," *Managing the Non-Profit Organizations: Practices and Principles*, ed. P. Drucker (New York: HarperCollins, 1990) 171–85.

12. "A Recipe for Presidency: Three Veterans Talk Turkey about Their Job," *In Trust* (Easter, 1991) 12–17.

13. L. B. Smedes, ed., *Ministry and the Miraculous: A Case Study at Fuller Theological Seminary*, with a foreword by David Allan Hubbard (Waco: Word, 1987).

I
METHODOLOGY

1

DOING OLD TESTAMENT
THEOLOGY TODAY

Robert L. Hubbard, Jr.[1]

On July 10, 1965, David Hubbard delivered the annual Tyndale Old Testament Lecture in Cambridge, England.[2] The lecture ("The Wisdom Movement and Israel's Covenant Faith") sought to show possible links between these two areas of Israelite thought, areas that scholars tended not to interrelate. Through the eyes of hindsight, it is apparent that he spoke as an OT theologian in the context of the postwar Biblical Theology Movement.[3] The contrast, however, between the state of OT theology then and today could hardly be more stark. As Hasel says, "Old Testament theology today is undeniably in crisis. . . . Though it is centuries old, OT theology is now uncertain of its true identity."[4] At the heart of the crisis lies an uncertainty about the proper way to do OT theology. Complex methodological issues dog the steps of anyone who attempts to write an OT theology. Nevertheless, the church desires—indeed, needs—to hear the OT's theological voice afresh today. Thus, this essay proposes a working model of how to do OT theology today. One will appreciate it better, however, if one understands the larger methodological discussion out of which it emerges. It is with this discussion, therefore, that we begin.

The Problems

Why do scholars disagree about how to do OT theology? First, the very complexity of the OT itself makes the doing of OT theology difficult. Decades of exegetical work have unearthed a perplexing theological diversity within the OT. Indeed, today scholars speak not of the OT theology but of its "plurality of theologies."[5] For example, OT writers seem to have different theologies of God, the OT's leading character. Thus, one psalmist confidently affirms that Yahweh never slumbers nor sleeps (Ps 121:4) while another prays "Awake, O Lord! Why do you sleep?" (Ps 44:23, NIV [Heb. 23]). Further, the OT seems ambivalent over whether he is the only God (1 Kgs 18; Isa 44:6) or one among other divine beings (Exod 20:3; Ps 82:1, 6).[6] Finally, the OT portrays his relationship to the world in radically different ways. Exodus portrays God as a great sovereign dramatically initiating events and giving commentary, but Esther shows no obvious signs either of his presence or his activity. The data here can be multiplied many times.

A related problem concerns the unity of the OT itself. Scholars have spilt much ink debating what is the "center" (die Mitte)—the central theological theme or idea—that binds the OT as a whole.[7] Initially, scholars proffered a series of single concepts as its center. So, Eichrodt structured his landmark OT theology around the idea of "covenant," Vriezen around that of "communion" (i.e., God's relationship to people and the world).[8] As critics pointed out, however, such single conceptual rubrics usually failed to incorporate adequately all of the OT, particularly its wisdom literature (e.g., Job, Proverbs, and Ecclesiastes). For example, one asked Eichrodt how Israel's wisdom thought theologically related to his covenant center since the word "covenant" in wisdom literature never refers to God's relationship to Israel (Job 5:23; 31:1; 41:4 [Heb. 40:28]; Prov 2:17).

Recognizing the inadequacy of a single center, other scholars suggested motifs or themes as centers. Fohrer proposed a dual center, "the rule of God and the communion between God and man," Smend the covenant formulary "Yahweh the God of Israel, Israel the people of Yahweh."[9] Schmidt suggested the first commandment ("You shall have no other gods before me," Exod 20:3, NIV; Deut 5:7), while Zimmerli chose Israel's confessional phrase "You . . . Yahweh" (Deut 26:10).[10] For von Rad, on the other hand, the center is the theology of history held by the so-called Deuteronomist. The reason, he claims, is that only that theology expresses the heart of the OT, namely, its story of salvation history constantly driven onward by the word of God.[11] By contrast, Herrmann argued for the entire book of Deuteronomy as a good center since, in his view, it treats all the main subjects of OT theology.[12] Again, various scholars argued that God—whether as holy, universal lord, present, etc.—constitutes the OT's theological center.[13] Many other voices contribute to this chorus.

Unfortunately, the OT's theological complexity continues to escape the confines of all suggested centers. This fact alone implies that the OT has no such single center. So, instead of a "center," Knierim proposes that one seek to systematize the OT's various theologies in accordance with the priorities and subordinations intrinsic to the OT itself. In his view, one should proceed from what he perceives to be its "ultimate vantage point—the universal dominion of Yahweh in justice and righteousness."[14] By contrast, Hasel argues for a "multiplex canonical" approach, one flexible enough to handle the canon's diversity.[15] Finally, one must mention the "canonical" approach of Childs, whose starting point is the final form of the Bible.[16]

The second problem facing the OT theologian concerns the definition of the task. Traditionally, scholars defined OT theology as an exclusively historical and descriptive enterprise.[17] That is, its purpose is to analyze the OT through objective, scientific means and to articulate "what it meant" to those who first wrote it. Also, its "articulations" usually depend heavily on the literary theories derived from modern historical criticism. For example, to discuss creation in Genesis 1–2, von Rad compared the theologies of the so-called Yahwist and the priestly writer.[18] Finally, this approach delegated the discussion of "what it means"—i.e., its normative application for today—to systematic theologians and homileticians. In the last two decades, however, a growing consensus has affirmed that OT theology is—or, in the case of some scholars, must be—both historical and theological.[19] By "historical and theological" they mean that it must articulate both "what it meant" and "what it means." In other words, discussion of OT theology's normative application is an integral part of the theologian's task.

The final problem is how theologically to relate the OT to its canonical partner, the NT. At one extreme, Bultmann flatly said that the OT was no longer revelation for Christians, while, at the other, van Ruler boldly called it "the true Bible" and the NT its "explanatory gloss."[20] A far more common and less extreme approach is to relate the two testaments under the schema of promise/fulfillment.[21] Most Christian scholars incorporate some form of this approach in their OT theologies. I concur with that consensus as will become apparent below. For now, the above survey of problems has brought us to consider my proposed framework for doing OT theology.

Doing OT Theology: Assumptions

The present approach to OT theology rests on certain assumptions about the nature of the task and of the material for theological reflection. First, it assumes that the task of OT theology is a specifically Christian task. The very words "OT theology" presuppose the Christian canon with its "old" and "new" sections. Hence, because of its canonical tie to the NT, it will look quite a bit different from a "theology of the Hebrew Bible" despite the fact that both approaches use the same Hebrew scriptures.[22] Thus, the task of OT theology is a branch of Christian theology, that large enterprise that seeks to articulate what Christians believe and how they are to live.

This presupposes, of course, that the OT is both a complete entity in itself as well as a distant partner in conversation with the NT and the Christian church.[23] As an "entity in itself," it may be the subject of theological reflection apart from the NT. Such reflection in isolation aims to hear its own unique testimony to the God of Israel, the same God that the Christian church claims to worship and serve. However, since the OT is the NT's "distant dialogue partner," that "reading" of it will have a particularly Christian stamp. A Christian "reader" presumes that there is a historical and theological connection between the life and history of ancient Israel and the life and ministry of Jesus Christ. Thus, while guarding against common mistakes—e.g., to read NT theology back into the OT, to judge the OT by NT standards, etc.—the Christian interpreter inescapably hears the OT with Christian ears. In this respect, the present approach departs from scholars like McKenzie, who self-consciously approach OT theology "as if the NT did not exist."[24] Instead, it self-consciously aims to understand Israel's faith both on its own terms as well as in the light of the Christian faith.

This means also that the theologian's primary context is the Christian community of faith, which treasures the OT as part of its scripture.[25] Given the nature of the Bible, that only makes good sense. The OT, after all, originated in one community of faith—i.e., Judaism—and formed the foundation of another community of faith—i.e., Christianity. Thus, the theologian labors within a context of faith, the circle of committed believers that includes both those who compiled the OT as well as those who acknowledge its authority today. This stance, however, has risks as well as benefits. The benefit is that it frees the theologian to give the OT a more sympathetic hearing than would a so-called objective, scientific historian. By identifying with the faith of ancient Israel, the theologian can plumb its depths—depths that the unsympathetic historian might dismiss or find offensive.

On the other hand, such sympathetic identification runs two risks. First, the theologian may be inclined toward selective rather than comprehensive theological reflection. The temptation is to ignore the OT's more troublesome aspects in favor of those of personal interest or those deemed especially relevant to one's generation.[26] Against this risk, however, stands the community's commitment to obey the whole of scripture. That conviction opens the possibility that at least some community members may challenge others to reckon with all of the OT, not just the more comfortable (or comforting) parts. A second risk is that the theologian's prior faith commitment may obscure the hearing of the text. The theologian might read in Christian theology where none is present, or might misconstrue theology that clashes with personal preconceptions. Against this risk, however, stand the views of other scholars, particularly those of radically different religious commitments or even non-commitments. If heard sympathetically, those outside the circle of faith provide those within it much-needed correction.

Second, this approach assumes that the task of OT theology is both descriptive and normative. That is, it describes both "what the text meant" as well as "what it means." Thus, it rigorously pursues the descriptive task—a rigorous analysis of the theologies of biblical literature, whether of individual texts, books, or other literary entities, in their original historical contexts. To understand the OT better, it compares and contrasts its views with those of other ancient Near Eastern religions from Israel's historical neighborhood.[27] In the past, the rigid historicism of some higher critics led them to disregard or explain away biblical claims to transcendent divine intervention in human history. As Hasel points out, however, while claiming "objectivity," such a method actually wears its own dogmatic philosophical blinders and, hence, cannot reckon adequately with scripture.[28]

Indeed, the present writer would argue that a method that takes the text at face value, transcendent claims and all, may be the more truly objective one since it leaves all options open, even the possibility of supernatural activity in history. In actual fact, read straightforwardly, the Bible does present God as very much involved directly in the day-to-day world. Only a method that reckons with the OT's "faith" dimensions can be truly "historical exegesis"—that is, one that does full justice to "all levels of meaning present in the text."[29]

On the other hand, the present approach affirms that the discussion of prescriptive implications is integral to the task of OT theology.[30] This is consistent with the faith-community context described above. On the one hand, it assumes that by its very nature the Bible makes claims on its readers—witness its countless commands and prohibitions. To do it justice requires that one attempt to show what these commands and prohibitions (and the rest of scripture) have to say about contemporary life in that community and in its surrounding world. To not do so would be to fail to treat the full dimensions of the OT's theology. Granted, the theological diversity of the OT makes the task a complex one; nevertheless, the theologian must tackle it.[31] On the other hand, it also assumes that the community desires to hear a word from its Lord through the older testament. However strange that word may sound to modern ears, the desire to hear and obey it remains strong. Indeed, only its voice can protect that community from straying into God-dishonoring paths.[32]

As for the nature of the material for study, the present approach affirms that the Hebrew scriptures should be the object of theological reflection.[33] Only the final form of the text is theologically authoritative. This assumption sets aside two views commonly proposed as solutions to the OT's theological diversity. It counters those who would apply a "canon within the canon"—i.e., some biblical part, dominant theme, etc.—to relativize or relegate to unimportance some aspects of that diversity.[34] It also opposes those for whom the object of theologizing is the tradition process that eventually produced the canon.[35] Instead, the assumption here is that OT theology must preoccupy itself with the full range of theological perspectives evident in the present biblical text rather than select one from among them as a standard against which to compare the others.

One must ask, however, what constitutes the unity of the OT. The very collection of the OT's diverse materials into a single canon itself implies that some sort of communality links them. One can first set aside several unpromising responses to the question. Obviously, its unity is not a structural or organizational one; the failed search for the "center" of OT theology confirms that it has no obvious internal architecture. Further, one might speculate that an as-yet-undefined inner theological unity holds its diverse elements together, but so far one cannot speak of it with any certainty.[36] So, a better approach is to describe its unity metaphorically.

The OT is best compared to a collection of paintings of a landscape or to a multi-generational family picture album.[37] Like a collection of paintings, the OT portrays the same religion from various angles, during different time periods, in varied styles, with varying focuses of attention. Its diversity beckons the reader simply to enjoy each portrait individually, to delight in the wide range of insights, and to find one relevant to personal needs, rather than to attempt to unify them. The family-picture-album metaphor, by contrast, underscores both the "family resemblances" that the OT's diverse theologies share as well as their development over time.

When compared to family and non-family (i.e., to other religions) the family's shared features—e.g., the same God (however conceived), nation, view of humanity and the world, etc.—become apparent. By flipping through the pages, the reader can identify each member and appreciate each on his or her own terms. At the same time, one can see the changes in traits through history and marvel at the resulting family tree. In sum, one may enjoy the individuality of each theology as well as the diversity of all family members.

OT Theology: Its Structure

How should one structure an OT theology? Should one pursue a "systematic theology of the OT" (Eichrodt, Knierim), a cross section of "topics" (McKenzie, Childs, Dyrness), or a "multiplex" approach (Hasel)?[38] While no single approach has yet won acceptance, a consensus among scholars concerning several general guidelines seems evident. First, scholars generally agree that the structure and the categories used to describe the OT's parts must derive from the OT itself. So, for example, most reject the use of the traditional God-Man-Salvation three-part structure of systematic theology because the OT itself reflects no such structure.[39] To be "OT" theology, its structure and categories must approximate as closely as possible the structure and categories of the OT itself. Second, it must let the OT speak on its own terms without the influence of the NT. As Childs puts it:

> The task of OT theology is . . . not to Christianize the OT by identifying it with the NT witness, but to hear its own theological testimony to the God of Israel whom the church confesses also to worship.[40]

In that sense, one may agree with McKenzie that one should write an OT theology "as if the NT did not exist."[41] For a Christian, of course, this is a difficult assignment, one to which we shall return below. Thus, one might modify McKenzie's statement along this line: one should write an OT theology, not "as if the NT did not exist" *today*, but rather "in the ever present recognition that it originally existed and found its meaning apart from the existence of the NT." The point is that the OT should somehow have its own say free of outside influences, at least at first. Third, though about the OT, such a theology must at the same time relate to NT theology. In other words, it must contribute to the larger subject of "biblical theology," the theology that comprises both testaments.[42]

As its structural starting point for an OT theology, the present approach first plots the literature of the OT along a chronological time line.[43] At first glance, this may sound surprising in light of the heavy stress placed earlier on the canon. Why choose a historical framework over one that follows the structural contours of the canon? First, this framework conforms to the content of the canon itself. Granted, its main structural parts are "Torah," "Prophets," and "Writings." Granted also, their contents may have a complex compositional pre-history. Nevertheless, from Genesis to 2 Kings the canon presents a continuous story from creation to the Babylonian exile.[44] Second, the historical framework provides a convenient and necessary way, on the one hand, to understand the OT's diverse theologies in light of their own original contexts, and, on the other, to reckon with their conflicting views. In other words, the present approach stresses that one best comprehends these theologies in a historical context.[45]

The reference above to "the literature" requires clarification. It refers to books commonly accepted as original wholes (e.g., Ruth, Lamentations, Chronicles, etc.) or blocks of material within books about whose time of composition scholars generally agree (e.g., early poems [Exod 15; Judg 5]; the Joseph Story [Gen 37–50]; the Succession Narrative [2 Sam 9–20; 1 Kgs 1–2]; Prov 25–29, etc.). The reason for separating them from the text's "final form" is to permit their varied theological perspectives to come to the fore. Granted, to date sections within biblical books is only slightly less speculative and risky than to date the final forms of the books themselves. That difficulty, however, should not deter the theologian from ordering the materials along a historical time line. At the same time, however—and this is a crucial point—one must also incorporate the final form of books into this chronological scheme. The reason is that, as Childs has shown, the finished books themselves, whatever their compositional history, reflect theological perspectives of specific historical contexts and communities of faith with which one must reckon.[46]

Thus, the content of an OT theology must treat original books, originally independent texts, and the final forms of books in chronological sequence—to the extent, of course, that one can know it. Once done, two more important steps follow. First, one must analyze the unique theologies of each book or text-block in light of its historical setting. Second, one needs to reckon with the different, even conflicting, theological slants that may emerge. To bring the conflicts vividly to life, one may visualize each slant as a different theologian arguing for his or her position in an imaginary "debate" with the others. For example, undoubtedly a wide variety of theologians in Jerusalem about 612 B.C.—the prophets Jeremiah, Zephaniah, Nahum, and Habakkuk; the temple priests; the wisdom sages; and the deuteronomic theologians—pondered the theological significance of the end of the Assyrian Empire. The canon simply juxtaposes their words; the theological task is to sort out the relationship, perhaps even the priorities, among their views.[47]

In each time period, however, the OT theologian needs to keep a sharp eye for the major themes that emerge. One may reasonably expect each main theological perspective to have major and minor emphases. Though in any given case scholars may differ about where the line between "major" and "minor" lies, one may yet expect a consensus to emerge among them at least on most of the major themes. Once recognized, an OT theology needs to trace these themes along the chronological time line, to the extent that the materials permit.[48] In a sense, this requires the theologian to step back and—to return to one of the metaphors suggested above—survey the OT's larger theological landscape as a whole.

Now, in this longitudinal survey, one may expect to face a complicated picture. Some themes may emerge in one historical period and enjoy development in later ones while others, like conceptual shooting stars, may dominate one historical horizon, only to vanish completely from view. Still others may appear, seem to vanish for ages, then unexpectedly reappear down the line. In sum, the theologian must simply portray the resulting theological landscape as it actually is, neither tailoring the themes to fit some a priori scheme nor discarding those as "unimportant" whose appearance seems only fleeting.

Once the theologian has tracked the main themes throughout OT history, analysis of the entire landscape follows. One must ask, Does it show any kind of pattern, system, or flow? Does it imply that certain theological motifs enjoy more priority or prominence than others? Can one explain why certain motifs dominate the whole picture while others, perhaps temporarily dominant, die out? In the end, one may find within the OT a "systematic theology of the OT"—a system of interconnected, already-prioritized beliefs (or perhaps polarities).[49] One cannot determine ahead of time what that system might be—or even if there indeed is a system. The point is, having walked carefully through the theological "trees," from a distance one may observe something striking—a pattern, order, or system—about the whole theological "forest."

OT Theology: Its Relationship to the NT

The present approach claims to be a Christian one that considers the entire Bible as the OT's ultimate canonical context. Hence, in the end, the Christian OT theologian must explain how OT theology relates to the NT. This step launches one on especially treacherous waters where sweet Siren voices tempt well-meaning theologians to founder on rocks. One subtle temptation is to use the OT simply as a foil for the NT. In other words, one presents OT theology simply to highlight how NT theology has superseded, if not far exceeded, it. In effect, the well-known law/gospel dichotomy of traditional Lutheran and modern dispensationalist theologies does that. More subtly, those who view the unity of the testaments exclusively in terms of promise (OT) and fulfillment (NT) imply the superiority of the latter over the former. Both tend to denigrate the older testament in favor of the newer. The opposite temptation is subtly to elevate the OT and, by implication, to denigrate the NT. As noted above, van Ruler takes the OT as the true revelation, the NT simply as its historical footnote. In a truly "biblical" theology, neither testament should dominate the other. However one fine-tunes their interrelationship, both contribute to the larger Christian theological task.

Several general guidelines concerning the relationship between the testaments need to be kept in mind. First, one must remember that, compared to the OT, the NT has a narrower focus. It does not set aside, revise, or update the OT rather, its primary preoccupation is to interpret the significance of the Christ-event and to set up the fledgling Christian church on a solid footing. Hence, it focuses on the person and teaching of Jesus, the principles of church life and ministry, and the personal conduct of believers. So, one must view the NT as both a historical sequel (perhaps even climax) to the OT as well as the latter's theological supplement. But the point is that the NT does not see itself as the replacement of the OT, so the latter retains full authority for Christians.

Second, however, a well-intentioned desire to retain the value of the OT and the unity of the testaments should not blind one to the glaring differences between them. That is, besides fulfilling the OT, the NT goes beyond it.[50] Consider these two examples: because of Christ's once-for-all self-sacrifice, Christians need no longer perform the numerous animal sacrifices that the Israelites performed; today the people of God are dispersed throughout all nations rather than concentrated in geographical Israel. Most important, Jesus does more than simply fulfill OT prophetic hopes—He actually exceeds their expectations by radically reforming Israel's religion and by inaugurating a new era of God's dealings with humanity. Fourth, the principle of analogy is the key link that unites the testaments. In other words, both share analogous concepts with each other— e.g., a self-revealing creator-God, a people of God, gifts given to them by God, concepts of salvation, etc. Indeed, the NT regards its analogous ideas as the continuation and culmination of its OT counterparts.

Fifth and finally, one must define how Jesus Christ relates to the OT since He is the heart of the NT. Obviously, Christians regard Him as the fulfillment of some OT theological ideas. For example, he brings the ancient blessing of Abraham to all nations (Gal 3:14), realizes the long-expected Davidic ideal (e.g., Ps 2; Isa 9:6–7; 11; cf. Matt 1:1, 6), and offers the supreme, final atoning sacrifice (John 1:29; Heb 9:26–28). Again, Christ gives the entire Bible, including the OT, a new center in two respects. On the one hand, Christ is the key figure of Bible history—the hero who turns it from a long, sad tragedy into an eventual resounding triumph for God's ancient purposes. According to the Bible, human history turns on the double fulcrum of his incarnation and second coming. He also is the goal of history—the one toward whom Israel's history pointed, the one toward whose future kingdom present history marches.

On the other hand, Christ provides a new, final interpretive key for the Bible. Christians view everything within the Bible from the point of view of Christ. If Christ is the goal of Israel's history, then one must interpret that history in light of his later life and work. If he is the final sacrifice, then ultimately one will understand OT sacrifices best in light of his death. If he personally embodies the wisdom of God (Col 1:15–17; 2:3, 8; cf. 1 Cor 1:30), then one must ultimately comprehend OT wisdom on his terms. In sum, while interpreting the OT in its own historical context, the Christian OT theologian must view its theologies in the larger canonical context of which Christ is the key.

How can one relate the two testaments together theologically? The present approach suggests that one view the relationship as an extension of a concept noted above. That is, it conceives of the OT-NT relationship as a series of parallel theological trajectories moving from one testament to the other. Each of these trajectories tracks the course of a specific OT theological theme—e.g., God, election, promise, covenant, sacrifice, human kingship, kingdom, justice, wisdom, worship, etc.—into the NT.[51] The course and width of each trajectory varies with the subject matter concerned. Some will flow directly into the NT and broaden into rich, complex theological streams. The theologies of promised universal blessing and the promised New David illustrate this kind of trajectory. Moving from OT to NT, the theme of the blessing of all nations through Abraham's descendants (Gen 12:1–3) joins the theme of the new Davidic ruler (e.g., Isa 11) to form the major, multifaceted NT theology about the messiahship of Jesus. In other words, this case involves the convergence of two OT theologies, their fulfillment by Christ, as well as their substantial expansion in the NT.

On the other hand, with some trajectories the NT seemingly assumes the full validity of their OT theologies and adds virtually nothing to it. The theology of justice offers an example. It seems likely that, had one asked Jesus or the apostles, "How should Christians practice social justice?" their reply would be, "Go back and read the law of Moses and prophets like Amos. We really have nothing to add." One could make a similar case for OT proverbial wisdom. The NT needed no "Book of NT Proverbs" because the old one still served the church well. The above examples only illustrate two of the multiplex relationships between the theologies of the OT and the NT. But that is the point—to track the course and nature of the theological trajectories. To do so is to determine the theological unity of the Bible, to do not just "OT theology" but "biblical theology."

Conclusion

In an article on "Hope in the OT," David Hubbard concluded by asking whether Christians could learn anything from the OT's view of hope since Christ had fulfilled it. Had "that final Word," he wondered, rendered the OT "penultimate words empty?"[52] One might ask the same question of OT theology. Has NT theology made OT theology obsolete, or at least less relevant? The present paper answers the question in the negative and suggests how Christians may do OT theology today. The task is difficult and tricky but well worth the attempt. Certainly, today's church, fraught with self-doubt about its identity and groping to find ways to address its surrounding cultures, would do well to hear afresh the ancient theological voices of the OT. In fact, far from emptying them, "that final Word" has set those "penultimate words" in a larger historical context, a context that permits readers to enjoy their meaning as never before.

NOTES

1. I have probably known David Hubbard longer than anyone else in this volume has—more than forty years. Of course, I have had the simple advantage of being his nephew! To borrow from a recent song, he has been "the wind beneath my wings"— my encourager, teacher, counselor, and professional inspiration. I offer him this essay as an expression of my profound gratitude. It is the least I can do to repay an enormous personal and professional debt.

2. D. A. Hubbard, "The Wisdom Movement and Israel's Covenant Faith," *TynBul* 17 (1966) 3–33.

3. On this movement, see B. S. Childs, *Biblical Theology in Crisis* (Philadelphia: Westminster, 1970) 13–87; but cf. J. D. Smart, *The Past, Present, and Future of Biblical Theology* (Philadelphia: Westminster, 1979) 22–30, who denies its existence.

4. G. Hasel, *Old Testament Theology: Basic Issues in the Current Debate* (Grand Rapids: Eerdmans, 1991) 1. For the history of the discipline, see H.-J. Kraus, *Die Biblische Theologie: Ihre Geschichte und Problematik* (Neukirchen: Neukirchener, 1970); and J. H. Hayes and F. Prussner, *Old Testament Theology: Its History and Development* (Atlanta: John Knox, 1985).

5. R. P. Knierim, "The Task of Old Testament Theology," *HBT* 6 (1984) 25 (my italics), for whom that plurality is "the theological problem of the Old Testament."

6. The examples come from J. Goldingay, *Theological Diversity and the Authority of the Old Testament* (Grand Rapids: Eerdmans, 1987) 2; cf. his full discussion (1–28). See also the discussion of various theological "polarities" in P. D. Hanson, *The Diversity of Scripture: A Theological Interpretation*, OBT 11 (Philadelphia: Fortress, 1982) 14–82.

7. Cf. R. Smend, *Die Mitte des Alten Testaments*, BET 99 (Munich: Chr. Kaiser, 1986) 40–84; Hasel, *Old Testament Theology*, 139–71.

8. W. Eichrodt, *Theology of the Old Testament*, OTL, 2 vols. (Philadelphia: Westminster, 1961–67) 1:11–18, 36–69 (henceforth *TOT*); Th. C. Vriezen, *An Outline of Old Testament Theology*, 2d ed. (Newton, MA: Branford, 1970) 8, 160. For other single ideas, see Hasel, *Old Testament Theology*, 141–42.

9. G. Fohrer, "Der Mittelpunkt einer Theologie des Alten Testaments," *TZ* 24 (1968) 163 (cf. also 161–72); idem, *Theologische Grundstrukturen des Alten Testaments* (Berlin: de Gruyter, 1972); Smend, *Die Mitte*, 73–84, esp. 74–75.

10. W. H. Schmidt, *Das erste Gebot: Seine Bedeutung für das Alten Testament* (Munich: Chr. Kaiser, 1969) 11; W. Zimmerli, "Alttestamentliche Traditionsgeschichte und Theologie," in *Probleme biblischer Theologie: Gerhard von Rad zum 70. Geburtstag*, ed. H. W. Wolff (Munich: Chr. Kaiser, 1971) 632–47, esp. 639–41; cf. idem, *Old Testament Theology in Outline* (Atlanta: John Knox, 1978).

11. So the assessment of Hasel, *Old Testament Theology*, 145–49; cf. G. von Rad, *Old Testament Theology*, 2 vols. (New York: Harper & Row, 1962–65) 1:340–44 (henceforth *OTT*). Most scholars believe the Deuteronomist is responsible for compiling and editing the books of Deuteronomy to 2 Kings.

12. S. Herrmann, "Die konstruktive Restauration: Das Deuteronomium als Mitte biblischer Theologie," in *Probleme biblischer Theologie: Gerhard von Rad zum 70. Geburtstag*, ed. H. W. Wolff (München: Chr. Kaiser, 1970) 155–70.

13. For other views and bibliography, see G. Hasel, "Major Recent Issues in Old Testament Theology 1978–1983," *JSOT* 31 (1985) 37–40.

14. Knierim, *HBT* 6 (1984) 43; cf. the critical responses in *HBT* 6 (1984) by W. Harrelson ("The Limited Task of Old Testament Theology," 59–64), R. E. Murphy ("A Response to 'The Task of Old Testament Theology,'" 65–71), and W. S. Towner ("Is Old Testament Theology Equal to Its Task?" 73–80); cf. also Knierim's reply to his critics ("On The Task of Old Testament Theology," 91–128).

15. Hasel, *Old Testament Theology*, 11–14, 194–208; cf. B. C. Birch, "Old Testament Theology: Its Task and Future," *HBT* 6/1 (1984) vi ("future, viable approaches... are likely to be multi-valent").

16. B. S. Childs, *Old Testament Theology in a Canonical Context* (Philadelphia: Fortress, 1985) esp. 1–19.

17. Cf. K. Stendahl, "Biblical Theology, Contemporary," *IDB* 1:418–32. For an overview of the following discussion with critique, see Hasel, *Old Testament Theology*, 28–38.

18. *OTT* 1:139–51.

19. E.g., Childs, *Biblical Theology in Crisis*, 139–47; R. E. Clements, *Old Testament Theology: A Fresh Approach* (Atlanta: John Knox, 1978) 20, 191, whose concern is that OT theology be a branch of theology, not of historical criticism.

20. R. Bultmann, "The Significance of the Old Testament for the Christian Faith," in *The Old Testament and Christian Faith*, ed. B. W. Anderson (New York: Herder & Herder, 1969) 8–35; A. A. van Ruler, *The Christian Church and the Old Testament* (Grand Rapids: Eerdmans, 1971) 72, 74 n. 45.

21. E.g., W. C. Kaiser, Jr., *Toward an Old Testament Theology* (Grand Rapids: Zondervan, 1978).

22. For the recent Jewish discussion of OT theology, see Hasel, *Old Testament Theology*, 6–7, 34–37 (with bibliography).

23. I owe this and some of what follows to Childs, *Old Testament Theology*, 7–12; cf. also Hasel, *Old Testament Theology*, 111–12, 201–2; Goldingay, *Theological Diversity*, 186–87.

24. J. L. McKenzie, *A Theology of the Old Testament* (Garden City, NY: Doubleday, 1974) 319; cf. R. Rendtorff, "Must 'Biblical Theology' Be Christian Theology?" *Bible Review* 4 (1988) 40–43.

25. C. H. H. Scobie, "The Challenge of Biblical Theology," *TynBul* 42 (1991) 47 (with bibliography); Clements, *Old Testament Theology*, 193; cf. S. E. Fish, *Is There a Text in This Class? The Authority of Interpretive Communities* (Cambridge: Harvard, 1980) 171–72, who argues that communities are the only contexts in which to interpret texts.

26. Cf. Goldingay, *Theological Diversity*, 129; Hanson, *The Diversity of Scripture*, 4 ("we are pleading for an openness to the total address of Scripture, lest we select only what reinforces our present views and exclude the possibility of growth").

27. Unlike the Biblical Theology Movement, however, the goal of such study is simply to come to understand the OT's theology, not to prove its uniqueness or even superiority over other ancient faiths; cf. Childs, *Biblical Theology in Crisis*, 44–50, 70–77.

28. Cf. Hasel, *Old Testament Theology*, 198. Concerning the problem of history and the OT, see his discussion (ibid., 115–38).

29. R. Knierim, "Criticism of Literary Features, Form, Tradition, and Redaction," in *The Hebrew Bible and Its Modern Interpreters*, ed. D. A. Knight & G. M. Tucker (Philadelphia/Chico, CA: Fortress/Scholars Press, 1985) 125.

30. So B. S. Childs, "Interpretation in Faith: The Theological Responsibility of an Old Testament Commentary," *Int* 18 (1964) 443–44; cf. idem, *Old Testament Theology*, 11, 12.

31. For guidance, see the "evaluative or critical approach" of Goldingay, *Theological Diversity*, 97–133; cf. P. Stuhlmacher, *Historical Criticism and Theological Interpretation of Scripture* (Philadelphia: Fortress, 1977) 85 ("we must again learn to ask what claim or truth about man, his world, and transcendence we hear from these texts").

32. Cf. Childs, *Old Testament Theology*, 17: "As the history of exegesis eloquently demonstrates, a Christian church without the Old Testament is in constant danger of turning the faith into various forms of gnostic, mystic, or romantic speculation."

33. Childs, ibid., 6; cf. S. Fowl, "The Canonical Approach of Brevard Childs," *ExpTim* 96 (1985) 173–76; Clements, *Old Testament Theology*, 20, 155, 191. For criticism of

Childs, see J. Barr, "Childs' Introduction to the Old Testament as Scripture," *JSOT* 16 (1980) 12–23; J. Barton, *Reading the Old Testament* (Philadelphia: Westminster, 1984) 77–103; implicitly, Hanson, *Diversity of Scripture*, 108–13.

34. E.g., the Book of Deuteronomy (Herrmann) or the deuteronomic theology of history (von Rad).

35. Cf. H. Gese, "Tradition and Biblical Theology," in *Tradition and Theology in the Old Testament*, ed. D.A. Knight (Philadelphia: Fortress, 1977) 301–26, for whom the object of theology is the tradition-formation process. For an assessment of Gese, see J. H. Schmid, *Biblische Theologie in der Sicht heutiger Alttestamentler* (Giessen/Zurich: Brunnen Verlag/Gotthelf, 1986) 28–99.

36. Cf. Eichrodt, *TOT* 1:490 ("unchanging truth hidden under its bewildering diversity"); McKenzie, *A Theology of the Old Testament*, 29, 35 (the experience of the reality of Yahweh); and Hasel, *Old Testament Theology*, 167–71, 205–7, who seems to assume the possibility and calls for its discovery.

37. For what follows, cf. Goldingay, *Theological Diversity*, 29, 33, who also suggests comparisons to a symposium, a battle, a landscape, a person, family resemblances, and common human anatomy (12, 33, 115, 167). Cf. also D. L. Baker's diagram of OT theology as an elliptical cylinder with Christ as its center, God and Israel as two foci, and key themes (e.g., election, etc.) as concentric layers (*Two Testaments, One Bible: A Study of Some Modern Solutions to the Theological Problem of the Relationship between the Old and New Testaments* [Downers Grove: InterVarsity, 1977] 386).

38. Cf. Eichrodt, *TOT* 1:27–28, 32–33; Knierim, "The Task of Old Testament Theology," 44–45, 47–48; McKenzie, *A Theology of the Old Testament;* Childs, *Old Testament Theology;* W. Dyrness, *Themes in Old Testament Theology* (Downers Grove: InterVarsity, 1979); Hasel, *Old Testament Theology*, 111–14, 194–208.

39. Cf. Hasel, ibid., 39–40 ("most have discarded [it] as an out-moded model"), 42 (critique). The same criticism applies to Eichrodt's three-part structure of "God and the People, God and the World, and God and Man" (*TOT* 1:33).

40. Childs, *Old Testament Theology*, 9.

41. McKenzie, *A Theology of the Old Testament;* Childs, *Old Testament Theology*, 319.

42. Goldingay, *Theological Diversity*, 187 ("ultimately biblical theology will be the Christian scholar's concern"); cf. Childs, *Old Testament Theology*, 14–15.

43. Similarly, J. Høgenhaven, *Problems and Prospects of Old Testament Theology* (Sheffield: JSOT, 1987) 95.

44. Cf. Childs' thesis (*Introduction to the Old Testament as Scripture* [Philadelphia: Fortress, 1979] 232–37) that the canonical shape of the "former prophets" aimed to stress the fulfillment of the prophetic message.

45. See the fine discussion in Goldingay, *Theological Diversity*, 29–58.

46. This, of course, is one particular strength of his programmatic *Introduction to the Old Testament as Scripture.*

47. I owe this example to Knierim, "The Task of Old Testament Theology," 28–29. Goldingay, *Theological Diversity*, 29–58, 97–133, offers a helpful approach to sorting out conflicting views.

48. So Hasel, *Old Testament Theology*, 204–5.

49. This is precisely the task that Knierim ("The Task of Old Testament Theology," 47) set for OT theology; cf. also Goldingay, *Theological Diversity*, 112. On polarities, see ibid., 191–97, 212–17; Hanson, *The Diversity of Scripture*, 14–82; and the survey in Hasel, *Old Testament Theology*, 86–94 (with bibliography).

50. For what follows, cf. Baker, *Two Testaments: One Bible*, 368–72. See also his principles for the proper use of typology (266–70). Cf. also Kraus, *Biblische Theologie*, 314–21, 380–87.

51. So also Hasel, *Old Testament Theology*, 204–5; cf. F. F. Bruce, *The New Testament Development of Old Testament Themes* (Grand Rapids: Eerdmans, 1968).

52. D. A. Hubbard, "Hope in the Old Testament," *TynBul* 34 (1983) 59.

2

FROM EXEGESIS TO PROCLAMATION

Elizabeth Achtemeier

The primary purpose of this essay is methodological. It is intended to discuss the way in which the preacher moves from exegesis to sermon formation in preparing to preach from the Old Testament. Before taking up methodological considerations, however, it is necessary to set forth some basic presuppositions apart from which it is impossible to preach a biblical sermon.

The Relation of the Text to History

In preparing a sermon, everything depends upon the convictions with which the preacher approaches the text, and there are a number of contemporary approaches that can lead a preacher astray.

The first of these is to divorce the text from the history in which it is embedded. One thinks immediately of structuralism, which looks in the text for ahistorical structures and symbols, applicable to all times. Or a deconstructionalist approach, which disconnects the language of the text from any historical context and finally from any meaning for any time. But neither of these approaches is used by many preachers.

Rather, one of the most frequent methods of sermon preparation has been that of the thematic sermon, in which the preacher looks for suprahistorical "truths" or eternal "principles" in the text. A truth or theme is lifted out of its context in Israel's historical existence and applied without further ado to the life of the congregation. Thus God's real action within the history of Israel is ignored, and the Bible is turned into a set of principles for better living.

Certainly one of the enormous contributions of historical critical scholarship has been to set biblical texts in their actual time and place in the ancient Near East, and to illumine the linguistic, geographical, sociological, political, historical, and religious factors involved in them. Though carried on as disinterested science, historical criticism has therefore served to emphasize that God has acted and spoken his word into real history, at particular times and places, to actual people inhabiting the Fertile Crescent. The preacher cannot ignore this historical actuality and claim to be speaking the Bible's message.

A second approach to the text that can lead a preacher astray is to consider the text only in its historical context; as a word spoken and having meaning only in the past, or as an event concerning past Israel alone. This is the hermeneutical virus that is eating at the life of many of our mainline churches today. The view widespread among many religious writers and leaders is that all biblical texts are historically conditioned, reflecting only ancient cultures and beliefs. They reflect merely the thought of those cultures, and those cultures are separated from us by time and societal differences. Therefore, is the argument, the biblical texts have no authority for our faith and action today.

This is an attitude prominent among feminist theologians, who have abandoned the Bible as the product of a patriarchal society, but it is an attitude found also among many liberal mainline church leaders, who consider the Bible's views to be outdated. Indeed, historical critics have sometimes contributed to this erroneous approach by viewing the biblical text only as a historical artifact to be studied and placed in its proper chronological position in the history of religions.

The History of Religions School was very prominent in the opening decades of our century, and it finally led to a loss of the OT as a revelatory part of our canon. The OT was viewed as primitive, outdated, superseded by the higher spiritual developments, teachings, and institutions of Christianity. Thus, for all practical purposes, the church discarded the OT and returned to a revived Marcionism, which had its evil outcome in Hitler's persecution of the Jews.

Even when they give lip service to the authority of the Scriptures, many lay people still are influenced by this view and consider the OT to be outdated and irrelevant for the life of the church; thus there is widespread reluctance among church congregations to study the OT. Obviously, preachers do nothing to overcome such attitudes when they find themselves, while constructing a sermon, unable to move in a legitimate fashion from the past of an OT text to the present life of the congregation.

The fact is, of course, that any text in the Bible never concerns the past only. Rather, through that text, the holy and living God continues to work and to speak in the present. The text is the medium of the revelation of God, which means that the text is the medium of the action of God. Revelation, in the Bible's understanding, is never simply the conveying of new information about God. Rather, revelation is the creation of a new situation. "If any one is in Christ, [that person] is a new creation" (2 Cor 5:17, RSV). Revelation is an event, which brings about a changed life and circumstance.

One can see this working of God through the biblical text so clearly in a passage like Deuteronomy 26:5–9, for example, which is a confession of faith recited by the Israelite worshiper on the occasion of bringing the offering of first fruits to the temple. The worshiper in that passage begins to tell the story of Israel's life with God, from the time of Jacob on. And as the history of the patriarchs and the exodus, of the wilderness wanderings and of the entrance into the land is recited, that history becomes present event for the worshiper, as indicated by the change in the pronouns used: "And the Egyptians treated us harshly, and afflicted us, and laid upon us hard bondage" (v. 6, RSV).

The same thing happens when we recite the story of the Last Supper. We tell the history, "On the night that he was betrayed, our Lord took bread . . . ," and suddenly we are there, sharing in that meal and hearing that one of us will betray him to be crucified.

The texts of the Bible tell of actions and words of God in the past, which then become present. Through the history of revelation in the past, the living God reveals himself here and now.

To be sure, such revelation is given only to faith, and there is no way that simply hearing the recitation of a biblical text can ensure that revelation. God makes himself known only to faith. But certainly, it is the story of the Bible itself that inspires faith, as countless converts who have come to faith by reading or hearing the Bible preached could testify. "Faith comes from what is heard, and what is heard comes by the preaching of Christ" (Rom 10:17, RSV). Unless the preacher therefore has that faith from previous experience of the biblical Word, he or she has no business preaching.

In other words, the conviction absolutely necessary for biblical preaching is the belief that though the Bible comes out of an ancient culture, separated from our life by centuries and by custom, it nevertheless is the medium through which the living God speaks to his people in their present situation. Apart from that conviction, the biblical text will remain a dead letter from the past, without interest or authority.

The Old Testament as Israel's Book

The second basic presupposition that we must hold as we preach from the OT is that the OT is directed to Israel, the covenant community of God's chosen people. Unless we therefore have some connection with Israel, the OT is not our book, and it is not revelation spoken to us. We cannot escape the OT's context in Israel's concrete, historical community.

Preachers sometimes make the mistake, when they are preaching from the Book of the Old Covenant, of equating Israel with the United States of America. Thus some prophetic text addressed to the nation of Judah is interpreted as addressed to the U.S.A. But our country is not the chosen, covenant people of God, despite the civil religion abroad in our land, and despite the fact that Abraham Lincoln called us "God's almost chosen people." The U.S.A. is a secular, pluralistic state, with a multitude of religious beliefs and nonbeliefs, and it has not as a nation been elected by God or entered into covenant relation with him.

The parallel to Israel in the OT is rather the Christian Church, as the NT repeatedly recognizes. The Church alone can lay claim to Israel's title of being also an elected, covenant community, because the Church alone has been joined to Israel by the work of Jesus Christ. As Ephesians 2 states, Christ "has made us both one," and the Church now has become a member of "the commonwealth of Israel." Or, as in Romans 11, we wild gentile branches have been grafted into the root of Israel. Thus Paul can call the Church "the Israel of God" (Gal 6:16) and "the true circumcision" (Phil 3:3), who have not replaced the Israel of the OT, but rather become one with the Israel of faith (Rom 11). But this union of the Church with the covenant people of the OT has been achieved only through the work of Jesus Christ.

It follows, therefore, that the OT will be heard properly only in the context of the covenant community of faith, that is, in the Church. It is the habit of some theological professors of the Bible to absent themselves from the life of their local churches, but they have thereby cut themselves off from the one context in which the Bible can truly be heard.

It is also true, however, that for Christians, the OT can properly be heard only through Jesus Christ, because it is only through him that the

OT is addressed to us Christians. Most sermons from the OT implicitly acknowledge this fact. When preaching primarily from some text of the OT, many preachers are in the habit of giving a general statement of the gospel at the end of the sermon, in order to make the sermon a Christian proclamation.

It has always been my contention, however, that the gospel is not given us in general; it comes to us only through the specific words and deeds recorded for us in the NT. Every sermon from an OT text should, therefore, include a specific NT text paired with the Old.

This does not mean that the major portion of the sermon will not be taken from the OT or that the NT message will overshadow that of the OT for the OT brings to us its own revelation of the living God, and that revelation is absolutely essential to the fullness of the gospel. For example, according to the NT itself, we do not know who Jesus Christ is, apart from the OT (e.g., Luke 24:44; Matt 1:1). It is in the traditions of the theologies of the OT that our Lord is presented to us as Messiah, Son of God, Son of David and of Abraham, Suffering Servant, Son of Man, Shepherd-King, new Moses, high priest Melchizedek, true vine, redemption price, new covenant, new temple, place of rest, incarnate Word.

Similarly, apart from the OT we do not know who we are in the church as "the Israel of God," for only from the OT do we learn who Israel is and what she is to do. Apart from the OT, we have no full understanding that God is working out a holy history that spans all time, from creation to the coming of the kingdom. And apart from the OT, we cannot fully know that God is Creator and Lord of all nature and history.

Furthermore, we receive all of these things only through God's act in Jesus Christ, by which we join covenant with Israel. The OT is given its final interpretation by that act of God in Christ. The pairing of OT and NT texts is therefore essential for preaching from the OT.

The Pairing of OT and NT Texts

Although the lectionary now always includes texts from OT, Gospels, and Epistles, many preachers who are not used to the method find great difficulty in pairing texts from both testaments and using them together in a sermon from the OT. Once the method is practiced and mastered, however, it can add enormous power to preaching, not to mention greater theological integrity.

There are a number of ways of joining OT and NT, and I am sure that Daniel Fuller's article, (in the following pages) will further elucidate the methodology. Probably the best-known approach is to pair texts on the basis of promise and fulfillment: the OT text contains a promise that is then seen to be fulfilled in the NT text. Congregations and preachers have long been acquainted with such pairing—note for example our custom at Christmastime of reading from Isaiah's promises—"For to us a child is born . . . ," Isa 9:6, RSV)—and understanding them to have been fulfilled in Christ. The Gospel according to Matthew continually draws on this scheme, sometimes in a surprising and thought-provoking manner (see, for example, Matt 2:15). The Fourth Gospel uses it (John 19:36–37), as does Paul (Gal 3:6–9).

One of the great values of a promise-fulfillment understanding is that it recognizes the over-arching span of God's sacred history that is still being worked out in our time and in our lives. We are seen to be the heirs of the promises that God made to Israel (Gal 4:7, RSV).

This understanding of promise and fulfillment should also be applied to texts that we would not normally consider in such a scheme, especially texts from the prophets. For example, when God says to Israel in Amos 3:2, "You only have I known / of all the families of the earth; / therefore I will punish you / for all your iniquities" (RSV), the preacher should ask how that promise is being fulfilled in our present lives. And the same question should be asked about all of the prophetic words such as Amos 8:11–12 or Jeremiah 2:4–13. Have these things spoken by the prophets come to pass for us also? What text in the NT speaks of the fulfillment of the prophetic judgments on Israel as judgments come also upon us? John 3:19? The story of the crucifixion? Preachers need to ask these questions and search the Scriptures for their answers.

A second method of pairing OT and NT texts is to relate them on the basis of analogy, and this is probably the method most useful when preaching from an OT narrative. The preacher asks how Israel's situation in relation to God is analogous to the Church's situation and ours in relation to him. Certainly, both OT and NT times and societies are very different from ours, and yet our relation to God is very much like those relations found in the Bible, and the preacher can draw analogies between them.

Indeed, according to the biblical history, the life of the Christian church parallels the life of Israel in many respects. Both Israel and the Church have been redeemed out of slavery, long before they have done anything to deserve it: Israel was redeemed from bondage in Egypt; we are redeemed from slavery to sin and death. Both Israel and the Church are elected as God's treasured possessions, among all the peoples of the earth. Both of us are brought to the table of covenant, where in gratitude, we promise to serve God alone and to be obedient to his will. Both Israel and the Church are made kingdoms of priests and holy nations, set apart for God's purposes as mediators of the knowledge of God to all the rest of the world. Both of us are on pilgrimages, traveling toward a promised place of rest and looking for an eternal kingdom of love and justice. Both Israel and the Church are accompanied by God every step along the way.

In other words, Israel's story in the OT is our story as members of the Christian church. We can identify with it. The preacher, therefore, has ample opportunity to talk about our life with God by talking about the life of Israel.

Let us look at only one example. In Numbers 14:1–10, after the spies have brought back reports about conditions in the promised land, the Israelites cry out, "Let us choose a captain, and go back to Egypt" (v. 4, RSV). In other words, they want to forget all about their redemption. "Back to Egypt!" is the cry. "Back to slavery! Never mind that we are God's elected people, chosen to serve his will in the world. Forget the exodus! Forget the covenant! Forget that we have been redeemed!"

That is very much the same attitude that Paul finds in the Galatian church in 1:6–9 or 3:1–4 or 5:1. "For freedom Christ has set us free," he writes; "stand fast therefore, and do not submit again to a yoke of slavery" (RSV). But, of course, we are tempted to fall once again into slavery, aren't we? Faced with the lure of society's faithless ways, or with temptations to abandon our faith, or with sufferings that severely test our trust, we just want to forget all about being Christians. "Never mind the cross! Forget what God has done in Christ. Forget our redemption! Back to slavery!" Thus, Israel's story is our story, and can powerfully illumine it. There is no need in such analogous pairing to apply the text to our situation. The text mirrors our situation; it tells of our condition.

A third method of pairing texts in the OT and NT is to choose those that share motifs common to both. Literally hundreds of motifs, traditions, symbols, and metaphors join the testaments together and point to God's ongoing activity through two thousand years of sacred history. Many of these are well known: in both testaments we find redemption, covenant, bread from heaven, water of life, the Word, circumcision, light, life, the way, and all of the common titles for God, as King, Shepherd, Redeemer, Savior, Lord, Warrior, Judge, and so forth.

But the testaments share other motifs that are not so well known. For example, in Jeremiah 2:20, the prophet proclaims to Judah, "Long ago you broke your yoke / and burst your bonds; / and you said, 'I will not serve'" (RSV). In Matthew 11:29, our Lord picks up that figure of the "yoke" and invites us, "Take my yoke upon you, and learn from me" (RSV). Again, in Isaiah 28:16, the prophet promises that the new Jerusalem of the future will be built upon the cornerstone of faith, and in 1 Peter 2:6, Christ Jesus has become that cornerstone.

Sometimes such motifs are used to draw contrasts. In Jeremiah 25:15–29, the prophet is given the cup of the wrath of the Lord's judgment, which all nations are forced to drink, but in 1 Corinthians 10 and 11, that "cup" becomes a cup of blessing and our participation in the blood of Christ. Again, in Genesis 4:10, the blood of murdered Abel cries out to God from the ground, but in Hebrews 12:24, the blood of the new covenant in Jesus Christ "speaks more graciously than the blood of Abel" (RSV). In drawing such contrasts between the testaments' common motifs, however, the preacher must be careful not to ignore or devalue the OT. Without the judgment announced in Jeremiah 25 and Genesis 4, the contrasting salvation in 1 Corinthians 10–11 and Hebrews 12 would have no meaning. Even by way of contrast with the NT, the OT serves an indispensable function in illumining the condition of our sinful lives.

Finally, sometimes texts are paired simply to let the text in one testament illumine the text in the other. For example, Paul writes in Romans 6 that we are slaves of sin. The stories of the OT can graphically illustrate that condition—the story of Israel's slavery in Egypt, or the story of her captivity in Babylonia. Or Jeremiah 13:23 (NIV) sums up the condition in two sentences: "Can the Ethiopian change his skin / or the leopard his spots? / Neither can you do good / who are accustomed to doing evil." And Hosea 5:4 does the same: "Their deeds do not permit them / to return to their God. / For the spirit of harlotry is within them, / and they know not the LORD" (RSV). Preaching about the sinful condition of Israel can give entrance into an understanding of our similar condition. To give another example, who cannot recognize our ingratitude from the story of Numbers 11:4? We laugh over Israel's blindness in that passage until we realize it is also ours.

The more thoroughly the preacher knows the whole Bible, the easier it becomes to pair texts from the two testaments, but a center-column cross-reference Bible can also be of enormous help in putting texts together. Certainly, much of the direction the sermon takes will depend on what text from the NT is used in partnership with the OT, for the two texts interpret one another as they mutually interact.

Let us now turn more specifically to sermon construction.

The Foundation of the Sermon

The basic message of the sermon is taken from the thought of the biblical text, which has been revealed through careful exegesis and prayerful meditation. How simple that sounds, and yet how frequently preachers ignore it! For example, I recently heard a sermon based on Psalm 107:43, "Whoever is wise, let him give heed to these things; / let [mortals] consider the steadfast love of the LORD" (RSV). The key to that verse is the parallelism between "these things" and "the steadfast love of the LORD." In short, "these things" are evidences of that steadfast love, and all of them are detailed in the preceding forty-two verses of the psalm. They concern God's deliverance of those wandering in desert wastes, of those delivered from prison and illness, of those saved from storms at sea, of those oppressed, and so forth. But the preacher never mentioned such acts of God's deliverance. Instead, he preached about what he thought were contemporary evidences of God's steadfast love. The meaning of the text was forgotten in the rush to relate it to modern life.

It cannot be repeated too often or over-emphasized that every major point in a sermon is to be based on the thought of the text in its context. The text's meaning dictates the thought of the sermon; the text's function determines the function of the sermon; the text's message shapes the viewpoint of the sermon.

For example, suppose that we are preaching from Habakkuk 1:1–11. The prophet complains to God in 1:1–4 that Judah's life is full of violence and wrong, that the influence of the wicked overcomes the righteous, and that obedience to God's law is slacked and justice never goes forth. The prophet asks how long God will allow such conditions to prevail. The answer in 1:5–11 is that God will correct Judah's sinfulness by bringing the Babylonian army upon them in judgment—certainly neither the expected answer to the prophet's prayer nor a pleasant one. But the preacher using this text cannot waver from its message: God corrects sin sometimes by judging nations and destroying them—a profound view of how God's sovereignty operates in human history. Applied to the Church as the parallel to Israel, it is also a sobering message concerning the sinful life of the Church. But the meaning of the text dictates the message of the sermon. Otherwise the sermon is not biblical.

Even the briefest texts can yield plenteous fruit if carefully studied. For example, let us look at Zechariah 2:1–5, which describes the third vision given to the prophet in 519 B.C., when Jerusalem was still in ruins after the Babylonian captivity. The passage is promissory: God is going to make a new Jerusalem. Further, in a few brief sentences, the text makes four important points: the new Jerusalem will not be like the old city; it will have no human limitations on its population; its one source of defense will be God alone; and its one claim to glory will be the presence of God in its midst. That is a marvelous basis for a sermon! Suppose we pick up the motif of Jerusalem or Zion, which both hymnody and the NT have used as a name for the Church (cf. Heb 12:22; 1 Pet 2:6; Rev 14:1). We then have in this passage a description of what the life and nature of the Christian church are to be. And if we pair the text with 1 Corinthians 3:10–23, we are also allowed to add the point that Jesus Christ is the foundation of that new Jerusalem which the Church is called to be. But the point is that the texts have determined the content of the sermon, and it surely is a sermon that very much needs to be preached.

The Expansion of the Basic Message

Although every major point of the sermon is taken from the biblical text(s), it is also true that most of those points need to be developed further in order to make up a full-length sermon. Certainly, in the example given immediately above, the thought of the new Jerusalem was made relevant to the present by linking it with the motif of the Church as Zion. We have seen, in the discussion of pairing texts, how such pairing helps in the development of a sermon. But there are other ways of expanding on the thought of a sermon, and we need to mention them.

We might say that in sermon development, the text is brought into two conversations. First of all, it is set into conversation with the rest of the canon. Pairing texts is such a conversation, as is the discovery of common motifs: the text is linked with other portions of the Bible. But tradition-criticism can also play an enormous role in this regard. For example, in Psalm 46:1–3, we have the affirmation of faith that God is our refuge and strength, though the earth change and the mountains shake in the heart of the sea. The description of the tumult of the waters in these verses alerts us that they are not ordinary waters. And indeed, in the center-column cross reference, we find similar passages cited in Psalm 93:3–4 and Jeremiah 5:22. The latter reference especially reminds us of the creation story, and further investigation in a Bible dictionary or concordance reveals that what we are dealing with here in Psalm 46 are the chaotic waters, the great *tĕhôm*, the dark, evil chaos of Genesis 1. In short, Psalm 46 is using the chaos tradition that is so prevalent throughout the Bible. Israel and we, as the new Israel, are threatened with the disorder and darkness and death inherent in the chaos that can engulf our world. How well we know this in our atomic age! And how well we know it in our broken and tragic life-situations! But "God is our refuge and strength, / a very present help in trouble. / Therefore we will not fear . . ." (Ps 46:1–2, RSV). "In the world you have tribulation; but be of good cheer, I have overcome the world" (John 16:33, RSV). The faith of the psalmist is affirmed and completed by the promise of our Lord. Tradition-criticism can help us shape and fill out the entire sermon.

So too can the use of a center-column cross-reference Bible help us enlarge on the thought of individual verses in the text. The cross-references indicate where the verse is quoted elsewhere in the Bible, or where similar words and thoughts appear. For example, Malachi 4:5 promises that before the final Day of the Lord comes, God will send Elijah to urge repentance. That verse is cross-referenced with Mark 9:11–13, in which Jesus states that Elijah has come, and with Matthew 11:14 in which Jesus identifies John the Baptist with Elijah. Could it be, therefore, that the final warning has been given and that now in the coming and second coming of Jesus Christ the Day of the Lord is upon us? By using the cross-reference, which allows the Scriptures to interpret the Scriptures, meanings are clarified and the content of the sermon is filled out.

Similarly with the use of a concordance, key words in a text can be enlarged upon. For example, Jeremiah 2:13 speaks of God as "the fountain of living waters." The phrase "living waters" cannot be found in a concordance, but "living" can be and under that heading is listed Psalm 42:2: "My soul thirsts for God, / for the living God" (RSV). This suggests immediately a sermon on our thirst for God, in the context of Jeremiah 2:4–13. Or under "living" in the concordance, we find the phrase, "living water[s]," occurring in Jeremiah 17:13; Zechariah 14:8; John 4:10; 7:38; and Revelation 7:17. The connection of the Jeremiah text with John 4:10 and 7:38 is immediately suggested: Jesus Christ has become the fountain of living waters, who will satisfy all our thirst and give us eternal life, over against our desperate situation pictured in Jeremiah 2:4–13.

Texts set in the context of the canon as a whole by these devices almost always expand their own meanings, so that the preacher need not want for additional content to the sermon.

The second conversation into which any text should be set is that of conversation with the congregation, and this becomes enormously important in enlarging the content of a sermon. The sermon is not being preached to people devoid of presuppositions, thoughts, and feelings; the text is encountering living situations in the lives of the listening people, and all of those situations play a part in how the people will receive the text. The preacher, therefore, is the meeting point between the text and the congregation, and the preacher should never listen to a text simply for himself or herself alone. Rather, the preacher should listen to the text on behalf of the congregation.

This "priestly listening"[1] prompts many questions that should then be asked of the text. Among the major points that the text has set forth, are there those that the congregation will doubt are true? If so, the sermon may have to deal with those doubts. Is the text's view of God and the world radically different from the views held by the congregation? If so, the sermon may have to discuss those differences and overcome them. Indeed, a useful device in enlarging the thought of the sermon is to contrast the text's views with those of the congregation's secular world.

One caution is necessary here, however. Some preachers dwell so long on the sinful world's views and actions that they then give scant time to the message of the biblical text. It is easy to tell what is wrong and sinful in our society; it is much harder to tell at length just what God is doing about it. But the actions and purposes of God, revealed through the text, should form the major content of the sermon, and it is this concentration on God that distinguishes great biblical preaching from mediocre run-of-the-mill sermons.

The preacher may ask other questions of the text. With what characters in the text does the congregation identify? Only with the faithful? Should they, therefore, be led to see that they (along with the preacher) are among the unfaithful instead?

Are there attitudes, thoughts, and feelings portrayed in the text that remind the congregation of themselves, and so can those form the congregation's entrance into understanding the text?

Are there historical situations or theological terms in the text that need to be clarified? Most congregations are woefully ignorant of the historical setting of any text in the Bible, and sometimes that setting needs to be explained. Similarly, few congregations know the biblical meaning of common theological terms such as "redemption" or "grace" or "blessing," and often a preacher will have to explain the meaning of such terms or use synonyms that clarify their meaning. One of the great failures of the pulpit in the last fifty years has been to educate congregations, and thus erudite teaching from the pulpit has become a pressing necessity in our time. Sermons should not take on the form of lectures, and often meanings and historical contexts can be set forth in a sentence or two. But there should also be much greater utilization of biblical stories as the illustration of meanings. Modern congregations have heard that God is love; they have a pressing need to hear the stories of the exodus and wilderness wanderings as examples that spell out the nature of that love.

A preacher may ask the question, "If this text is true, what are the implications for me and my congregation?" Or the opposite may be asked: "If this text were not true, what would that mean for our lives?" Sometimes the importance of God's words and actions revealed in a text can be emphasized by spelling out what our lives would be like without them. What would it mean for us if God had never called Abraham, for instance? Or what kind of God would we worship if he had never sent Israel into exile? Meditations on questions such as these, and indeed on all of the questions we have raised, can furnish a preacher with profound sermon material.

Outlining the Sermon

After a preacher has decided on all of the major points from the text to be used in the sermon, has paired the OT text with one from the NT, and has listened to all of the points from the texts in conversation with the canon and the congregation, the task becomes one of outlining the sermon in full, either on paper or in his or her mind.

A number of contemporary homileticians object to sermon outlining, because they believe that it leads to static sermons or to sermons divorced from the texts themselves. And there is no doubt that such has been the case in the past history of preaching in this country. We would do well to burn all of the books and periodicals containing suggested sermon outlines for preachers; their only contribution has been to prevent preachers from wrestling with the biblical texts for themselves and their congregations.

If, however, a preacher has worked diligently with the biblical text(s), as we have suggested above, there is no substitute for clarifying in his or her own mind the whole course that the sermon is going to follow, before the preacher ever starts to write. By outlining the entire sermon, the preacher can have a clear idea of where the sermon is going, what its function is, and how its separate points hold together, without repetition of its points and with a steady movement forward toward the climax. Otherwise, preachers are far too prone to begin writing with only an initial opening and perhaps the first point in mind. They then often find themselves uncertain as to how to proceed, because they are not clear about what they really want to say in the sermon. Or they repeat the same point over and over, because they have not developed the sermon in their own minds. Or the sermon drives forward toward no climax and ends in a confusing mishmash of several unrelated topics. Sermon construction is an art, and only the clearest and most comprehensive initial thought on the preacher's part will master the art.

In constructing the sermon outline, major points are set down first. Introduction and conclusion are then added. The introduction may start with the text or it may start with some situation in the congregation's life, but it is intended to introduce the subject at hand and to awaken immediate congregational interest. If the congregation hears nothing that concerns it in the introduction, the preacher will have lost the listeners. Or if the introduction has no relation to what follows, the congregation will be confused from the start. The major weakness of most introductions, however, is that they are too long. Rarely should an introduction occupy more than two-thirds of a page of sermon manuscript. The preacher should introduce the topic at hand and then immediately get on with it.

Conclusions may sum up the thought of the entire sermon or they may drive home the main message. They should call forth the desired response on the part of the congregation. And they should always be in a positive, not a negative, form. It is not very helpful to leave a congregation with a question or with an indecisive conclusion. The gospel message should be affirmed, so that the congregation wants to respond to it—by renewed faith, by repentance, by praise, by determination to undertake some action, by whatever response the sermon is designed to prompt. Above all, the conclusion should not introduce a new biblical text or a new point not previously discussed in the sermon. This latter is probably the most common error heard in sermon conclusions. The task is to conclude, in a convincing manner, the message that has been proclaimed. Introducing a new point or a new biblical quotation is like starting all over again.

Writing the Sermon Manuscript

If the sermon outline has been fully and carefully constructed, the task of writing out the sermon manuscript is incomparably easier, but the sermon should be written out in full. Many preachers are tempted to let the outline suffice and to preach from that, and some preachers can do so very well. However, most preachers who write only an outline say things on Sunday morning that they did not intend to say, they use language that is not very powerful or artful, and they usually become distracted from worshiping with the congregation because they are thinking about the sermon content. Fully written manuscripts help eliminate all of these tendencies. To be sure, when the sermon is actually preached, the preacher may take into the pulpit only the outline or brief notes—although there is nothing wrong with having the whole manuscript at hand. But by writing out the sermon in full, everything has been thought through carefully. Language has been shaped to the best of the preacher's ability; appropriate illustrations have been inserted at proper points; the whole has been constructed to move forward steadily toward the desired conclusion and response. The preacher is then free to worship with the congregation and to offer up the sermon to God to be used to God's glory and for his purpose.

When writing the sermon manuscript, the preacher should speak it aloud to him or herself, so that the sermon is an oral and not a written presentation. The rhythm and pace of spoken language are different from those of written prose, and only if the preacher writes oral prose is it going to be actually directed to the congregation.

Preachers also need to keep in mind that preaching is direct address to a gathered people. It is not the learned discussion of some subject or the private meditation of the homiletician. It is addressed to the people, concerning their lives, dealing with their thoughts and feelings, leading them through an experience of the immediate action of the living God. Indeed, preaching is not even talking about some biblical text. It is the text speaking to both the people and the minister, bringing its word of judgment or salvation, comfort or discomfort, strengthening or questioning, forgiveness or condemnation into the minds of God's people and writing that Word on their hearts and transforming them to accord with the Word spoken. Preaching is the act of the living and present God in the lives of his gathered people on any given day or Sunday. If it is effective, that is God's doing; the preacher is his servant—as Paul says, we are "stewards of the mysteries of God," stewards of those mysteries now handed down to us in the Holy Scriptures. And above all else, "it is required of stewards that they be found trustworthy" (1 Cor 4:1–2, RSV).

NOTE

1. L. Keck, *The Bible in the Pulpit: The Renewal of Biblical Preaching* (Nashville: Abingdon, 1978) 53–68.

3

THE IMPORTANCE OF A UNITY
OF THE BIBLE

Daniel P. Fuller

Increasingly of late there has been a call for seminaries to modify their teaching of the theoretical disciplines in order to provide a more solid basis for the practice to be carried out in the churches. As James Smart, formerly professor of biblical interpretation at Union Seminary, New York City, has said,

> Consistently for years there has been an underestimating of the distance between these two contexts [seminary and church] in which the Bible is interpreted, as though it were a very short and easy step the seminary graduate has to take from one to the other . . . . Scholars and churchmen must come awake to the fact that some of the most capable students have not been making that journey very successfully from school to church, from fact to faith, from historical record to sermon text, from cultural artifact to Christian revelation.[1]

As Smart saw it, the basic problem was how seminaries should handle biblical theology, because this discipline underlies the systematic theology on which church practice is based. "There are unsolved problems of methodology and understanding that must be faced and worked through if that future [for biblical theology] is to be a healthy and fruitful one . . . . The problems are gigantic. The literature is enormous."[2]

So, for Smart if the step from seminary to church was to become easier, biblical scholars would have to tackle afresh these unsolved problems. But no less daunting is the flood of literature on biblical exegesis that is continually pouring forth in English, French, and German. Most biblical studies professors can only stay on top of the literature for their specialty, e.g., the Pentateuch, prophets, or the synoptic Gospels. Some super-achievers, however, can also keep abreast of major happenings in one or two adjacent fields. George Ladd, for example, is cited with high approval by Smart as one who had read well enough "to make a significant contribution in . . . the mainstream of twentieth-century theological discussion," which he did by writing a biblical theology on the whole New Testament.[3]

In doing this Ladd implied that there was a basic unity in the NT writings. This pleased Smart because a unified NT would make it easier to take the step from the biblical interpretation of the seminaries to that of the churches. Presumably, Smart would have liked to see a biblical theology that would also have embraced OT theology, for this would have eased the step even more. Many reviewers of Ladd's book, however, criticized him for implying the unity of the NT, for critical scholarship was stressing apparent diversity even within single books of the NT. So the outcry against a biblical theology of both testaments would be far greater, even though the churches have such a great need for it. Only a few professors like James Smart, whose academic title sanctioned him to work in both testaments, would even consider the task. Yet such might well never even consider it, given the immense task of reading all that is constantly being published on all parts of the Bible.

Richard Muller, my former colleague and now professor of historical theology at Calvin Seminary in Grand Rapids, shares Smart's concern for the training of tomorrow's ministers. Muller believes that all ministry in the church must be based on systematic theology. "If seminary study is to have any coherence and if it is to issue forth in a coherent ministry, theology must make sense as a whole."[4] Like Smart, Muller believes the major problem is how the exegesis leading to biblical theology is to be handled. He believes there must be recourse to more than the historical-critical method typical of modern biblical studies in interpreting the text:

> What presently stands in the way of a unified approach to theological study . . . is the modern critical approach to the text of Scripture. Inasmuch as modern critical methods focus primarily on the meaning of

the text in its ancient historical situation, they can create barriers . . .
to the attempt to draw text and interpreter together and to bring the
ancient meaning to bear, with contemporary significance, on the
present situation.[5]

To offer some help in solving this problem, Muller recommends that
seminaries supplement the historical-critical method in biblical exegesis
with a consideration of the exegesis of the church in earlier centuries.
For example, in texts such as Matthew 11:27, where Jesus refers to himself as God's Son, some modern exegetes who do not take historical dogmatics into account understand this to mean Jesus' experience in his
humanity of "filial" relationship to God. But "the doctrine of the Trinity
[set forth in the early church] . . . provides a solution to the theological
difficulties [for such an understanding of Jesus] in such texts as the prologue to John or the various Pauline texts indicating Christ's heavenly
preexistence and divinity."[6] In other words, being aware of how the Church
practiced exegesis in earlier times will broaden the modern exegete's
horizon as to the possibilities of a text's meaning.

As a Biblical Studies scholar I welcome this suggestion. Naturally much
more must be said fully to address the problem about which Muller speaks.
For example, there must be a hermeneutic that reins in Biblical Studies'
excessive fascination with seeing evidence as supporting diversity and thus
fragmentizing the text. And any leads for developing a unity of the Bible—
an entire biblical theology—should be followed, for this would help the
Bible win back control in carrying out the churches' ministry tasks. This
article proposes some steps toward achieving these *desiderata*. Its thesis is
that the Bible's unity is found in the goal intended by the sequence and
climax of its redemptive events.

Locating the Bible's Unity in Redemptive History

In no other literature besides the Bible do some forty authors or editors, writing in a period of over a thousand years, in places and cultures
as widely separated as Rome and Babylon, succeed in developing a body
of literature that even at a first inspection gives an indication of being a
unity. Early in this century an OT scholar contrasted the Bible with the
scriptures of some other religions as follows:

The Koran, for instance, is a miscellany of disjointed pieces, out of
which it is impossible to extract any order, progress, or arrangement.

> The 114 Suras or chapters of which it is composed are arranged chiefly according to length—the longer in general preceding the shorter. It is not otherwise with the Zoroastrian and Buddhist scriptures. These are equally destitute of beginning, middle or end. They are for the most part heterogeneous materials, loosely placed together. How different everyone must acknowledge it to be with the Bible! From Genesis to Revelation we feel that this book is in a real sense a unity. It is not a collection of fragments but has, as we say, an organic character. It has one connected story to tell from beginning to end; we see something growing before our eyes; there is plan, purpose, progress; the end folds back on the beginning, and, when the whole is finished, we feel that there again, as in primal creation, God has finished all his works, and behold, they are very good.[7]

More detailed evidence that the Bible is a unity based on a redemptive history comes from a careful scrutiny of its contents. To begin with there is in most biblical books a great anticipation of the blessings God will bring to pass in the future. In Numbers 14:21 and Habakkuk 2:14, for example, God promises that one day "the earth will be filled with the knowledge of the glory of the Lord" (rsv). To know and experience God in his glory or praiseworthiness—this is the climactic point toward which the Bible points. Thus, the psalmist expressed his great desire as follows: "One thing have I asked of the Lord, / that will I seek after; / that I may dwell in the house of the Lord / all the days of my life, / to behold the beauty of the Lord, / and to inquire in his temple" (Ps 27:4, rsv). To see God is also the blessing promised to the pure of heart in the sixth beatitude (Matt 5:8). Similarly, God's final blessing for his people comes when "[he] himself will be with them" (Rev 21:3, rsv).

Standing in the way of the enjoyment of this blessedness, however, is the curse God has put on humankind because of their sin in worshiping the creature rather than the creator. The Bible, therefore, spells out the way in which God works progressively to deliver people from sin and its curse. Oscar Cullmann, the foremost recent advocate for understanding the Bible as a redemptive history, has said that "sin, apart from which all salvation history is totally unintelligible, stands at the beginning of salvation history and determines its further development."[8] And it is the steps by which God overcomes the problem of sin that make the Bible's history a redemptive history.

Thus, soon after Adam and Eve had succumbed to temptation, God gave them the heartening promise that someday righteousness would triumph over sin and its consequent miseries (Gen 3:15). And when Noah was born, it was revealed to his father Lamech that his son would play a specific role in God's work of delivering the world from evil (Gen 5:29). Then, as Noah and his family were starting out anew after the flood, God gave them the so-called power of the sword (Gen 9:6–7). This was indispensable for administering justice and suppressing the evil that had previously been unchecked and would have destroyed the human race.

But why had God allowed sin to become so rampant? Why did he not give the power of the sword sooner so as to avert the flood and the necessity for Noah's sons to begin anew in carrying out the creator's command to "be fruitful and multiply, and fill the earth"? (Gen 9:1, RSV; cf. 1:28). In answer Gerhardus Vos proposed that God's purpose in so acting was

> to bring out the consequences of sin when left so far as possible to itself. Had God permitted grace freely to flow out into the world and to gather great strength within a short period, then the true nature and consequences of sin would have been imperfectly disclosed. Man would have ascribed to his own relative goodness what was in reality a product of the grace of God. Hence, before the work of redemption is further carried out, the downward tendency of sin is clearly illustrated, in order that subsequently in the light of this downgrade movement the true divine cause of the upward course of redemption might be appreciated.[9]

Thus, by stretching out redemptive history to allow violence to fill the earth after the Fall, God ensured that the tremendous potency of sin would be unmistakably recognized. As people see this destructive force revealed with such clarity, they appreciate more fully what God has done in beginning to suppress it by giving Noah's sons "the power of the sword."

What happens at Genesis 12 also stretches out the span of time involved in redemptive history because, as will be seen, this "delay" helps people to appreciate God's glory more fully. Instead of evangelizing the many peoples of earth at Genesis 12, God now singles out Abraham from one of these nations and proceeds to build a new people from his posterity alone. God thus continues to work almost exclusively with this new people until Jesus commands his Jewish disciples to take the gospel to all the peoples of earth (Matt 28:18–20). Why had God "allowed all the nations to walk in their own ways" (Acts 14:16, RSV) in the meantime—about two millennia? Romans 9:6–11:32 helps answer this question by outlining redemptive history from the patriarchs in Genesis (Rom 9:6–13) down to the full conversion of ethnic Israel at Jesus' second coming (11:25–26).

The beginning of this answer lies in the fact that most of Abraham's physical descendants through Jacob are not "the children of God" (Rom 9:8). Only a small remnant of ethnic Israel—7,000 in the days of Elijah, for example—is "chosen by grace" (Rom. 11:5). According to Romans 11:25–26, "a hardening has come upon part of Israel, until the full number of the Gentiles come in, and so [then] all Israel will be saved; as it is written, 'The Deliverer will come from Zion, / he will banish ungodliness from Jacob'" (RSV). In the meantime the great majority of Israel glory in their distinctives as Jews and in their possession of the law (Rom 2:17–23). Consequently, they fail to submit to God's righteousness (Rom 10:3) in two ways. First, they regard his commandments not as a law of faith, like a doctor's prescription, but as a law of works—a job description (Rom 9:32a)—although God is not "served by human hands, as though he needed anything" (Acts 17:25, RSV). Second, they have "stumbled over the stumbling stone" (Rom 9:32b, RSV), which is Jesus Christ at his first coming. There is no conjunction introducing 9:32b—an asyndeton—and this emphasizes the connectedness between these two failures.

The OT itself teaches that most of Israel will be rebellious against God for a large segment of her future history. According to Numbers 14:20–24, Israel in Moses' day lacked Caleb's "different spirit" (v. 24) and Joshua's "Holy Spirit" (27:18). As a result they joined with the ten unbelieving spies sent to the promised land and refused to enter it. Elsewhere, the OT clearly teaches that Israel as a whole remains unregenerated until the last part of redemptive history (Deut 30:6; Jer 31:31–34; Ezek 36:22–28; 37:14). And Leviticus 26:40–45 affirms that it was because of Israel's "uncircumcised heart" that she was to be banished to other lands. Nevertheless, God will remember his covenant with the Israelites to return them to their land "when their uncircumcised heart is humbled" (RSV). So the foundational understanding of Romans 9:6–11:32 that Israel is unregenerate until the distant future is clearly taught in the OT as well. Thus, there is no necessity to interpret the OT in the light of the NT in regard to Israel's continued hardness of heart—a fact that has much significance for constructing a unity of the Bible.

Another element establishing this unity between the testaments is Romans 9:32, where Israel's rejection of the law as a law of faith is equated with her rejection of Jesus. This means that the NT regards the teaching of justification by a faith that works in love (Gal 5:6) as a continuation of the message God was giving Israel from the beginning. In Exodus 20:6, for example—right in the middle of the Decalogue—God declares that he shows ". . . [*hesed*] to thousands of those who love me and keep my commandments" (RSV). One scholar speaks of *hesed* "as bestowing mercy and cordiality beyond what is expected."[10] So the English word *mercy* comes close to the meaning of the Hebrew. From everyday life we know that, although it is never merited or earned, mercy is conditional. It is an act of mercy for a head of state to pardon a criminal. But the criminal has to accept this pardon in order to benefit from it, and this is difficult, for it is an implicit admission of guilt. That is why John Ehrlichmann, one of the conspirators in the Watergate scandal of the 1970s, refused a pardon. "In accepting a pardon I would be admitting guilt," he explained.[11] Thus, Exodus 20:5 declares that as the condition for enjoying God's mercy, people must love God and keep his commandments out of an obedience of faith. (This obedience could not be that of works, for mercy is never earned.) So the condition for receiving mercy—the obedience of faith— is the same for both testaments.[12]

To understand the obedience of faith as the condition for receiving the blessings of God's mercy is to move a step closer to grasping why God prolonged redemptive history by working just with Israel and allowing the Gentile nations to go their own ways from Genesis 12 until after Jesus' ascension. And one can also see why, in God's plan, most of Israel contin- ues to reject God's righteousness and will do so until Christ's second com- ing. Romans 11:17–24 gives the perspective for understanding this elon- gation of redemptive history. In this passage Paul likens ethnic Israel to a cultivated olive tree and pictures Israel's unbelief in refusing to submit to God's righteousness as the cause for so many Jewish branches being torn from the tree to wither on the ground. These withered branches repre- sent God's punishments against Israel's unbelief, consisting first in her tumultuous history in the land, continued in her subjugation to other nations, and climaxing in her banishment from Jerusalem to live as for- eigners among Gentile nations, where many Israelites have suffered greatly over the centuries.

And these punishments are to be a lesson for Gentile believers, who are represented as wild olive branches grafted into the cultivated olive tree in place of Israel. Far from feeling smug and superior, these Gen- tiles are to view the withered Israelite branches as an example of how God punishes unbelief. They are to realize that "[Israelite branches] were broken off because of their unbelief, but you [Gentile branches] stand fast only through faith. So do not become proud but [fear]. For if God did not spare the natural branches, neither will he spare you" (Rom 11:20– 21, RSV). They are to fear the unbelief of not remaining in God's kind- ness by resting in his "precious and very great promises" (2 Pet 1:4, RSV), which then removes fear. Thus, because of God's punishments against Israel the Gentiles are brought to realize how important it is for them to humble themselves and commit their lives to God's grace.

The NT is not alone in this teaching. The OT also declares that God's punishments against Israel for failure to comply with the law of faith are for the instruction of the Gentiles. "I have set [Israel] in the center of the nations, with countries round about her. And she has wickedly rebelled against my ordinances . . . I will execute judgments in the midst of you in the sight of the nations . . . and any of you who survive I will scatter to all the winds. . . . You [Israel] shall be . . . a warning . . . to the nations round about you, when I execute judgments on you, in anger and fury. . . . " (Ezek 5:5–6, 8, 10, 15, RSV; cf. Deut 29:22–28; 2 Chr 7:19–22; Jer 22:8–9).

The Romans 9:6–11:32 passage also teaches that all ethnic Israel will be saved near the end of redemptive history. After "the full number of the Gentiles [is] come in . . . [then] all [ethnic] Israel will be saved" (Rom 11:25–26, RSV). The OT likewise teaches Israel's conversion in the distant future. Several passages speak of ethnic Israel's receiving "a new heart" at some time after she has been scattered among the nations (Deut 30:6; Jer 31:31–34; Ezek 36:22–28; Lev 26:40–45). So in Romans 11:32 Paul sums up his sketch of redemptive history by saying, "God has consigned all men [Jews and Gentiles] to disobedience, that he may have mercy upon all [Gentiles and then Jews]" (Rom 11:32, RSV).

Romans 9–11, of course, sets forth only some of the crucial aspects in redemptive history. Other important aspects are in the primal history of Genesis 1–11, in the cultic worship of Israel, in the sign of the covenant, and in the theme of the kingdom of God, which first becomes emphatic with the inauguration of the Davidic covenant (2 Sam 7:8–15). More prominent in the NT than the covenant theme is the "kingdom of God," although these two key themes appear in both testaments and are complementary ways of representing God's saving action in redemptive history.

The subject of redemptive history finds a place in most biblical books. In some of the OT wisdom literature, however, there is no explicit reference to it. The purpose of a book like Proverbs, for example, is to codify the nature of life and wise living that so often can be inferred simply from everyday events. Ordinary experience alone shows, for example, that a soft answer is best suited to cool down another's anger (Prov 15:1). And since such wisdom is universal, it is not surprising that Arabian and Egyptian proverbs too appear in Proverbs. As F. F. Bruce has observed, this happens because "wisdom, in short, is a gift with which the Creator has endowed [all] mankind."[13]

Proverbs also teaches, however, that "the fear of man lays a snare, / but he who trusts in the LORD is safe" (Prov 29:25, RSV). To affirm that safety for the unknown future belongs to those trusting God requires divine revelation. Likewise, there has to be revelation for Job to say, after losing wealth and health, "The LORD gave, and the LORD has taken away; [but] blessed be the name of the LORD" (Job 1:21, RSV). In order to affirm that one will go on enjoying great blessings from God alone, one has to know more than can be inferred from this visible world. Such revelatory teachings regarding the future cohere with those of other biblical books that affirm that God is working in the world to manifest his glory. So while these books do not specifically allude to redemptive history, they are nevertheless at home with books that do.

The Historicity of Redemptive Events

If the sequence of events in the Bible's redemptive history is to be made the framework for a unity of the Bible, however, something will have to be said about the historicity of these events. In fact, as Oscar Cullmann sees it, no effort should be spared in getting back to a redemptive event's historicity. He has said, for example, "If I project my inquiry concerning the origin of the oral Gospel tradition behind the time of the Gospel writer, I come up against the events of Easter. However these events are to be evaluated, I must make an effort to explore them historically if I am ultimately to trace the origin of the oral tradition back to them."[14] And Cullmann believes that the facts surrounding Jesus' resurrection—the empty tomb and the appearances—are indeed "open to historical investigation."[15] "The [actual] occurrence of Jesus' resurrection, which is not itself accessible to historical investigation, and is not itself described in the Gospels, is linked with facts at least theoretically provable within the historical framework—the resurrection appearances and the empty tomb."[16] So Cullmann affirms the actual bodily resurrection of Jesus himself not because anyone had direct knowledge of this event itself but because it is necessarily linked with events potentially capable of historical verification.

He, therefore, affirms the historicity of the center of redemptive history—the bodily resurrection of Jesus—by working inward from the controllable outside ring of the redemptive events of the empty tomb and the resurrection appearances. But Cullmann also goes in the opposite direction from this outside ring and affirms the historicity of redemptive events both back to creation and forward to future ones. "Within the Bible, an essential item of all salvation history is the fact that the revelation of saving events and *how they are linked together* in the divine plan was disclosed to definite witnesses."[17] Furthermore, "It is an unrelinquishable

NT conviction that things inaccessible to empirical investigation really happen in that province which corresponds with historically verifiable events."[18] So, for example,

> the creation story . . . still assumes a quite different character [from the timeless mythologies from which it was derived]. As a result of its association with the historical [historisch]—i.e., historically controllable] central portion, which is at the same time significant for the whole saving process . . . the account of creation now fulfills the function of indicating the solidarity of creation with man and its tie to salvation history which comes to pass because of human sin.[19]

Cullmann also clearly affirms the historicity of the Fall somewhere back in time. "Even though we stress the non-historical [nichthistorisch] account of the first man's sin we still maintain all the more firmly that this story offers a revelation just as the historical [historisch] events of the Bible do. It is not revelation about the sinful situation of man, but revelation about an original event in which man resisted his divinely appointed destiny."[20] For Cullmann, however, it is not necessary to insist on a one-to-one correspondence between the biblical narrative and what really happened. As to the destruction of Pharaoh's chariots in the Red Sea, he says, for example, "Even if research comes to the conclusion that in this case the historical core was nothing more than the destruction of a band of chariots, this event is not irrelevant as one of the causes of the kerygma which has effects that extend right into the NT."[21]

So, in this manner Cullmann insists on the "event-character" for each happening in the sequence of redemptive history, and affirms that "the sequence of events must be allowed to stand."[22] Following this lead one is able to draw significance from the chronology of Genesis 5. We know that its time span back to the origin of human sin fits in with the general understanding of the original readers and of pre-scientific humanity up until a century or so ago. The recent findings of paleontology, however, have caused us moderns to regard the origin of human sinfulness as much earlier than that chronology would permit. But in following Cullmann one would say that the function of Genesis 5 in putting an interval between the Fall and the flood is as operative in the scientific as it was in the pre-scientific era. What is important is not the amount of time it took evil to show its terrible power and awfulness, but that there was a sufficient interval for evil to reach its apex.

Implications for Today

The foregoing material sketches in some essentials for an exegetical procedure capable of yielding a system of biblical theology, an essential foundation for the practice of ministry. It has indicated how to tackle some of the "gigantic problems" of exegesis, for example, how grace is conditional but not earned, and how to establish the historicity of the Bible's redemptive events.

But how can biblical studies handle the great torrent of expository literature that pours out continuously in at least three languages? The answer is that most biblical studies professors should continue to be specialists in various parts of the Bible. But should not each seminary also have a biblical studies professor like James Smart, with a title like "professor of biblical interpretation," that sanctions him or her to grapple with the interpretation of the whole Bible? Such a professor would seek help from his or her specialist colleagues to keep aware of important developments with regard to the Pentateuch, the Johannine writings, and so on. But that professor's distinctive task would be to work with a biblical book's literary units to see if they might not meld naturally into a "whole" or unity.

Assuming such a hermeneutical stance would provide a counterpoise to the fragmentizing mood characterizing much of biblical studies today. Thus an interpreter would be disinclined to try to go behind the material of the final redactor now explicit in the biblical text. Nor is this preference contrary to the historical-critical method. To the contrary, much endless speculation could be avoided by this preference, and it is well to remember von Rad's statement, agreeing with the Jewish dictum, that "basically we are dependent only on [the redactor of the Hexateuch], on his great work of theology, as we receive the Hexateuch at all only from his hands."[23]

Great care, of course, must be exercised to honor the intentional meanings of various authors and redactors in their various life situations. But great care must also be exercised not to agree too quickly that what seems contradictory in separate authors really does fail to cohere. In the introduction to his 1522 edition of the NT, Luther declared that James was an epistle of straw for saying that "A man is justified by works and not by faith alone" (James 2:24), whereas Paul said "A man is justified by faith apart from the works of the law" (Rom 3:28). But the interpreter concerned with the unity of the Bible will want to weigh the possibility that Paul's term "works of the law" represented a complete violation of the law's demands rather than an attempt to comply with them.[24] If this possibility proves correct, then Romans 3:28 would not be excluding obedience to the moral law from faith. Neither would it be in conflict with James 2:24, especially when Paul himself said that "faith working [itself out] through love [is everything]" (Gal 5:6).

Analogy-of-faith hermeneutics has long been teaching that the way to receive God's forgiveness is found basically in Paul and John and only obscurely in James and the Synoptic Gospels, though such a procedure is manifestly arbitrary. But if it can be shown that the teachings of each of the canonical books makes its distinctive contribution to the others in a natural way, then the concept of the unity of the Bible would have integrity. And this would greatly facilitate the step from the biblical interpretation of the seminary to that of the churches.

NOTES

1. J. Smart, *The Past, Present, and Future of Biblical Theology* (Philadelphia: Westminster, 1979) 94–95.
2. Smart, ibid., 156–57.
3. Smart, ibid., 155, citing G. E. Ladd, *A Theology of the New Testament* (Grand Rapids: Eerdmans, 1974).
4. R. Muller, *The Study of Theology* (Grand Rapids: Zondervan, 1991) xii.
5. Muller, ibid., 35.
6. Muller, ibid., 135–36.
7. J. Orr, *The Problem of the Old Testament* (London: James Nisbet, 1907) 31–32.
8. O. Cullmann, *Salvation in History* (New York: Harper and Row, 1965) 311. He also said (292), "An outline of a dogmatics or ethics of a redemptive history ought to be written someday."
9. G. Vos, *Biblical Theology* (Grand Rapids: Eerdmans, 1948) 56.
10. H. Stoebe, *"hesed," THAT* 1:614.
11. J. Ehrlichman, *Witness to Power* (New York: Simon and Schuster, 1982) 410.
12. For a more detailed consideration of "the obedience of faith" see my *Gospel and Law* (Grand Rapids: Eerdmans, 1980) 65–120, 199–204, and *The Unity of the Bible* (Grand Rapids: Zondervan, 1992) chs. 17–21 and the Appendix.
13. F. F. Bruce, "Theology and Interpretation," in *Tradition and Interpretation*, ed. G. W. Anderson (Oxford: Clarendon, 1979) 404.
14. Cullmann, *Salvation in History*, 94.
15. Ibid., 139.
16. Ibid., 143.
17. Ibid., 114 (italics added).
18. Ibid., 143.
19. Ibid., 144.
20. Ibid., 145.

21. Cullman, *Salvation in History,* 95.
22. O. Cullmann, "The Connection of Primal Events and End Events with the New Testament Redemptive History," in *The Old Testament and Christian Faith* (New York: Harper and Row, 1963) 123.
23. G. von Rad, *Genesis* (Philadelphia: Westminster, 1961) 41.
24. D. P. Fuller, *The Unity of the Bible* (Grand Rapids: Zondervan, 1992) 471–478.

II
THE OLD TESTAMENT

The Torah

4

IMAGES OF YAHWEH: GOD IN THE PENTATEUCH

David J. A. Clines

Preliminaries

There are three kinds of data we could use in constructing a picture of God in the Pentateuch. The first is what the character God says about himself. To some readers it might seem a very reliable type of information, for here it might appear that it is God himself who is talking about himself. But we need to realize that when the narrative says for example, "The LORD ... proclaimed, 'The LORD, the LORD, a God merciful and gracious, slow to anger, and abounding in steadfast love and faithfulness'" (Exod 34:6, NRSV), this self-description does not consist of the words of God himself (what language does *he* speak?) but of the words of the narrator (in Hebrew). These are no more than words put in the mouth of the character God by the narrator. Such sentences of self-description contribute to our overall picture of the character God, of course, but the words in the mouth of God have no privileged status compared with words spoken directly by the narrator in describing God's motives and actions.

Perhaps the second kind of data—what the narrator says about God—will be more useful. They will at least be words to which the narrator is committing himself, being his own words, and not words he is ascribing to one of his characters. Of course, one cannot always safely assume that the narrator is reliable even in biblical texts, for he is sometimes ironical and, in that respect at least, not a safe guide to the reliability of his words. But assuming that the narrator is a reliable one, we can take it that the descriptions the narrator gives us of the character God are material for our construction of a picture of God in the Pentateuch.

The only problem here is that there are not many such descriptions of God on the part of the narrator. We learn from the narrator in Genesis 6:6 that the Lord was "sorry that he had made man on the earth, and it grieved him to his heart," and we find in Exodus 24:17 that "the appearance of the glory of the LORD was like a devouring fire" (NRSV). But there are very few sentences like these, describing his appearance, his feelings, his character, in the whole of the Pentateuch. We could hardly construct a very rounded picture of God on the basis of what the narrator tells us directly and descriptively about him.

The third kind of data is the account of what God does and says throughout the narrative. Here we have a much more plentiful source of knowledge about the figure of God in the Pentateuch. The problem with this source, however, is that its significance for the picture of God is at times far from clear. It is a risky business even in everyday life to make inferences from a person's actions to their character; but in everyday life we usually have the possibility of cross-checking our provisional conclusions with the person himself or herself, of approaching other people for other points of view, and of seeing many repeated or similar actions. In the case of the character God, as of characters everywhere, all these possibilities are foreclosed to us. If we are to consider the character "God in the Pentateuch" we shall be shut up to the evidence that the Pentateuch provides. We shall not be thinking about a real "person," and we shall not be able to check our evidence from the Pentateuch with other evidence. The picture that results will be at times tantalizingly ambiguous, and there will be tensions and incompatibilities in it that cannot be thoroughly resolved. It is simply impossible, for example, to say why it is that the character God does not allow Moses into the promised land,[1] or indeed what most of the motives and intentions of the character are.

As a result, the thrust of the present essay must not be toward developing some unified and coherent portrait of the God depicted in the Pentateuch, but toward bringing to the surface some of the materials, contrasting and inconclusive though they may be, that contribute to the portraiture.

The Pentateuch as a Novel

Let us think of the Pentateuch as a novel.[2] Not that it is a work of fantasy, and not that it must be declared "untrue" if it does not at every point report historical actuality with the utmost fidelity. Like *War and Peace* and *Adam Bede*, the Pentateuch has its own truth and its own credibility even when it recounts events some people may not think actually happened, like a snake talking or a universal flood. Like a novel, it reports the inner thoughts of its characters, which no one else could ever have heard, and it recounts the dialogue of persons whose actual words had been long since forgotten when the author was writing. Like a novel, it transports its readers through space and time, makes them witnesses to the behaviors and changing motivations of its characters, and, on the whole, avoids the didactic and the dogmatic, insisting that its readers judge for themselves the persons and the acts they encounter in its pages.

Above all, the Pentateuch is a novel in that it is a machine for generating interpretations, to use Umberto Eco's phrase. There are so many complex strands in it, so many fragmentary glimpses of its personalities, that we cannot reduce it to a single coherent graspable unity that all readers will agree upon.[3] This chapter will, therefore, do no more than develop some possible readings of the Pentateuch. And these variant readings will not be just the result of the willful imposition of readers' prejudices upon the text, for, like all texts, the Torah must, as Rabbi Ben Bag Bag long ago said it did, have all its interpretations enshrined within it: "Turn it and turn it again, for everything is in it."[4]

God as a Character

Let us next think of the God in the Pentateuch as a character in a novel. God in the Pentateuch is not a "person"; he is a character in a book. And there are no people in books, no real people; for books are made, not procreated. Even when the characters have the same name as real people and remind us vividly of the real people whose names they bear, they are still made of paper. Even if I should write my autobiography, the readers of my book will not be encountering me, but only the fictive character I have chosen to create in my writing.[5]

The point, obvious though it is, is worth making in this connection if we are to speak honestly about the God in the Pentateuch. For if we were to imagine that the God of whom it speaks so extensively is identical with the "true God"—the God who is worshiped and theologized about—we might have some serious theological problems on our hands, and at the very least we should be tempted to modulate what we read in the text of the Pentateuch in order to harmonize it with what we already believe we know of the "true God." No doubt there is a serious question here, namely what the relation is between the God who is a character in the book and the "real God," but we cannot begin to address it until we have systematically made a distinction between the two. How else could we approach the issue of their relationship?

Reading With and Against the Grain

Most readers of the Pentateuch, especially the Jewish and Christian communities, approve of the story the Pentateuch tells. They think it was a good idea to create the world, to destroy it with a flood, to choose one family and nation as the principal object of divine blessing, and to give them the land of Canaan as their homeland. They are in general sympathetic to the Hebrew people, and tend to believe that what was good for the Hebrews is what should have happened. In short, most readers of the Pentateuch have subscribed to the ideology of the text; they have read with the grain of the text.[6]

But it is not difficult to think how differently the narrative could sound if one read against the grain, from the viewpoint of an Egyptian or a Canaanite, for example, or even from the perspective of a Jewish or Christian reader who was squeamish about killing or held very strict views about lying. Since the text itself offers very many bases for such readings, it is hard to think of a reason why we should not make reading against the grain one of our normal strategies for approaching the text. It may be a way of disclosing to us a wider range of possibilities in the text.

We need not suppose that reading against the grain of the text is a sign of disrespect for the text. What is disrespectful to the text is to assume that it will say what it is we would like it to say. Nor is it harmful to the church or the synagogue to hear of readings against the grain. We should not assume that "believing communities" always want to hear, or should hear, only the ideology of the text being rehearsed. Perhaps they also need to know what their texts are capable of, what unorthodox and unconventional meanings they can suggest, and what a large element of choice there is in any decision to take the text's perspective as the definitive word.

The Dialectic of the Text

I have just now been describing a dialectic that we can set up between the text and the reader, when the reader takes up a position, or starts out from a position, that is not shared by the text. There is another kind of dialectic to which we can pay attention, however. It is a dialectic that is immanent in the text, a dialectic between the elements of tension in the text itself. In the Pentateuch such a dialectic comes to expression in such questions as: Is God merciful or vengeful? Does God wish to reveal himself or conceal himself? Is God directing the course of human history or not? Without probing very far beneath the surface of the text of the Pentateuch, we soon form the impression that the text says quite different things on these subjects at different moments, that there is at the very least a tension in the text, and at the most there is irreconcilable conflict.

The possibility of such dialectical relations in our texts needs to be in our minds when we address the issue of "God in the Pentateuch." Perhaps we will at the end of the day uncover some grand harmonizing truth that brings the poles of tension together and enables us to create some unitary vision of our topic. But even if that should happen "at the end of the day," we shall have in the meantime to give weight to elements that pull apart from one another, or else we shall never know that there is any unitary statement for which to seek.

Dialectic Readings

God and Noah

Here is a very simple example of the dialectic readers may find themselves involved in with their text. The issue can be framed in this way: Is the story of Noah a story of God as savior or of Noah as savior?

The ideology of the text has some plain outlines. According to the text, all humans deserve to be wiped out by a flood because of their wickedness, but Noah finds favor in the eyes of the Lord (Gen 6:8). God tells Noah how he can escape the flood, God commands him to make an ark, God sends him into the ark, God shuts him in, God remembers him, and God tells him to leave the ark when the waters have subsided. In short, God saves Noah (and, with him, humanity) from the flood.[7]

Readers, however, might well find themselves asking, But what does God actually do to save Noah from the flood? If this is a story of some "saving act" of God, let us say, how exactly does God act in order to save Noah? The answer has to be that God merely tells Noah what to do. God does not do anything himself to save Noah; he tells Noah how to save himself. Compared with some of the "mighty acts of God" in the Pentateuch, such as the exodus from Egypt when the Lord fights for the Hebrews and they have to do nothing but "only to keep still" (Exod 14:14), there is no saving act of God at the flood at all. So is it a story about God at all, if it is not about anything he does? Is it perhaps a story about the achievement of a great hero, who saves humanity from extinction by keeping alive his family in a boat? To be sure, the deity has warned the hero of the coming of the flood and has given him instructions about the ark that must be built if the flood is to be survived. But the actual saving acts are those of Noah, who even in his six-hundredth year is building the ark, collecting all the animals and stocking it with food—singlehandedly (the verbs in 6:16–21 are all in the singular).

The ideology of the text does not contain this second reading, I would say; the text does not authorize it, nor does it encourage us to read it that way. But then neither does it disallow it, for it gives us all the data by which we may develop this reading against the grain. And once we have encountered such a reading, it is hard to forget it, hard to expunge the memory of its possibility from our consciousness, hard to adhere any longer to the idea of a univocal meaning of the text—hard, in short, to be sure what it is the text wants to say about God. The possibility of reading against the grain makes for a plurality of interpretations.

God and the Exodus

Here is another example of a dialectic reading of the Pentateuch. It seems to be both a case of a reader reading against the grain and of a tension that is immanent in the surface of the text. In a word, the text represents the exodus from Egypt as a great act of deliverance on God's part. The day of the exodus is called the day when "the LORD brought you out from there by strength of hand" (Exod 13:3, NRSV), and the moment of victory over the Egyptians is recalled as the time when "horse and rider he has thrown into the sea" (15:21, NRSV). It is to be commemorated in time to come as the day when "[b]y strength of hand the LORD brought us out of Egypt, from the house of slavery" (13:14, NRSV). The text has persuaded its readers that it is telling of a mighty deed of salvation.

What the text never says, in this connection, is that it was the Lord who brought them into Egypt in the first place. In the Book of Exodus, the presence of the Hebrews in Egypt is regarded as a given, and the only questions are whether, how, and when the Lord will remove them from the house of bondage. The story of the exodus begins only when the Hebrews groan under their hard labor. Then the Lord remembers his covenant with Abraham, Isaac, and Jacob (Exod 2:23–24)—which is to say, the narrative of Genesis 12–36. No one in Exodus, in other words, seems to remember the events of Genesis 37–50, chapters that have told us how the Hebrews happen to be in Egypt in the first place; and no one seems to remember Joseph's words to his brothers: "So it was not you who sent me here, but God" (Gen 45:8, NRSV), and "Even though you intended to do harm to me, God intended it for good" (50:20, NRSV). It is evidently not only the new Egyptian king who knows not Joseph (Exod 1:8), but the narrator also. And his character God seems to regard the presence of the Hebrews in Egypt as nothing more than an unfortunate accident that has happened to them; he never acknowledges that it is his own deliberate design.

Now it makes a difference (does it not?) whether the deliverance from Egypt is a sheer act of divine grace in conformity with the covenant to the forefathers, or whether it is a way of undoing the damage done to the Hebrew people by engineering their descent into Egypt in the first place. Regardless of how we resolve this question, or whether we resolve it at all, we are left with an equivocal picture of "God in the Pentateuch." A tension immanent in the larger text of Genesis through Exodus has led to a reading that in some respects goes against the grain of the smaller text of the opening chapters of Exodus.

God and the Plagues in Egypt

In at least one place there is an evident tension, on the surface of the text, regarding the behavior of God during the affair of the Egyptian plagues. There is little doubt that the general intention of the text is to represent God as the savior of the Hebrew people from the Egyptians: in Exodus 3:17 he says, "I declare that I will bring you up out of the misery

of Egypt, to the land of the Canaanites" (NRSV), and in 14:13 Moses says
to the people, "Do not be afraid, stand firm, and see the deliverance that
the LORD will accomplish for you today" (NRSV). But the text also contains
a quite contrary view of God's activity: in 5:22–23, after the Hebrews have
been compelled to find their own straw to make bricks, there is a question of Moses, "O LORD, why have you mistreated this people? Why did
you ever send me? Since I first came to Pharaoh to speak in your name,
he has mistreated this people, and you have done nothing at all to deliver your people" (NRSV).

This is not the question of an opponent of God, and it is not rebuffed
by God. Moses is not punished for asking it, and God effectively concedes
the truth of it by not denying it but changing the subject in his response.
Now, I hardly need to observe that the text does not mean us to accept
that this is how we should read the entire narrative of the plagues, as a
sequence of damaging actions of God against the Hebrews; and the narrative as a whole ensures that we ultimately forget about this objection of
Moses, or almost so. But the question does open a window into the narrative, another angle of vision that enables the divine actions to be interpreted in another way from that of the text as a whole. This question of
Moses invites us as readers to consider the whole plagues narrative from
an alternative perspective; and even if we do not come to accept this perspective in the end, a little note of ambiguity has been introduced into
the portraiture of God.

There is another point at which the text, less overtly, introduces ambiguity into the larger picture. The casual reader remembers that after each
of the plagues Pharaoh promises to let the Hebrews leave Egypt but sub-
sequently "hardens his heart" and changes his mind. More observant readers know that it is sometimes said that Pharaoh "hardens his heart" (as in
8:15 [Heb. 11], 32 [Heb. 28]; 9:34) and sometimes that "his heart is hardened" (as in 7:13, 14, 22; 8:19 [Heb. 15]; 9:7, 35), but (most interest-
ingly) that sometimes it is the Lord who "hardens Pharaoh's heart" (as in
9:12; 10:1, 20, 27; 11:10).

The first ambiguity that arises is whether in the cases where the hardening of Pharaoh's heart is spoken of in the passive ("his heart was hardened") we should understand it was the Pharaoh himself or God that did
the hardening. If it was God, then most of the heart-hardening that was
going on in the text was God's doing and not Pharaoh's. Of course, we can
never know which of these possibilities we should choose, but we can hardly
help wondering about it, especially because of the second ambiguity.

The second ambiguity in the portrayal of God here is a very tantalizing
one: it is the evidence in the text that God was working against his own

purposes by making the Pharaoh keep the people in Egypt at the very time that he was endeavoring to liberate them from Egypt (and publicly proclaiming that as his intention). Readers of Genesis have had occasion before this to wonder at the role of the deferrals of the promise, and at God's penchant for making things difficult for himself (like choosing a childless nonagenarian to be the father of a multitude of nations),[8] but never before have we encountered such an uncompromising conflict in the divine actions. How are we to read this dissonant behavior on God's part? Are we to say, The God of the Exodus is so powerful that he can remove every obstacle placed in his way—even those he in his omnipotence has put there himself (like an irresistible force getting rid of an immovable object); or, The God of the Exodus has difficulty in deciding whether he really wants these Hebrews to be out of Egypt, and defers the moment of their release as long as possible; or, The humiliation of the Egyptian king and the transforming of him from a free agent resisting God into a mere pawn in the divine hands is more important to God than achieving the freedom of the Hebrews at the earliest possible moment?[9] Or are we to go on inventing more and more explanatory accounts of the circumstances?[10]

As if aware of the oddity in God's behavior, the text addresses the problem by offering an explanation of God's hardening of Pharaoh's heart. In Exodus 10:1–2, the Lord says to Moses, "I have hardened his heart and the heart of his officials, in order that I may show these signs of mine among them, and that you may tell your children and grandchildren how I have made fools of the Egyptians and what signs I have done among them—so that you may know that I am the LORD" (NRSV). It is an explanation that bows under the weight of the problem. For, in the first place, if Pharaoh's heart had not been hardened and he had agreed to let the Hebrews go earlier, there would have been no need for "signs" to show Yahweh playing with ("making fools of") the Egyptians; can Yahweh mean that he simply wanted to enjoy the discomfiture of the Egyptians, and that the hardening of their hearts was his ploy to give a justification for his repeated assaults on them? And, in the second place, to say that he has hardened the hearts so as to give the Hebrews something to remember in later years is to suggest that there was no justification or necessity for the hardening of the hearts at the time. Can the text really be implying that the Hebrews would otherwise not have had enough folk memories to pass on to their children, not enough evidence that "I am the LORD"? And in the third place, we have to remember the angle of vision on this narrative opened up by Moses' earlier question, "Why have you mistreated this people?" (5:22, NRSV). That is to say, while Yahweh is having all this sport making a fool of Pharaoh, and while all these memories are being laid down in the national consciousness, the Hebrews are still at work in the brick kilns. Every day that passes in fruitless negotiations with Pharaoh is another day of slave labor for the people of God, even if the text does not draw our attention to the fact at this moment.

None of this is to say that we must read the text this way, fix our attention exclusively on the negative aspects that undermine it in some degree and ignore the larger picture, which is ungainsayably an account of God's deliverance of the Hebrews from Egypt. But whatever we do, the textual data remain, and the picture of God remains intriguing and ultimately unexplainable. If the narrator had set out to portray a deity whose purposes were not entirely clear and whose behavior was from time to time eccentric, a deity who operated under the self-professed slogan, "I will be what I will be," he might well have given us such a narrative as this.[11]

God and the Chosen People

Fundamental to the ideology of the Pentateuch is the idea that God has chosen the people of Israel from among all the nations on earth. The idea first becomes apparent in Genesis 12, though the language of choosing is not yet used. When the Lord tells Abram that he will make of him a great nation and that he will bless him and make his name great (12:2), he does not say that he will *not* make other men into ancestors of great nations, that he will *not* bless them or make their name great—but he implies it. The blessing to Abram has to be preferential and competitive or otherwise Abram's significance for the "families of the earth" (12:3, NRSV) is unintelligible.

Though the idea of Israel's election surfaces at various points in the Pentateuch, the language of God's "choosing" Israel becomes prominent only in Deuteronomy.[12] In Deuteronomy 4:37 and 10:15 it is tied up with God's "love" for the ancestors and his effecting of the exodus from Egypt; in 6:7 and 14:2 it is a choosing of Israel as God's own people out of all the peoples of the earth. The announcement of God's choice of Israel is hedged about, as the theologians do not tire of pointing out,[13] with safeguards against Israel's drawing improper implications from the fact: it was, for example, "not because you were more numerous than any other people that the LORD set his heart on you and chose you" (7:7, NRSV). We wonder, incidentally, whether any Israelites of whatever century needed to be told that they were not the most numerous people on the face of the earth; even without a state educational system or encyclopedias, did they really imagine Israel was a greater state than Egypt, Assyria, Babylonia, or Persia? Or, if they did, how does the author of Deuteronomy happen to know that they were not? Nonetheless, whatever the implications, there is no doubt that the Pentateuch represents God as the God of the Hebrews, God of the Hebrews, that is, in a way he is not God of the Egyptians or Hittites, for example (even if he is God of those nations in any sense at all).

This is all right if you happen to be an Israelite and have no dealings with Hittites. You know all you need to know, which is that Yahweh is your God. But if you happen to be a Hittite, or even a twentieth-century reader of the Pentateuch, how congenial is it to encounter in its pages a deity who is bound in this way to just one nation: the nation claims that he is their peculiar deity, and he professes that he has chosen them as his own peculiar people. What is the sense in this arrangement, what rationale is offered for it—especially since the Pentateuch regards God as the creator of the whole world? And above all, for our present consideration of God in the Pentateuch, what does this exclusivity say about the character of the deity represented here? The Pentateuch itself sees no problem here, nothing to be excused or justified; if anything, it makes a point out of there being no rationale for the choice of Israel as the people of God. But it does not realize that the very idea of one nation as a chosen people—leaving the rest of humanity unchosen—is itself problematic.

The time-honored language, and the sense of fitness that creeps over us through long acquaintance with the idea, must not be allowed to soften the sense of shock that such an example of nationalistic ideology must deliver. Nor should we blur the contours of this distinct figuration of God in the Pentateuch with some pacific harmonization or identification of this God with the deity we ourselves believe in—or, for that matter, patronize the God of the Pentateuch by excusing the myopia of his vision as a necessary stage in the progress of religion.

The grain of the text, in short, assumes the centrality of the Jewish people and portrays a God whose attention is concentrated upon that nation. So long as we stay with the ideology of the text, we experience no discomfort with the portraiture. But the moment we position ourselves outside the text and become conscious that our own identity is very different from that of the Hebrews, it becomes difficult not to take a more quizzical view of the character. If we do not actually approve of a universal deity having one favorite race, we are bound to take a different view of that deity's character from a reader who happily embraces the ideology of the text.

Unifying Readings

The readings presented above of the character God in the Pentateuch are meant only to be exemplary of the ambiguities and indeterminacy of the portrait offered by the text. They themselves, readings against the grain of the text, go against the grain also of the central tradition in biblical scholarship, which has generally striven for a harmonizing and unifying depiction of the character of the deity in the Old Testament, one indeed that maximizes the compatibility of the portrait with that of the God of the New Testament and of Christian theology. This standpoint is, of course, quite legitimate—provided only that it is recognized that, like all standpoints, it has to be chosen, and, when it is chosen, it restricts the range of vision.

In this section I will present some themes from the scholarly literature that treats the depiction of God in the Pentateuch; works like those of Gerhard von Rad, Walther Zimmerli, Claus Westermann or Bernhard W. Anderson.[14] To all these authors, it should be noted, "God" is not a character in a literary work called the Pentateuch but is a real being concerning whom the Pentateuch is written. So far as I can tell, the authors do not think the Pentateuch ever says anything untrue about this "real God" and, even as Christian theologians, they do not seem to find any inconsistency between the figure of God in the Pentateuch and the God of Christian worship and theology.[15]

1. God is present. The Pentateuch is not a story of human history in which God appears at the margins, making only occasional interventions like a *deus ex machina.* Even when the narrative does not foreground him,[16] he remains the story's dominant character. Very little is said in the Pentateuch of the nature of God in himself; it is always God in relationship with humans, involved in the events of family or national history. Westermann, for example, says that "[t]he story told in the Old Testament is not a salvation history in the sense of a series of God's salvation acts, but rather a history of God and man whose nucleus is the experience of saving."[17] Nor is it a story of divine actions unilaterally injected into the course of human affairs, for "all of God's acts and speaking are directed toward eliciting a response."[18] Similarly, Anderson writes:

> Just as persons are known in the context of relationship, so God's self is revealed in his historical relations with his people. He is the God of Abraham, Isaac, and Jacob, not the God of speculative thought. He is known by what he has done, is doing, and will do—i.e., in the events of history.[19]

Beyond doubt, this is a fundamental aspect of the character God in the Pentateuch.

2. God speaks. God is the principal speaker in the Pentateuch. Most of the central chapters of the Pentateuch, from Exodus 20 to the end of Numbers, are the speeches of God. If you write down ten of the page numbers of the Pentateuch at random, and look them up to see if God speaks or is quoted on them, you will probably find, as I did, that on six out of ten pages there are words of God.

The significance of this speaking is variously understood by theologians. Sometimes it is seen as being God's *self-revelation.* The pervasiveness of God's speech is said to establish that the text "does not purport to be the record of human initiative in seeking for and discovering God" but rather "testifies to God's overture, God's initiative."[20] Sometimes the speech of God in the Pentateuch is seen as God's *summons* of Israel to obedience, God's announcement of his requirements. The Pentateuchal law, spoken by God to Moses, can indeed be regarded as a gift, but "[e]very gift implies an element of duty,"[21] and the words of God essentially impose duties upon their hearers. Sometimes the words of God are seen as *instruction,* the emphasis being on God's speech as guidance for life rather than as legal requirements. Sometimes it is stressed that the words of God that direct Israel's behavior are effectively part of his *salvation* of the nation. So, it is argued, the law must not be "separated from God's saving deed and absolutized. Because God encountered Israel as savior, he commanded to it his will."[22] Sometimes the words of God are seen as the *provisions of the covenant* that defines the relationship between God and the people.[23] No matter the precise significance of God's speaking, speech is a prominent element in the characterization of God in the Pentateuch.[24]

3. God promises. The OT as a whole has commonly been read by Christian interpreters as promise, to which the NT corresponds as fulfillment.[25] However appropriate or otherwise that may be for the OT generally, the theme of promise is certainly perceived as an important thread in the Pentateuch's depiction of God. Zimmerli, for example, sees God's promise to the ancestors in Genesis as "constitut[ing] the subject matter of the patriarchal history,"[26] so fundamental is it to the entire narrative. And I have argued myself that the theme of the threefold promise to the ancestors of progeny, land, and a divine-human relationship binds the whole Pentateuch together: Genesis develops the element of the promise of progeny; Exodus and Leviticus concern themselves with the promise of the divine-human relationship; and Numbers and Deuteronomy focus on the promise of the land.[27] We can safely say, therefore, that God is viewed in the Pentateuch as the one who promises.[28]

4. God saves. In the work of Gerhard von Rad in particular we find the Hexateuch (the Pentateuch plus Joshua) characterized as "salvation history" (*Heilsgeschichte*), that is, as a narrative of God's saving acts, or, as the "biblical theology" movement put it, "the mighty acts of God."[29] Von Rad found the core of the Hexateuch in the confessional statement of Deuteronomy 26:5–9, which he called Israel's Credo: "A wandering Aramean was my ancestor . . . . [W]e cried to the LORD, the God of our ancestors; the LORD heard our voice, and saw our affliction . . . . [T]he LORD brought us out of Egypt" (NRSV). In these words are recapitulated, said von Rad, "the main events in the saving history from the time of the patriarchs down to the conquest." The God of the Pentateuch is, thus, a God who delivers and saves.[30] To the same effect Westermann writes, "The experience of the deliverance at the beginning [i.e., at the exodus as the beginning of Israel's national history] means for Israel that Yahweh will remain Israel's savior. As he was the savior at the beginning, so his rescue continues to be expected, prayed for, and experienced. Yahweh is the saving God."[31]

5. God blesses. Westermann in particular has drawn attention to this aspect of the character of the God of the Pentateuch. On the first page of Genesis, God appears as the originator of blessing, that is, a general benevolence that is "universal and valid for all forms of life." Blessing differs from saving, according to Westermann. God's saving is "a special turning towards a particular group" and is experienced in "individual events or a sequence of events." Blessing, on the other hand, is a "quiet, continuous, flowing, and unnoticed working of God which cannot be captured in moments or dates,"[32] and which is directed toward humanity in general and not just toward Israel. The Pentateuch as a whole, though it consists for the most part of a story of salvation, that is, of the salvation of Israel, is nevertheless framed by two major statements of God's blessing: the blessing of the creator in Genesis 1–11, and "the blessing in Deuteronomy directed toward the people in the promised land."[33] It is hard to say, therefore, whether it is God's saving or blessing that is the more prominent in the Pentateuch; both must be given full recognition.

Here then have been five things that contemporary OT theologians find the Pentateuch to be affirming about God. Without question, all these statements about God are well attested in the Pentateuch, and many students and scholars would be content to conclude their account of the God of the Pentateuch with a catalogue like the foregoing—more developed and more sophisticated, no doubt, but essentially on these lines. But each of these statements, however "positive" or "constructive," deserves to be probed more critically, for each statement both implies and denies far more than is evident on the surface.

Conclusions

Reading against the grain implies that there *is* a grain. It implies that texts have designs on their readers and wish to persuade them of something or other. It implies that there are ideologies inscribed in texts and that the readers implied by texts share the texts' ideologies. But, as I have suggested earlier, readers are free to resist the ideologies of texts, and, what is more, texts themselves sometimes provoke readers into resisting them by manifesting tensions immanent within the texts themselves. All the same, there is no obligation to resist, nothing wrong in adopting the ideology of one's text. All that is wrong is not knowing and admitting that that is what one is doing or not permitting other people to resist the ideology of the text.

I do not want to deny that the five points in the previous section represent, with whatever measure of success, the ideology of the Pentateuch on the subject of God, that is to say, the grain of the text. But so that those who wish to accede to this ideology know what they are doing, and can recognize that they are making a choice when they do so, I shall offer a few reflections that go against the grain. Their effect will be, I think, to suggest that none of the five themes in the figuration of God in the Pentateuch that I have outlined above can be said to be unequivocally true about the character. Some qualification must always be added, even though our handbooks of OT theology uniformly devote themselves to exposition and refrain from critical evaluation of the portrait.

It is true that God in the Pentateuch is present, speaks, and saves. But, on the whole, it is true only if you take the position of Israel. If you adopt the point of view of the Egyptians or of the Canaanites, God is not experienced as a saving God, and the only words you will hear addressed to you are words of reproach and threat. If you are not Israel, you do not know the presence of God—not because of some defect in you but because you have not been chosen. It is perfectly true that the character God in the Pentateuch saves Israel from Egypt, but it is equally true that the same God destroys or humiliates the Egyptians, and ignores almost everyone else. The text does not wish us to think that, or, if it allows us to know it, it wants us to suppress that knowledge and concentrate on the deliverance of Israel. But when the deliverance of Israel is effected precisely through the destruction of the Egyptian soldiers, when what is deliverance from one point of view is death from another, must we succumb to the text's ideology and suppress part of the reality to which it bears witness?[34]

The election of Israel is, without question, a thorny problem for the character of God in the Pentateuch. Some writers have thought to ameliorate matters by emphasizing that Israel's election is not thought to be an end in itself but for the purpose of bringing benefit to the other nations. Bernhard Anderson, for example, writes that "the deepest insight into Israel's election or special calling is that God has chosen Israel to be the historical agent of world-wide blessing." But he has to go on to say, "Admittedly, Israel did not always understand her [sic] calling in this universal perspective."[35] The fact is that Israel (or shall we say in the present context, the narrator of the Pentateuch) seems to give a very low priority to this "deepest insight," for it is very difficult to see how the Israel of the Pentateuch brings blessing to anyone at all,[36] and does not rather spell disaster for all the nations with which it comes into contact. Genesis 1 and 9, indeed, speak of God's blessing upon humanity in general, and Westermann especially wants to give the idea of universal blessing parity of place with the idea of particular salvation for Israel.[37] But the Pentateuch does not support his view, for it consistently privileges Israel and marginalizes the other nations.

If we now turn our attention to the theme of God promising in the Pentateuch, again the realities in the text do not allow a clear and unambiguous statement. There is no doubt that the divine promises to the patriarchs are fundamental for the dynamic of the Pentateuchal narrative: God promises progeny, a relationship, and land, and the narrative presses towards the realization of these promises. But it would be unacceptably short-sighted to depict the God of the Pentateuch as making promises without also asking whether or to what extent those promises are fulfilled whether within the Pentateuch or beyond its confines. He promises to make Abram into a "great nation" (Gen 12:2), but has this happened in the course of the Pentateuchal narrative?

The promise of the land has certainly not been realized by the end of Deuteronomy, and the divine-human relationship is decidedly less stable than we had imagined when it was first promised to the patriarchs. But perhaps this is the point at which we should question the notion of the "Pentateuch" as an independent literary work, and invoke the entity that we can call the "Primary History": that sequence of historiographical narrative that runs from Genesis to the end of 2 Kings.[38] Yet if the boundaries of that work are to form the horizon within which we consider the promises and their fulfillment, the news is even worse than if we restrict ourselves to the first five books. For by the end of the narrative of the Primary History, Israel has lost the land and has been thrown out of God's presence (2 Kgs 24:20). Further, the threat of Deuteronomy 4:27 that Israel is to be scattered among the other nations with only a few of its members surviving has been fulfilled. Perhaps we might then reflect that even the exile is not the end of the story—though it is the end of the history; perhaps the promises even now still await their fulfillment. But whatever historical moment we fix on to take our soundings in order to discover whether the promises have been fulfilled, we find an ambivalent situation. In short, in the Pentateuch God makes promises, indeed, but if we are properly to appreciate the character of this Pentateuchal God we need to be able to determine whether there is any truth in these promises; and the answer is certainly not straightforward.

It is the same with the speaking of God. There is no doubt that the God of the Pentateuch is not a distant, uninterested, or uncommunicative God. But if we are to say anything more than bland generalities we have to flesh out what this speaking consists of. Here again there are ambivalences. For as well as the words of moral guidance he speaks to Israel in the Pentateuch there is, for example, an oracle about Esau and Jacob, that "the elder shall serve the younger" (Gen 25:23, NRSV). We may well find ourselves asking, Why should the traditional rights of the firstborn be overturned at this point? Why should a man who cynically buys a birthright for the price of a meal be divinely authorized to keep it? Is it possible in any case to "buy" a birthright, and why in any case should one of them "serve" the other, considering that they are brothers? Or, to take another example, what is one to make of the amazingly elaborate instructions given by the character God for the construction of the tabernacle and for the performance of sacrifice in his honor? What kind of a deity is it that wants to specify to this degree precisely how he is to be worshiped and what will count as legitimate and illegitimate expressions of reverence for him? What kind of a person, we might ask, is so concerned for his own honor and lays so many constraints on the responses of others to him?

There are no straightforward answers to such questions. The God of the Pentateuch is a complex and mysterious character, passionate and dynamic but by no means conformable to human notions of right behavior. He is not very lovable, but he must be obeyed. He has his plans, but they are not infrequently deflected. He does not do very much explaining, and he relates to people mostly by a system of threats and promises. He has his favorites, and he is fiercely loyal to them. He is hard to please. But which of all these characteristics should weigh heaviest in the scales? Different readers will decide the matter differently. The Pentateuch is a machine for generating variant readings of the character of God, and the answers it gives will be shaped by the kinds of questions we allow ourselves to address to it. None of our readings will be disinterested; all will enshrine our own ideology.

NOTES

1. Numbers 20:12 says it is because Moses "did not trust" in the Lord; but it proves impossible to tell how his action of striking the rock evidenced a lack of trust.

2. The "novel" is not just a modern genre, of course, for the ancient novel is well attested; see G. Anderson, *Ancient Fiction: The Novel in the Greco-Roman World* (Totowa, NJ: Barnes and Noble, 1984); T. Hågg, *The Novel in Antiquity* (Berkeley: University of California Press, 1983); B. E. Perry, *The Ancient Romances: A Literary Historical Account of their Origins* (Stather Lectures, 1951; Berkeley: University of California Press, 1967). I am not arguing that the Pentateuch is a novel of this kind from the point of view of its genre, but only that it is not improper to regard it as having some elements in common with the novel.

3. Some readers may wonder how this squares with the claim implied in the title of my book, *The Theme of the Pentateuch*, JSOTSup 10 (Sheffield: JSOT, 1976). It does not. I now think that there is more than one way of saying "what the Pentateuch is all about," though I still think that the theme of the fulfillment and non-fulfillment of the threefold promise is one fruitful way of talking about the Pentateuch.

4. *Pirqe ʾabot* 5.22.

5. The point is further helpfully developed by Dale Patrick in chapter 1 ("The Characterization of God") of his book *The Rendering of God in the Old Testament*, OBT 10 (Philadelphia: Fortress, 1981) 13–27.

6. I have used the image (which I did not invent) of reading with and against the grain in my paper, "The Story of Michal, Wife of David, in Its Sequential Unfolding," in *Telling Queen Michal's Story: An Experiment in Comparative Interpretation*, ed. D. J. A. Clines & T. C. Eskenazi, JSOTSup 119 (Sheffield: JSOT, 1991) 129–30. The reader might consider also the image of moiré, "the meaningful but unstable and reticulating patterns in shot silk" (George Steiner, *On Difficulty and Other Essays* [Oxford: Oxford University Press, 1978] 40).

7. Cf. the account given of Genesis 1–11 by Gerhard von Rad as "a story of God with man, the story of continuously new punishment and at the same time gracious preservation"; the Flood Story itself he characterizes with the sentence, "God transferred man . . . to a newly ordered world" (*Genesis*, OTL, rev. ed. [London: SCM, 1972] 153). There is no doubt in von Rad's mind who is the hero of the story.

8. See L. A. Turner, *Announcements of Plot in Genesis*, JSOTSup 96 (Sheffield: JSOT, 1990); D. J. A. Clines, "What Happens in Genesis," in *What Does Eve Do to Help? And Other Readerly Questions to the Old Testament*, JSOTSup 94 (Sheffield: JSOT, 1990) 49–66.

9. On this last reading, see D. M. Gunn, "The 'Hardening of Pharaoh's Heart': Plot, Character, and Theology in Exodus 1–14," in *Art and Meaning: Rhetoric in Biblical Literature*, ed. D. J. A. Clines, D. M. Gunn, & A. J. Hauser, JSOTSup 19 (Sheffield: JSOT, 1982) 72–96.

10. The issue in the narrative is often cast as the problem of causality (i.e., who caused the hardening of Pharaoh's heart?), but the reader will see that I am not setting the problem up in these terms, which deflect attention from the truly critical problems in the text for the portrait of God. Nevertheless, I cannot forbear quoting some sentences from a standard work that show how badly this issue too stands in need of critical reformulation: "[T]he biblical writers speak of God's hardening men's

hearts.... At the same time they avow men harden their own hearts.... They found no apparent inconsistency in ascribing this activity both to God and to men. For men, by acting in accordance with their own self-will, were carrying out the divine purpose" (V. H. Kooy, "Harden the Heart," *IDB* 2:524). On this I might comment, first, that it is not the end of the matter to say that "the biblical writers ... found no ... inconsistency"; perhaps they should have, and perhaps we do. And in the second place, does it resolve the issue to say that humans acting freely are carrying out the divine will, unless we are prepared to say also that God acting freely is carrying out human will?

11. The divine self-description in Exodus 3:14 could well be translated, "I will be what I will be," and some commentators have rightly remarked on the note of concealment in this formulation; e.g., W. Zimmerli, *Old Testament Theology in Outline* (Edinburgh: T. & T. Clark, 1978) 20: "In this figure of speech resounds the sovereign freedom of Yahweh, who, even at the moment he reveals himself in his name, refuses simply to put himself at the disposal of humanity or to allow humanity to comprehend him."

12. Cf. A. D. H. Mayes, *Deuteronomy*, NCB (London: Oliphants, 1979) 60: "What is really distinctive in Deuteronomy is that the whole life of the people is regulated from the point of view of its relationship with Yahweh, and the basic element here is that Israel was chosen by Yahweh."

13. E.g., E. Jacob, *Theology of the Old Testament* (London: Hodder & Stoughton, 1958) 110–11.

14. Especially G. von Rad, *Old Testament Theology*, 2 vols. (Edinburgh: Oliver & Boyd, 1962) 1:129–305 ("The Theology of the Hexateuch"); Zimmerli, *Old Testament Theology* C. Westermann, *Elements of Old Testament Theology* (Atlanta: John Knox, 1982); B. W. Anderson, "God, OT View of," IDB 2:417–30.

15. Von Rad (*Old Testament Theology*, 1:148), for example, even thinks that "it is a bad thing for the Christian expositor completely to disregard [the cosmology of Genesis 1] as obsolete," since "[i]n the scientific ideas of the time theology had found an instrument which suited it perfectly" (contrast *Old Testament Theology*, 1:344, where von Rad does regard the Deuteronomist's conception of history as defective; but somehow the motive behind this defect turns out to be the very thing that gives the Deuteronomist's work its "theological grandeur"). T. E. Fretheim has correctly remarked on how the portrait of God in OT scholarship "bears a striking resemblance to the quite traditional Jewish or Christian understanding of God regnant in synagogue or church" (*The Suffering of God: An Old Testament Perspective*, OBT 14 [Philadelphia: Westminster, 1984] 17).

16. R. L. Cohn, "Narrative Structure and Canonical Perspective in Genesis," *JSOT* 25 (1983) 3–16, has shown how God increasingly retreats into the background throughout Genesis 12–50.

17. Westermann, *Elements*, 10–11.

18. Westermann, ibid., 27.

19. Anderson, "God, OT View of," 418.

20. Anderson, ibid., 419. Anderson is speaking of the OT in general, it should be noted. To take another, not uncharacteristic, example, G. von Rad deals with the speeches of God to Moses at Sinai (the "Law") under the rubric of "The Divine Revelation at Sinai" (*Old Testament Theology*, 1:187–305).

21. Zimmerli, *Old Testament Theology*, 109.

22. Westermann, *Elements*, 176.
23. Cf. R. E. Clements, *Old Testament Theology: A Fresh Approach* (Atlanta: John Knox, 1978) 110: "*Tôrâh* is the comprehensive list of instructions and stipulations by which Israel's covenant with God is controlled."
24. Cf. also Patrick, *The Rendering of God*, 90–100 (ch. 6, "God's Speaking").
25. See, for example, Clements, *Old Testament Theology* 131–54 (ch. 6, "The OT as Promise").
26. Zimmerli, *Old Testament Theology*, 29.
27. Clines, *The Theme of the Pentateuch*, esp. p. 29.
28. See also Walther Zimmerli, *Man and His Hope in the Old Testament*, SBT 2/20 (London: SCM, 1971) 42–69.
29. Cf. G. E. Wright, *God Who Acts*, SBT 8 (London: SCM, 1952). On the "biblical theology" movement, see B. S. Childs, *Biblical Theology in Crisis* (Philadelphia: Westminster, 1970), and J. Barr, "Biblical Theology," *IDBSup*, 104–11.
30. For some brief criticisms of von Rad's conception of "salvation history," see, for example, Westermann, *Elements*, 14–15, who points out that God also acts for punishment as well as for salvation, and that an ongoing activity of "blessing" also needs to be taken account of (see the next point).
31. Westermann, *Elements*, 37.
32. Westermann, ibid., 102–3.
33. Westermann, ibid., 103–4.
34. As an example of the prevailing agreement to regard the exodus as an "act of God" but to ignore the fact that it did any harm to anyone, see P. D. Hanson, *Dynamic Transcendence: The Correlation of Confessional Heritage and Contemporary Experience in a Biblical Model of Divine Activity* (Philadelphia: Fortress, 1978) 28–35.
35. Anderson, "God, OT View of ," 429.
36. Joseph's providing food for the Egyptians is the one evident exception (cf. Gen 47:25), but even this benefit must be set against the fact that in order to do so he deprives the Egyptians of their animals and land and "made slaves of them from one end of Egypt to the other" (47:21, NRSV).
37. Westermann, *Elements*, 85–117 (Part III, "The Blessing God and Creation").
38. See D. J. A. Clines, "The OT Histories: A Reader's Guide," in *What Does Eve Do to Help?*, 85–105.

5

IMAGES OF ISRAEL: THE PEOPLE OF GOD IN THE TORAH

Frederic W. Bush[1]

The concept of "the people of God" is one of the most important in the Pentateuch and in all of Scripture.[2] Indeed, that concept is just another way of stating the promise to the patriarchs, which functions so centrally in the progress and development of the whole Pentateuch. In one of the most insightful ways in which this promise has been analyzed, D. J. A. Clines affirms that

> the promise has three elements: posterity, divine-human relationship, and land. The posterity-element . . . is dominant in Genesis 12–50, the relationship-element in Exodus and Leviticus, and the land-element in Numbers and Deuteronomy.[3]

Clearly, the Pentateuch's concept of the people of God involves all three of these elements. Clines goes on to demonstrate that "the theme of the Pentateuch is the partial fulfillment—which implies also the partial non-fulfillment—of the promise to or blessing of the patriarchs."[4] Hence, the very theme of the Pentateuch itself is the partial fulfillment of the promise of the people of God. The present essay, thus, will follow this partial fulfillment to see what it means to be the people of God.

The People of God in Promise (Gen 12–50)[5]

The Unconditional Grace and Initiative of God

The story of the people of God begins with the call of Abraham and God's promise to him of posterity (Gen 12:1–3). Literarily, the call and promise are sudden and abrupt, so to speak, catching Abram in mid-course without any indication of time, place, or circumstances. Also, outside the brief, familial facts given in the few preceding verses (11:26–32), it does not even identify Abram. This throws the divine choice into bold relief—stark and inexplicable—and emphasizes that it is God's sovereignty, not human initiative, that brings the people of God into existence. The subsequent Abrahamic cycle (12:4–25:18) strikingly underscores the role of Yahweh's initiative in the fulfillment of the promise. After repeatedly reminding readers of Sarah's infertility (11:30; 16:1–2; 17:17–18; 18:10–14), the story credits Isaac's birth to Yahweh's intervention: "Yahweh took note of Sarah . . . and did what he promised" (21:1 author's trans.). Hence, as Goldingay says, the people of God

> is not merely a natural entity. A special act of God creates it. . . .
> It is not even that God makes an already existent people his own;
> he brings a people into being. They only exist as a people be-
> cause of an act of God.[6]

The primary and most important OT metaphor for the relationship between God and his people was the covenant (*bĕrît*).[7] It appears in the Abrahamic covenant of Genesis and in the Mosaic covenant of Exodus-Deuteronomy. Covenant also becomes the primary symbol in the period of the monarchy to describe the relationship of God with his people through the Davidic kingship (2 Sam 7; Ps 89). Later, the prophets use it to picture God's relationship with his people (e.g., Hos 6:7; 8:1; Isa 33:8; Jer 11:8, 10; 34:13), and Jeremiah employs it as a metaphor for what God will do after the judgment that is coming (Jer 31:31–34). Though an ambiguous metaphor with complex historical roots, the covenant is essentially an "obligation" or "commitment" to certain requirements or courses of action, often given sanction by an oath sworn in a solemn religious ritual.[8] Unlike the well-known "parity" covenants made between humans in the ancient Near East, however, the covenants between God and his people did not involve mutual agreements contracted by equal parties.[9] Rather, they are exclusively instituted by God; he is the only subject of the standard expressions for covenant-making.[10]

Two different divine-human covenants emerge in the Pentateuch. We might call the first a "covenant of promise," since in this type God takes upon himself the obligations of the threefold promise to the patriarchs. (For the second type, "covenant of obligation," see below.) Genesis 15:7–21 exemplifies the covenant of promise.[11] In a haunting scene conducted in terrifying darkness (v. 12), smoke, and fire (v. 17), God performs a mysterious oath ritual. He himself passes between the halves of the slain animals, symbolically validating his covenant promises.[12] Strikingly, the covenant's content centers on the element of land in the promise. The other example of this type (Gen 17:1–22), however, lacks an oath ritual. Instead, God simply reiterates his promise of posterity (vv. 2, 5, 6, 16, 19, 21) and personal relationship with Abraham's descendants ("to be God to you and to your descendants after you," v. 7; cf. v. 8c).[13] Now this is what is important in these two examples: both emphasize the promise itself, not a required lifestyle that Abraham must follow.[14]

Hence, the existence of the people of God—i.e., as descendants, land, and a divine-human relationship—rests exclusively on a covenant of promise, a divine dispensation of grace and blessing confirmed by oath. That is, ultimately it depends only on the character of the gracious God who makes it.

The Responsibility of the People of God

The Pentateuch also powerfully stresses that the promise is dependent on the faith and obedience of the people of God. For example, the prologue of Genesis 17 (vv. 1–3a) makes the covenant promise discussed above consequent upon Abraham's lifestyle. God commands him to "walk about before me and be whole" (v. 1 author's trans.), i.e., to live in God's presence wholly and completely.[15] And the Hebrew syntax clearly makes the covenantal promise of v. 2 a consequence of that command: "walk . . . so that I may confirm my covenant . . . ."(author's trans.)[16] Other passages also condition the promise on Abraham's obligation to live a life worthy of his calling (Gen 18:18–19; 26:3–5 [to Isaac]). Two major passages, however, give the necessity of Abraham's response its greatest stress.

Genesis 15:1–6 sets forth the other side of the coin of Yahweh's commitment to Abraham that vv. 7–21 articulate. To Yahweh's promise of great reward (v. 1) Abraham responds (vv. 2–3) in frustration over God's failure to provide him progeny so far: "What good is your reward while I continue childless . . . and a member of my own household will be my heir!" (author's trans.). Significantly, after God reaffirms that Abraham will have a son and many descendants (vv. 4–5), the narrator comments about Abraham's response: "He put his faith in Yahweh and he accounted it to him as righteousness" (v. 6, author's trans.). The comment stresses that Abraham has moved from disbelieving protest to an act of faith. Thus, we learn that the proper attitude of the people of God is faith and trust in the promise-giver (even when the promise is seemingly perversely postponed!). Further, the remark underscores that God regards Abraham's trust as righteousness. Thus, we learn that at the most basic level it is trust in God that makes one well pleasing in his sight (i.e., righteous).[17]

Genesis 22:1–19, however, presents the decisive portrayal of the obedience of faith required of the people of God. Indeed, the narrator himself prefaces his story with a summary of its theme, i.e., a test of Abraham (v. 1a). As v. 12 shows, the test is to determine whether Abraham maintains "fear of God," an expression that does not connote fright but awe and resultant obedience.[18] In between, the haunting, mysterious story unrelentingly follows Abraham's obedience to an incredible, seemingly impossible demand—to sacrifice the son of promise, his beloved Isaac, as a burnt offering. Just as Abraham holds the ritual knife over Isaac's prostrate form (v. 10), God stops the sacrifice. Through an angel from heaven, he declares, "Now I know that you fear God, because you have not withheld from me your son, your only son" (v. 12, NIV). By his complete obedience, Abraham passes the test of faith, and God renews all three elements of the patriarchal promise (v. 17).

Thus, we learn that the promise of the people of God depends not only on God's prevenient, unconditional grace but paradoxically also on the faith and obedience of the people of God themselves. Later God praises Abraham for obeying his requirements, commandments, decrees, and laws (26:5). We learn little, however, about all that that obedience entails. In the later Mosaic covenant, God spells out exactly what those requirements are.

The People of God in Formation (Exodus-Deuteronomy)

The Responsibility of the People of God

As Clines notes, Exodus and Leviticus emphasize the divine-human relationship element of the promise.[19] And the primary metaphor for that relationship is the second type of covenant, one we might call a "covenant of obligation" since in it God imposes upon his people the obligation to obey its stipulations. While still in Egypt, God promised Moses, "I will take you as my own people and I will be your God" (Exod 6:7, NIV). Later, at Mount Sinai, he announces the obligations of being God's people: "So now, if you will pay very careful attention to my voice, and keep my covenant, then you will be my own special treasure" (Exod 19:5, see notes). It is by keeping God's covenant that Israel will become his people, his own "special treasure" among all the peoples.[20] The subsequent narratives expand upon that announcement by detailing the specific elements of the covenant.

First, the covenant requires Israel to obey the stringent stipulations stated as basic principles in the Decalogue (Exod 20:1–17) and applied to daily life situations in the "Book of the Covenant" (Exod 20:22–23:33).[21] Second, the people bind themselves to keeping these stipulations with a blood oath (Exod 24:1–11). Though other interpretations are possible, the ritual probably parallels that of the covenant oath in Genesis 15.[22] Thus, the bloodshed chillingly symbolizes Israel's acceptance of the covenant and its requirements. Third, the covenant provides for severe judgment even to the point of rejection by Yahweh for violations of its stipulations. The announcement of the covenant (Exod 24:5–6) opens with a conditional clause that makes the covenant's special relationship dependent on Israel's obedience. This conditional statement also implies that if the people do *not* abide by the covenant's terms, they will cease to be

God's own "special treasure." After all, the Decalogue portrays Yahweh as a "jealous God" (ʾēl qannā ʾ) who will not tolerate the adoration due him to be given to other gods by his people (20:5). That punishment will follow such disobedience becomes abundantly clear later when God announces his destruction of Israel for her apostate worship of the golden calf (Exod 32:9–10). The curses for disobedience in Leviticus 26 and Deuteronomy 28 also confirm the certainty of divine judgment for disobedience.

Thus, the Mosaic covenant of obligation held over the heads of the people of God a desperately serious threat: if they failed to keep the covenant stipulations, terrible judgment—even utter destruction—would fall upon them.[23] Though rooted in God's initiative and grace, the covenant held the people of God responsible for living a life worthy of their calling. To be specific, the covenant demands that Israel live as a "holy people" (Exod 19:6), i.e., that they live a lifestyle that reflects the nature of the holy God who has called them. It is this quality of life that the Pentateuch's various "codes of law" articulate.

This is not the place to review the contents of those remarkable collections, but the reader should understand several important points.[24] First, as noted above, the Decalogue articulates the fundamental principles for living in fellowship with Yahweh. Hence, though comprehensive—the first four commands regulate relationship with Yahweh, the last six, relationships within the human community—it is not really "law" per se. It promulgates, not specific rules and their penalties, but "legal policy"—a broad statement of "those kinds of behavior which the community is willing to sustain by force."[25]

Second, the other "codes" apply this policy to concrete situations in community life. One particular feature bears special comment. Rather than promulgate a certain social order, the codes demand from the people of God a lifestyle reflecting the compassionate and merciful nature of their God. This assumption underlies the codes' frequent and radical concern to protect and enhance the well-being of those at the bottom of the social order—the widow, the orphan, the resident alien, the debtor, and the slave.[26] Frequently, the codes ground such concern either in the character of God (e.g., "for I am compassionate," Exod 22:27) or in Israel's past experience of deliverance (Exod 20:2; Deut 15:15). Given this constant emphasis, Hanson does not overstate the case when he observes,

> In fact, taken in its most fundamental and original meaning, the compassion of the Deliverer God Yahweh implied that this community was present in the world precisely as a home for the enslaved, the poor, the bereaved.[27]

The Grace and Unconditional Initiative of God

For all its stress on human responsibility, the Mosaic covenant still bears witness to the prevenient grace of God. Both the call of Moses and the exodus (Exod 1–15) supply supporting evidence. As is well known, these key events narrate how Yahweh delivered Israel from the harsh, terrible servitude she suffered at Egypt's cruel hands. It is important to note, however, that the deliverance came solely by the grace and unconditional initiative of God, just as had the call and election of Abraham. It was Yahweh who responded to Israel's "groaning" (Exod 2:25), who called Moses at the burning bush (3:10), who sent the terrible plagues (chs. 7–11) and opened up the sea (14:14, 17–18). In sum, Israel's birth as the people of God derived from God's gracious, unmerited initiative.[28]

The preamble to the Mosaic covenant also testifies to this fact. After Israel arrived at Mount Sinai, Yahweh prefaced his announcement of the covenant this way: "You yourselves have seen what I did to the Egyptians, and that I then lifted you upon wings of eagles and brought you to myself" (19:4, author's trans.).[29] Further, the Decalogue opens with a "formula of self-introduction" in which God identifies himself, first by his name "Yahweh, your God," then by the qualifier "who brought you out of the land of Egypt, out of the house of slavery" (Exod 20:2). The language used recalls his revelation of his name to Moses (3:13–15) and his promise (6:2–8). The point is that Israel's deliverance from Egypt by Yahweh, the Redeemer God, is the foundation for the following covenant obligations. Covenant obedience is grounded in God's prevenient acts of grace.

The Primacy of the Grace of God

The Pentateuch makes it clear that, while God works out his plan through human agents, these agents all too often lack integrity. No sooner had Israel escaped Egypt and set out for Sinai than the people of God fell into rebellion in the wilderness (cf. Exod 16:1–3; 17:3–7). Two incidents especially illustrate their faithlessness and disobedience. The first major rebellion was the apostasy of the golden calf (Exod 32–34). Literarily, the narrative falls between Yahweh's instructions concerning the tabernacle (chs. 25–31) and the tabernacle's actual construction (chs. 35–40). This placement is entirely appropriate, for the tabernacle is the place where Yahweh will be present in Israel (Exod 25:8; 29:45–46), and the rebellion threatens the covenant, the whole basis for Yahweh's presence with his people. The tabernacle can be built only after Yahweh deals with the rebellion. The text is ambiguous regarding exactly what Aaron made and how he did it. However, it clearly portrays the golden bull as a symbol of Yahweh and the apostasy as a particularly heinous violation of the second commandment of the Decalogue.[30]

But Israel did more than just seek to represent Yahweh, her mysterious, invisible God, in an image. She "got up to indulge in revelry" (32:6, NIV), probably a reference to orgiastic rites.[31] As Durham notes, "The contrast with the ritual and the communion meal of chap. 24 . . . is devastating . . . . The celebration of an obligating relationship in Exodus 24 becomes in Exodus 32 an orgy of the desertion of responsibility."[32] Hence, it is not surprising that the ensuing narrative frequently describes the people as "stiff-necked," an idiom meaning "obstinately sinful/rebellious" (32:9; 33:3, 5; 34:9; cf. Deut 9:6, 13; 31:27). Yahweh's angry reactions reflect how terrible a violation Israel has committed. In v. 7 he negates both their identity as "my people" (19:5–6) and his own identity as "Yahweh, your God, who brought you up out of the land of Egypt" (20:2). Instead, he orders Moses, "Go down, because *your* people, whom *you* brought up out of Egypt have become corrupt" (Exod 32:7, NIV). Worse, in vv. 9–10 he invokes the judgment of the covenant: "my anger will burn against them and I will bring them to an end" (author's trans.).

The second incident is the revolt against the taking of the land (Num 13–14). The rebellious nature of the people of God becomes the constant theme of the narrative, which reports Israel's journey from Sinai toward the promised land (Num 11:1–25:18). What makes this tale of unmitigated complaints, disaffection, and defiance seem so awful is its stark contrast with the consciously hyperbolic view of Israel as the holy and invincible army of God presented in Numbers 1–10.[33] About the nature of the people of God, Moses would say later, "From the day you left Egypt until you arrived here you have been rebellious against the Lord" (Deut 9:24). In the Numbers narrative, the turning point comes in the people's response to the report about Canaan brought back by Israel's spies. Initially, the spies return a favorable report: the land "certainly does flow with milk and honey" (Num 13:27). But then comes the "bad report": the inhabitants of Canaan are tall and powerful, their cities large and impregnable. By comparison, the spies felt themselves as puny as grasshoppers (13:28–33).

Hearing this, the people mourn, wishing they had never left Egypt (14:2a). Then they rebel, calling for new leadership to lead them back there (vv. 2b–4). Even the plea for confidence in Yahweh by Caleb and Joshua fails to turn back the tide of panicked public opinion (vv. 6–10). By making a golden calf to represent Yahweh, Israel sought "to shape

God into their own image."[34] Here "the people repudiate the power and faithfulness of God to fulfill his covenantal promises. In seeking another leader to return to Egypt, they have renounced God and his covenant with his people."[35] Again, Yahweh's reaction signals the radical nature of the rebellion. Though he assents to Moses' plea not to destroy the whole people (14:13–20), he swears an oath of judgment: "as I live . . . none of the men who . . . have put me to the test . . . shall see the land I promised. . . . They will meet their end in the desert; here they will die" (vv. 21–35 author's trans.). Except for Joshua and Caleb, all adult males twenty years and older are condemned to die in the wilderness (vv. 29–30).[36]

In sum, from the very moment of deliverance (Exod 15:24; 16:2–3) until the apostasy of the Baal of Peor (Num 25:1–18), the narrative unrelentingly depicts the people of God as "a stubborn and rebellious generation, whose heart was not loyal to God and whose spirit was not faithful to him" (Ps 78:8, author's trans.).[37] Now the question is, What happens to the relationship between God and his people when they violate the covenant? Do such violations cause an irreparable rupture in that relationship? If not, on what grounds can the covenant be restored? Here Exodus 32–34 instructs us on another important theme, the grace of God's forgiveness.

The Grace of Forgiveness

It is striking that, even amid his initial angry reaction to the golden calf apostasy (Exod 32:7–10), God's grace still shows itself. First, though harsh, his judgment is not absolutely final. Rather, he conditions his judgment, so to speak, on Moses' agreement: "Leave me alone so that I may . . . bring them to an end" (author's trans.)[38] Further, the judgment does not mean the end of his covenantal purposes: he will make Moses into a great nation (v. 10). As Childs notes, here we have "a profound paradox . . . which runs through the Bible. . . . The effect is that God himself leaves the door open for intercession. He allows himself to be persuaded."[39] The paradox reflects the character of Yahweh not only as a God of judgment but supremely as a God who is gracious and merciful. This is the theological truth that becomes the fundamental message of the whole story.[40] Without a moment's hesitation, Moses embraces the role of intercessor, step by step prevailing upon God's mercy in the context of his judgment.

Though God "changed his mind about the disaster" (v. 14, author's trans.), the rebellion has radically altered the divine-human relationship. God will now be present with his people only in his messenger, not personally

(32:34; 33:2). Israel will still go to the land, but the people of God will not know Yahweh's presence, only his absence. There will now be no need for the tabernacle. Yet even this awful prospect expresses God's mercy. He will not go with them because the presence of a holy God amid a sinful people constitutes a radical threat to them: "I am not going up in your midst lest I destroy you on the way" (33:3, author's trans.; cf. v. 5b). Further, since Yahweh is undecided about what to do with the people (v. 5d), the way is open for further intercession. So Moses seeks the full restoration of Yahweh's presence with them (33:12–16), and again Yahweh grants his request (v. 17). But the essential problem remains: How may Yahweh be present among an "obstinately sinful people" without destroying them?[41]

So Moses presses his intercession to its conclusion, asking to see God's "glory" (v. 18). Though an allusive way of speaking, in context "glory" clearly means Yahweh himself, his very presence.[42] God responds to this incredible request by revealing his essential character in the proclamation of his name. After instructing Moses to prepare for the renewal of the covenant (Exod 34:1–3), God descends to Mount Sinai and proclaims his name to Moses: "Yahweh! Yahweh! A God merciful and gracious: slow to anger and abounding in steadfast love and faithfulness, . . . who forgives iniquity, rebellion and sin; yet who by no means acquits the guilty" (34:6–7 author's trans.).

Though the paradox of concomitant mercy and judgment remains, clearly the emphasis falls upon God's grace, mercy, and forgiveness. A comparison of the above words with similar ones in the second commandment (Exod 20:5–6) proves very instructive. In Exodus 34, the theme of God's mercy comes first and in greatly expanded form. Further, 34:7a omits the condition of an obedient response as a requirement for receiving Yahweh's steadfast love ("to those who love and keep my commandments," 20:6). As Moberly notes, "this is of fundamental importance, for it means that Yahweh's mercy towards Israel is independent of their responding in the right way. *Even when Israel is disobedient* it is still the recipient of the divine goodness."[43] Finally, Moses presses for full restoration and forgiveness: "please, Lord, go in our midst. However much they are an obstinately sinful people, forgive us our iniquity and our sin, and take us as your own possession" (34:9, author's trans.).[44] The renewal of the covenant that follows (vv. 10–28) indicates unmistakably God's positive response. Here we have a theology of grace unsurpassed in the OT. Despite the people's grievous sin against the covenant, it has not come to an end. What is the basis of this remarkable forgiveness? According to 33:18–34:9, its grounds lie entirely in the character of God as merciful and gracious.

In conclusion, the story of the formation of the people of God (Exodus-Deuteronomy) gives detailed content to the faith and obedience that the patriarchal stories indicated was required of them. In the Mosaic covenant of obligation, they commit themselves on oath to be God's "holy people" by a quality of life that conforms to its various codes. But also, this story bears dramatic witness to their utter dependence, like Abraham, on God's free, gracious initiative and effectuation. This can be seen, first of all, in Israel's deliverance at the sea, the OT paradigm par excellence of salvation. Above all, however, it emerges in God's gracious accommodation to the repeated disobedience of his people—the grace of forgiveness rooted in Yahweh's own merciful character. As Childs puts it,

> Israel and the church have their existence because God picked up the pieces. . . . The people of God are from the outset the forgiven and restored community. There is a covenant—and a new covenant—because it was maintained from God's side.[45]

The People of God in Purpose (Gen 1–11)

Thus far we have traced the highlights of the partial fulfillment of the patriarchal promise from Genesis 12 to Deuteronomy. Our purpose has been to see something of what it means to be the people of God. But the beginning of their story lies in the much wider framework of the so-called "primeval prologue" (Gen 1–11). In that broad context, the people of God are part of the universal human community brought into being by God's creative activity. While the rich and varied fabric of this setting touches upon what it means to be the people of God in numerous ways, the most important elements relate to the purpose of their coming into being.

The Grace and Goodness of God in Creation (Gen 1–2)

In solemn, stately, repetitive rhythms, Genesis 1 sets forth God's creation of the world.[46] Rich in striking and sublime word pictures, the following narrative (Gen 2) introduces the story of human rebellion (ch. 3). Genesis 1 and 2 present the world as God created it—good, wholesome, and beautiful, with its climax being the creation of man and woman as responsible and blessed beings. In Genesis 1 God's climactic "evaluative word of approval" gave the entire creation the divine stamp of approval: "God looked at everything he had made and indeed it was very good" (1:31, author's trans.).[47] Genesis 2 confirms the goodness of creation by portraying the wholesome spiritual condition of man and woman. They live in God's own garden in peace and fellowship with him and, hence, in harmony with all the rest of creation. When faith formed by encounter with the gracious God whose name is Yahweh (Exod 34:6–7) considers creation, it can only affirm that no evil was laid upon the world at God's hand. This picture of creation's pristine goodness has implications for the people of God.

First, it teaches that they are to be his representatives on earth and to rule the world in his name. This is the inference that the text itself draws from their creation in God's image (v. 26, 28), whatever else that daring and striking metaphor may imply. Further, in Genesis 2 God gives humanity the task of working and caring for the garden. This directs the attention of both the community of faith and the rest of humanity to their obligation to be responsible stewards of the natural world God has created and entrusted into their care.

Second, in Genesis 2 only one "not good" casts a shadow over the garden scene's otherwise perfect harmony: "It is not good for the man to be alone" (2:18, NIV). He was not made to be an entity without need of others. True human life is life together. "Thus, the distinctively 'human' element as such does not appear in the individual; for existence-in-community is part of true humanity."[48] Hence, the essentially communal nature of what it is to be human is metaphorically expressed when God forms the woman from the man's own side. And in Genesis 1 the same reality is signaled when the author in 1:27 replaces "in the image of God" with "male and female": "God created *ʾāḏām* in his own image, in the image of God he created him; male and female, he created them" (author's trans.). In essence, Genesis 1 and 2 teach that humans cannot live as God intended if they live as isolated separate beings, but only if they live in the context of the shared experience of communal life. This communal nature of human life, so sadly marred by the selfish self-centeredness of sin, is what God desires to restore by calling into being the people of God, the community of faith.[49]

The Character of the Human Community (Gen 3–11)

In Genesis 3–11, the narrator moves to account for the world as it actually is, broken and disorderly, with human beings alienated and separated from one another and from God. He paints this dark picture by tracing the rise and development of human sin and rebellion. In chapter 3, the disobedience of the first man and woman leads to the disintegration of their primal unity and to their expulsion from the garden of God. Murder and bloody vengeance typify the next two generations (Gen 4:1–16, 17–23). This sad and sordid development, together with the story of the sexual union of women with the "sons of God" (6:1–4), which reveals a terrifying demonic element in human depravity, leads to God's evaluation of the depths of human sinfulness: "The LORD saw how great man's wickedness on the earth had become, and that every inclination of the thoughts of his heart was only evil all the time" (6:5, NIV). So, in the troubling story of the flood (Gen 6:4–9:29), God in judgment returned his creation to the watery chaos—its state before he separated land and sea (1:9–10).

Finally, the story of the Tower of Babel (11:1–9) depicts corporate human sin whose goal is expressly stated: "Come . . . let us make a name for ourselves and not be scattered over the face of the whole earth" (v. 4, author's trans.). That unmatched human pride, that defiance of God's creation ordinances (1:28; 9:1), leads to the final dissolution of humanity's primal unity: they are scattered into international disorder unable to understand each other's speech. This unrelenting tale of human sin and divine judgment would have been truly hopeless were it not for the presence of God's sustaining mercy and grace.[50]

The Primacy of the Grace and Unconditional Initiative of God

Surprisingly, the story of human sin in Genesis 3–11 is also the story of the grace of God. Though imposing severe judgment on Adam and Eve, God mercifully postpones his already-announced death penalty (2:17) until sometime in the future (3:19). Further, God himself clothes the guilty pair, enabling them to live with their shame (3:21; cf. 2:25; 3:7). Similarly, though banishing Cain to a restless existence, God places his mark of protection on him to prohibit his murder (4:13–15). Paradoxically, however, it is the flood story—the supreme symbol of divine judgment—that provides the supreme example of divine grace. After the flood, the narrator lets us hear God's inner thoughts (8:21–22). Strikingly, they echo his earlier musings before the flood (6:5–7), but they also modify them.

First, God accepts Noah's sacrifice and promises, "never again will I curse the ground because of humanity, however much the inclination of their hearts is evil from childhood" (8:21, author's trans.). The "however much" clause is virtually identical to the reason God gave for sending the flood originally (6:5).[51] In other words, God decided to treat his world with ultimate grace—to spare it and its creatures further cataclysmic judgment despite its sinfulness. Second, God decreed the uninterrupted continuation of nature's order: "As long as earth endures, seedtime and harvest, cold and heat, summer and winter, day and night will never cease" (8:22, author's trans.). As in Exodus 34, God's grace in judgment and mercy accommodates itself to human sin. Both stories testify that "in addition to judgment there is also mercy, a mercy which depends entirely on the character of God and is given to an unchangingly sinful people."[52]

Finally, the grace of God is supremely to be seen in the purpose that the narrative gives for the origin of the people of God. The biblical writer presents this purpose in two ways. The first is a literary device, the setting of the "prologue" (Gen 1–11) and the call and promise of Abraham (Gen 12:1–3) in sequence. It is striking that the Babel story concludes with God's judgment on humanity but without a word of grace.[53] Further, the story ends without a clear-cut break, but rather is succeeded by the genealogy of the descendants of Shem (11:10–26). This episode functions both as the conclusion of Genesis 1–11 and as the introduction to the story of Abraham. Therefore, the call and promise to Abraham—indeed, the whole subsequent pentateuchal story—serves as the word of divine grace. It is God's answer to the story of corporate human rebellion told by the primeval prologue, the story that reaches its climax in the Babel episode. Following Genesis 1–11, it reaffirms the validity of God's intentions for humanity.[54] Thus, the promise of posterity and land certainly recalls the blessing of God that underlies his command, "Be fruitful and increase in number; fill the earth and subdue it" (1:28, NIV). And the intimacy of the divine-human relationship in the covenant seeks to restore the intimacy that Adam and Eve enjoyed in the Garden of Eden.

The second way the author shows the purpose of the people of God is through the wording of the call and promise to Abraham (12:1–3), for it affirms that through him the blessing of God will extend to all humanity (v. 3). If Genesis 1–11 states the purpose implicitly, here it is stated explicitly (cf. also 26:4; 28:14): through the people of God and their story the world will ultimately be redeemed (Gal 3:8).[55]

In conclusion, this also demonstrates the full significance of the fact that the Pentateuch presents only the partial fulfillment of the promise of the people of God. Its ultimate fulfillment will wait for the Son of Abraham (Matt 1:1) who draws all people to himself (John 12:32) and whose death and resurrection will finally and fully unite the mercy and judgment of God. He will bring to a climax the story of the people of God, the long story of God's judgment and mercy whose early days the Torah dramatically portrays.

NOTES

1. It is a pleasure to dedicate this study to David Allan Hubbard, whose gracious and caring exercise of power and responsibility as President of Fuller Seminary has been a genuine reflection of the grace and lovingkindness (*hesed*) of God.

2. In what follows, *Pentateuch* replaces the more ambiguous term *Torah* to denote the whole contents of Genesis through Deuteronomy.

3. D. J. A. Clines, *The Theme of the Pentateuch,* JSOT Sup 10 (Sheffield: JSOT Press, 1978) 29.

4. Clines, ibid., 29. Clines (17–21) uses *theme* in a technical sense, i.e., that of "the conceptualization of the plot of" or "the central or dominating idea in" a literary work.

5. Strictly speaking, one should divide the text at Genesis 11:27 because of the genealogical formula, "This is the account [lit. *tôl̠dôt̠*, "generations"] of Terah. . ." (NIV). For our general purposes, however, the division by chapters will suffice.

6. J. Goldingay, *Theological Diversity and the Authority of the Old Testament* (Grand Rapids: Eerdmans, 1987) 62.

7. On the significance of the covenant, see Goldingay, Ibid. 172–81. For its ancient cultural background and function, see M. Weinfeld, "*berîth,*" *TDOT* 2:264, 278; P. Riemann, "Covenant, Mosaic," *IDBSup,* 192.

8. Goldingay, ibid., 178–81; Weinfeld, *TDOT* 2:255–56.

9. Cf. the discussion of parity covenants in G. Mendenhall, "Covenant," *IDB* 1:716–17.

10. E.g., *k̠arat̠ b̠e̠rît̠* (lit., "to cut a covenant"), et al.

11. M. Weinfeld compares the covenant with Abraham in Genesis 15 to royal grants of land made by kings to loyal servants ("The Covenant of Grant in the OT and the Ancient Near East," *JAOS* 90 [1970] 184–203; cf. idem, *TDOT* 2:270–72).

12. For the ritual's possible Mesopotamian background, see E. A. Speiser, *Genesis,* AB (Garden City: Doubleday, 1964) 113–14. For various interpretations of this rite, see G. von Rad, *Genesis,* OTL (Philadelphia: Westminster, 1972) 186 (a self-curse); G. Hasel, "The Meaning of the Animal Rite in Gen 15," *JSOT* 19 (1981) 61–78; G. J. Wenham, *Genesis 1–15,* WBC (Waco: Word, 1987) 332–33.

13. The text only mentions the promise of land once (v. 8), thereby setting it completely in the background.

14. Though Genesis 17 requires Abraham to practice circumcision (vv. 9–10), the text calls the rite the "sign of the covenant" (v. 11).

15. As a number of commentators have noted, the stress here is not so much on moral perfection, as the English translations "be perfect" or "blameless" imply, but rather on a life lived before God wholly and without reservations; see C. Westermann, *Genesis 12–36* (Minneapolis: Augsburg, 1985) 259; von Rad, *Genesis* 198–99.

16. A cohortative tense plus *waw* following an imperative regularly expresses result or purpose; cf. GKC §108d; R. Williams, *Hebrew Syntax* (Toronto: University of Toronto Press, 1976) §§187, 518; cf. NEB, REB.

17. For righteousness as "faithfulness to relationships," see G. von Rad, *Old Testament Theology,* 2 vols. (New York: Harper & Row, 1962–65) 1:370–83; idem, "Faith Reckoned as Righteousness," in *The Problem of the Hexateuch and Other Essays* (Edinburgh: Oliver & Boyd, 1965) 125–30.

18. T. Mann, *The Book of the Torah* (Atlanta: John Knox, 1988) 47; cf. H. Fuhs, "*yare*,"

TDOT 6:310; G. Coats, "Abraham's Sacrifice of Faith," *Int* 73 (1971) 397–98.

19. Clines, *The Theme of the Pentateuch*, 47–51.

20. The translation is that of J. Durham, *Exodus*, WBC 3 (Waco: Word, 1987) 256. From a possible Akkadian cognate word (*sikiltu*), Durham suggests (262) that the word "special treasure" (Heb. *s'gullâ*) connotes "the 'crown jewel' of a large collection, the masterwork, the one-of-a-kind piece."

21. Many scholars believe the Mosaic covenant may be patterned after well-known suzerain-vassal treaties, particularly those from Hittite sources. For an insightful treatment of it against this background, see D. Hillers, *Covenant: The History of a Biblical Idea* (Baltimore: Johns Hopkins, 1969). Cf. also K. Kitchen, "The Fall and Rise of Covenant, Law and Treaty," *TynBul* 40 (1989) 118–35, who believes the covenant draws on both treaty and ancient law-code forms.

22. Cf. Jer 34:17–20; B. S. Childs, *The Book of Exodus*, OTL (Philadelphia: Westminster, 1974) 505–6.

23. W. Zimmerli (*The Law and the Prophets* [New York: Harper & Row, 1965] 54–60) discusses this threat aspect of the Mosaic covenant; cf. Lev 26:25 ("a sword that shall execute vengeance for the covenant").

24. The "codes" include the Decalogue (Exod 20:1–17), the "Covenant Code" (Exod 20:22–23:33), the "Holiness Code" (Lev 17–27), and the "Deuteronomic Code" (Deut 12–26). For a survey of biblical law, see D. Patrick, *Old Testament Law* (Atlanta: John Knox, 1985).

25. Hillers, *Covenant*, 88.

26. E.g., Exod 22:21, 22–24, 25–27; 23:6, 9, 10–11; Lev 19:9–10, 33–34; 25:35–43; Deut 14:23–29; 15:4–11, 12–15; 24:12–15, 17–18, 19–22; 26:12–13; 27:19; etc.

27. P. Hanson, *The People Called* (San Francisco: Harper & Row, 1986) 49. See also Hanson's insightful study (42–52) of the so-called Book of the Covenant (Exod 20:23–23:33).

28. Hanson, ibid., 24.

29. For the grammar that makes this a preface to the announcement, see H. Brongers, "Bermerkungen zum Gebrauch des Adverbialen *w'* attāh im Alten Testament," *VT* 15 (1965) 293–94.

30. For discussion of details see the commentaries, especially Durham.

31. Cf. Gen 26:8; 39:14; R. Moberly, *At the Mountain of God*, JSOTSup 22 (Sheffield: JSOT, 1983) 196 n. 7. In Israel's polytheistic world, the bull was a symbol of fertility.

32. Durham, *Exodus*, 422.

33. Cf. the expression of the rebellion theme in Psalms 78 and 106. Concerning the nature and possible origin of the "murmuring tradition," see Childs, op. cit., 254–64.

34. A. Goldberg, *Das Buch Numeri* (Düsseldorf: Patmos, 1970) 66, cited from D. Olson, *The Death of the Old and the Birth of the New* (Chico, CA: Scholars Press, 1985) 227 n. 47.

35. Olson, ibid., 145.

36. In passing, one should observe another lesson for the people of God here, namely, the cost of apostasy. Three thousand die after the golden-calf incident; cf. Exod 32:25–29, 34; Ps 27:32–33.

37. As Childs says about the golden-calf episode, *The Book of Exodus*, (579–80), "embedded at the heart of the sacred tradition lies Israel's disobedience and rebellion. The OT understood this episode of flagrant disobedience, not as an accidental straying, but as representative in its character. The story of the divine redemption includes the history of human resistance and rebellion."

38. Childs (*The Book of Exodus* 567) recalls B. Jacob's comparison of this slightly lenient statement with the absolute finality of God's refusal to permit Moses to enter the land of promise (Deut 3:26).
39. Childs, ibid., 567.
40. Moberly, *At the Mountain of God*, 49–50.
41. Here following the insights of Moberly, ibid. 75–76; cf. Childs, *The Book of Exodus*. 595–97; Durham, *Exodus* 455.
42. Durham, *Exodus*, 450, 452.
43. Moberly, *At the Mountain of God*, 87–88 (italics his) as part of his fine discussion (87–90).
44. For the rendering of the Hebrew particle *kî* here as an emphatic concessive, "however much" or "although indeed," see Moberly, ibid., 89–90.
45. Childs, *The Book of Exodus*, 580.
46. Genesis 1 probably originated as an independent narrative but was editorially placed as the prologue to all that follows. This assumes that the *tôrĕdôt* formula (Gen 2:4a) introduces chs. 2–3 rather than concludes 1:1–2:3a; cf. Wenham, *Genesis 1–15*, 6; Clines, *The Theme of the Pentateuch*, 65–66.
47. Of course, the words "indeed it was very good" sound the final, climactic refrain of a series of divine evaluations: "God saw that it was good" (1:4, 10, 12, 18, 21, 25).
48. E. Brunner, *The Christian Doctrine of Creation and Redemption* (Philadelphia: Westminster, 1952) 64.
49. Cf. E. Brunner, *The Christian Doctrine of the Church, Faith, and the Consummation* (Philadelphia: Westminster, 1962) 26: "... faith is the will and the readiness to be with, to be with our fellow humans, communicative life. It is therefore in the nature of the case impossible that as a believer one should be or wish to remain a solitary .... It is just this living for one-self, this existence of a 'Monad without windows,' which is abolished by faith."
50. On the significance of the sin of the tower-builders as the capstone of Gen 2–11, see Clines, *The Theme of the Pentateuch*, 69–70.
51. For the translation of *kî* here as an emphatic concessive, see Moberly, *At the Mountain of God*, 91, 113–15.
52. Moberly, ibid., 90; cf. also Clines, *Theme* 76.
53. Von Rad (*Genesis*, 153) was the first one to see the relationship between Genesis 1–11 and Genesis 12.
54. For this and some of what follows, cf. Clines, *Theme*, 77–78; Wenham, *Genesis 1–15*, li.
55. See T. Mann, "All the Families of the Earth," *Int* 45 (1991) 351–52.

6

IMAGES FOR TODAY: THE TORAH SPEAKS TODAY

Walter C. Kaiser, Jr.

Is there any place for the first five books of the Bible in the life and experience of the Church of the late twentieth century? Or, as James T. Burtchaell asked: "Is the torah obsolete for Christians?"[1] Ever since the Reformation, these questions have had a special bite to them. Curiously enough, "The same founders who revived so learned a reverence for the Bible had made Romans and Galatians the rate of exchange for the whole of Scripture. All that was authentically Christian was seen as innovative, and as a breakaway from its Jewish antecedents."[2] Thankfully, this was not a universal conclusion, but the concept that the Pentateuch was practically synonymous with the concept of "law" only added fuel to this fire.

The Meaning of Torah

When the Hebrew word *tôrâ* was rendered in the Greek Septuagint as *nomos,* an incorrect (or at least an overly restrictive, narrow, and inadequate) translation arose. This, in turn, gave rise to the English rendering "law," the French *loi*, and the German *Gesetz*. Unfortunately, each of these translations continues to give credence to the notion that this portion of Scripture denotes merely formal regulations, often with ritual associations, to which those in the community who wished to attain redemption were subjected. This incorrect conclusion has led to the misguided inference that the Pentateuch must now be replaced in the life of the believing community, since legal instructions have now been exchanged for gracious acceptance and the material emphasis of the Torah has now been replaced with the spiritual tone of the New Testament.

Torah is much more than law. Even the word itself does not reflect static requirements that cover the whole gamut of human experience. Instead, *tôrâ* probably comes from the Hebrew verb meaning "to point [out the direction one should go]." That is why in the book of Proverbs its teaching is connected so frequently with a "path." God's law was meant to be a light on one's path: it was intended to point out which direction a person should go. Moreover, the legal sections of the Torah are a relatively small part of the Torah as a whole. And these laws, or directions, appear fully integrated within the total story and text of the Pentateuch, which traces the progress of God's word of promise to his people. To discuss one or more of these directions in abstraction and apart from the context of the story in which each occurs is to do a disservice both to the so-called law and to the context of the narrative itself.

While it is true that the perceived legal material is more prominent in the Pentateuch than it is in the wisdom or prophetic books, these directions in the Torah are more foundational to the rest of the Old Testament as the Torah establishes the grounds for the whole story of God's gracious dealings with his people. The wisdom and prophetic corpus usually merely allude to the legal guidelines set out in the Pentateuch. In the view of these prophetic and sapiential writers, the heart of the norms for the divinely directed life had already been laid out in the Mosaic revelation. Therefore, the rituals, ceremonies, and instructions supplied in the legal sections of the Pentateuch were not treated as if they were ends in and of themselves. Instead, they were perceived as means by which individuals could demonstrate how they attested to the reality of God's presence in the affairs of their everyday lives. Ceremonies, rituals, and guidelines only served as bridges over which mortals could meet with God. But to suggest that the means were the ends in themselves would be to totally confuse the two.

The Relation of Torah to Promise

Increasingly it is being recognized that the theme of the Pentateuch is the partial fulfillment and continued expectation of the fulfillment of the promise to or blessing of the patriarchs. This promise, which serves as the keystone, or as an arch over the first five books of the Bible, consists of at least three elements: a posterity, a divine-human relationship, and a land.[3] For example, the promise of a posterity or a "seed" appears some twenty-eight times in Genesis alone.[4] There is almost the same high frequency for the other elements of the promise.[5]

This gigantic theme of the promise did not cease when the narrative of the patriarchs came to a conclusion. In fact, it was only in the two focal points of the rest of the Pentateuch, viz., the exodus and the revelation of the law on Mount Sinai, that it became clear what the blessing of the promise and the pledged covenantal relationship would involve. Repeatedly, Israel was referred to in the episodes leading up to the exodus event as "my people." And the reason given for such a close relationship with God himself was the covenant that he inaugurated with the patriarchs (e.g., Exod 2:24; 3:6). Therefore, there is more than a mere setting of the scene or supplying of transitional materials between Genesis and the exodus event in Exodus 14. God would be a personal deity to them, they would also be his very own special possession, and, most amazingly of all, God would dwell, or tabernacle, in the midst of them.

If the emphasis of the books of Exodus and Leviticus was on the concepts of what it meant to be a "people" of God—for God to personally dwell in the midst of them—the emphasis of Numbers and Deuteronomy was on the promise of the land. It was clear that the element of the land did not appear at the conclusion of the Pentateuch. Rather, it was remembered as part of the pledge that Yahweh had given at the beginning of the narrative of the Pentateuch. Accordingly, Deuteronomy 34:4 recapitulated:

> The LORD said to [Moses], "This is the land I promised on oath to Abraham, Isaac and Jacob when I said, 'I will give it to your descendants'" (NIV).

How, then, did promise relate to torah? It was always a relationship that emphasized the priority of promise over torah. This may be demonstrated in a number of ways: for example, the election of Isaac was made solely on the basis of the purpose of God and not on the accumulated pious deeds of this son of Abraham. This is the precise point that the apostle Paul made when he appealed to Genesis 25:23 to show that God's selection between the twins occurred in the womb even before either son had an opportunity to do either right or wrong (Rom 9:11–12). The only reason left for the divine election of one and not the other was the purpose and will of God. Consequently, according to Genesis 21:8–21 and 25:23, there were no contributing factors of works or good deeds involved in God's decision. Once again, the existence of the promise precedes torah both in a temporal and in a theological sense.

Another case where the promise preceded torah can be seen in the conclusion to the story of the binding of Isaac in Genesis 22:16–18. The text reads:

> I swear by myself, declares the LORD, that because you have done this [obedience, in that you were willing to offer Isaac] and have not withheld your son, your only son, I will surely bless you and make your descendants as numerous as the stars in the sky and as the sand on the seashore. Your descendants will take possession of the cities of their enemies, and through your offspring all nations on earth will be blessed, *because you have obeyed me* (NIV, emphasis mine).

These were the words of promise already pledged in Genesis 12:1–3. Since the pledges issued here were already known, Abraham's obedience could not have been the basis for their repetition or initiation. The identical point must be made at the beginning of the story about Isaac (Gen 26:3b–5):

> I will be with you and will bless you. For to you and your descendants I will give all these lands and will confirm the oath I swore to your father Abraham. I will make your descendants as numerous as the stars in the sky and will give them all these lands, and through your offspring all nations on earth will be blessed, *because Abraham obeyed me and kept my requirements, my commands, my decrees and my laws* (NIV, emphasis mine).

The point must be stressed once again: this promise already was in effect. Thus, any obedience, merit, or so-called law-keeping on Abraham's part could not have resulted in his receiving this gracious pledge from God. Even though the words used here will become technical terms later on in the Sinaitic revelation and in Deuteronomy ("requirements, commands, decrees, laws"; *mišmᵉrôt, miṣwôt, ḥuqqôt, tôrôt*), they had not taken on these meanings as yet since that revelation had not been given according to the intention of the Pentateuch. Once more, all that can be said is that Abraham acted in accord with Yahweh's order of these as they had been revealed up to that point, but in no case was this exemplary obedience determinative in the communication of the promise any more than it had been in Genesis 22:18.

The Narrative Framework of the Pentateuch

If the promise-plan of God deserves to be recognized as the central theme of the Pentateuch, what is the framework that contains it? Surely there must be some middle way to regard the Pentateuch besides the two extremes of either anchoring it solely in the past or allowing it to be free-floating allegorized ideals to be used according to each individual's own preferences and subjective fancies! The best way to allow the Torah to speak to our day, vis-á-vis the two rejected extremes just mentioned, is to recognize that the Torah, i.e., the first five books of the Bible, is essentially a narrative. And this narrative is part of an ongoing story that embraces the whole of human history as told from the divine perspective. It is only by recognizing that this narrative has a beginning, a middle, and a temporary end (with the final end held over indefinitely until we come to the climax of the kingdom of God) that this literature can function in a time beyond its own.

Genesis 1–11

The narrative of the Torah did not begin with the patriarchs, but with the so-called primeval history of Genesis 1–11. In fact, there is no sharp disjunction or severe dissonance between what many view as the "universal history" of Genesis 1–11 and what others have dubbed the "salvation history" from Genesis 12 onward. Rather than contrast one another, the themes of the two units flow evenly into each other. Thus, it is incorrect to conclude that the universal history of Genesis 1–11 led directly and solely to judgment, while salvation history opened up an era of blessing. The problem with the method of telling the story by sharply dividing the two sections is that it fails to utilize the obvious connection between the focus of Genesis 1–11, viz., the "blessing of God," and the announcement of the promise to Abraham in Genesis 12:1–3, where the word "bless" or "blessing" *(brk)* occurs five times! The connection could not be more obvious and explicit.

Few will deny that the key motif of the opening eleven chapters was the "blessing" of God on the created order (Gen 1:22) and on the human pair

(Gen 1:28). This divine blessing was continued in 5:2 and picked up again after the flood story in 9:1. Moreover, the blessing theme was present even apart from the explicit use of the word "to bless" or the formula of "and God blessed them saying, 'Be fruitful and multiply, and fill the earth'" (RSV). The blessing of God was present, as Claus Westermann argued,[6] even in such prepatriarchal pledges as those of Genesis 3:15 and 9:27. But Westermann was not alone in noting this linkage of the promise between Genesis 1–11 and the patriarchal era. Both Zimmerli and Blythin called attention to the way "blessing" was associated with the concept of the promise in the patriarchal record.[7] Unfortunately, neither scholar carried this valid observation back to Genesis 1–11, nor did they notice that this emphasis also happened to fall just where the two epochs met in the canon.

In fact, so closely intertwined were both blessing and promise that many scholars have begun to look for ways to segregate them from each other. Albrecht Alt, for example, alleged that each patriarch originally had his own separate clan god: "The Shield of Abraham," "The Fear [or Kinsman] of Isaac," and "The Mighty One of Jacob."[8] For Alt, the choosing of Abraham and his seed had nothing to do with Yahweh, but instead went back to the religion of the gods of the father. Thus, it was alleged, there were two choosings (one for the patriarchs and one for Israel) from the three "clan gods" of the patriarchs and of Israel's Yahweh. These choosings were linked to two promises: the increase of the patriarch's posterity and Israel's possession of the land. Alt, surprisingly enough, divided the two and awarded the first promise of the descendants to the patriarchs; the second (of the land) he declared to be an editorial retrojection back to patriarchal times after Israel entered into the land.

Martin Noth, however, judged that both the promise of the land and the promise of progeny were very old, even though he gave greater prominence to Jacob than he gave to Abraham.[9] Von Rad agreed with Noth that this twofold promise went back to the time of the patriarchs.[10] In spite of this agreement, many still tended to associate "blessing" passages solely with the concerns of progeny and wealth, while promise passages were said to focus on the concern for the land. Such a division of the text, however, turns out to be very artificial and unnatural. The blessings were not, as some thought, individual and immediate, whereas the promises were corporate and future in nature. Instead, together the blessing-promises were addressed to those descendants of the present and future in the whole line of believers who had a historically representative individual in each generation (e.g., Abraham, Isaac, Jacob, David), who acted as an earnest (i.e., a down-payment) on what God would be and do in the future for the benefit of all who had not yet seen the end of this promised line.

Therefore, we conclude that the generous word of God was fulfilled in his "blessing" to man in both eras: "Be fruitful and multiply, and fill the earth" (Gen 1:28, rsv; 9:1, 7; 12:1–3; 35:11), and in his promise and portrayals of salvation in both eras, including a seed, a race, a land, a blessing to all nations, kings, etc. (Gen 3:15; 9:27; 12:1–3; 15; 17).

The Patriarchal Promise and the Mosaic Law

If there is one reason why the Torah is viewed as failing to speak to our day, it can be laid at the feet of the serious disjuncture that many have concluded exists between promise and law. But once again, the connections between the two sections are so very clear from the text itself. Most outstanding is the very formula that appears as a rubric for the Ten Commandments themselves: "I am Yahweh your God, who brought you out of the land of Egypt" (Exod 20:2, rsv). This formula of self-predication and self-revelation appears about 125 times in the rest of the OT. It is very similar to the formula of Genesis 15:7, also repeated often, though with less frequency: "I am Yahweh, who brought you out of Ur of the Chaldees" (rsv). Both formulae spoke of the grace of God; in no way were either of the two the result of any human efforts or merited favor on the part of any individual or group.

Moreover, the same elements that greeted the patriarchs' reception of the covenant were present at the reception of the covenant God gave at Sinai. For example, both record the presence of smoke and fire at the epiphanies connected with the giving of both covenants (Gen 15:17; Exod 19:18). Likewise, both continue to refer to "the God of my/your father" (Gen 26:24; 28:13; 32:10; Exod 3:6; 18:4). And when Israel was delivered from Pharaoh, the people sang, "Yahweh is my strength and my song, / and he has become my salvation; / this is my God, and I will praise him; / my father's God, and I will exalt him" (Exod 15:2, rsv). Even more directly to the point, the text of Exodus claims that what God did at the exodus and Sinai was a result of his remembering his covenant with Abraham, Isaac, and Jacob (Exod 2:24; 3:13, 15–16; 4:5; 6:3, 5, 8). Even the sevenfold emphasis on the rapid increase of people in Exodus 1:7–9 indicated that the blessing of multiplication pronounced in Genesis 1 and 2 had not been jettisoned.

However, what has troubled most theologians and readers of the Torah is not the continuity of the narrative, but rather the diverse nature of the materials of the two covenants: Sinai seemed to impose commands, demands, and obligations whereas the Abrahamic promise was filled with the gifts of free blessings. In fact, so strongly has this disjuncture been felt that some have pointed to other supporting lines of evidence. For example, von Rad pointed to Deuteronomy 26:5–9, which he regarded as the key credo of Israel, along with other credos such as Joshua 24:16–18, that confessed Israel's patriarchal beginnings, their oppression in Egypt, their wilderness wanderings, and their entrance into Egypt.[11] Von Rad's point was that the events of Sinai, which he regarded as the heart of the Pentateuch, were explicitly left out of these credos, thus proving that the Sinai events belonged to an older and separate tradition. Only later in the exilic period did it occur to anyone to link promise/gospel with law, according to this way of viewing the Torah.

Von Rad's analysis, however, was sharply challenged.[12] The fact was that the exodus from Egypt had been clearly connected with Sinai in Exodus 19:3–8 and 20:2–17. Moreover, the very credos that von Rad used to disassociate the Sinai revelation from the narrative of the Torah linked the deliverance from Egypt with the demands of the Sinaitic covenant; von Rad should have included all of Deuteronomy 26, not just verses 5–9, and all of Joshua 24, not just verses 16–18.[13]

Even admitting all of the connections traced thus far, the problem still remained: how were the demands of Exodus 20–Numbers 10 to be integrated, if at all, with the blessings and promises made in the prepatriarchal and patriarchal materials of Genesis? In my view, the best response to this query is to show how the same combination of promise and command existed in the patriarchal narratives as well. Commands, imperatives, and prohibitions were freely interspersed with the promises and blessings given to Abraham, Isaac, and Jacob. According to Premsagar, a list from Genesis would include:

12:1	"Go from your own country"
13:14	"Lift up your eyes and look"
15:1	"Do not be afraid"
15:9	"Bring me a heifer"
17:1	"Walk before me and be perfect"
22:2	"Take your son, your only son . . . and go"
26:2	"Do not go down to Egypt, but stay in this country"
26:24	"Fear not"
31:3	"Go back to the land of your fathers"
35:11	"Be fruitful and multiply"[14]

The conclusion that appears to be altogether fair is this: in each of these cases in the patriarchal situation, each command or prohibition was preceded or made in the context of promise. Thus, obedience was never the condition of the covenant for Abraham, Isaac, or Jacob. Instead, it was as Hebrews 11:8 put it: "By faith Abraham obeyed" (RSV).

Exactly the same point must be made for the Sinai legislation. The context for the Ten Commandments in Exodus 20 is the context of grace: God is the God who has just delivered Israel out of the hand of Pharaoh. Thus, the law is no less than the gift of God, as the psalmists rightly celebrate (Pss 1:2; 19:7–11; 40:8; 119). Promise did not oppose God's law, for both promise and law came from the same covenant-making God. Neither did the law promise a separate means, or even a hypothetical means, of salvation; it was only a means for maintaining fellowship with God, not the basis for initiating or establishing such a relationship. In fact, this same Sinaitic legislation was perhaps even more expansive in its explicit provisions for those who had failed to maintain fellowship with God than it was in describing what that standard was for holy living.

The Theology of Torah and the Law

What role, we ask then, did the law play in the development of the theology of the Pentateuch?[15] Here Schmitt offers an extremely stimulating starting point by arguing that the entire Pentateuch was a unified composition that focused on faith as its central theme.[16] At each of the crucial compositional seams throughout the Pentateuch, argued Schmitt, the "faith theme" *(Glaubens-Thematik)* appeared: Genesis 15:6 ("Abram believed the LORD, and he credited it to him as righteousness," NIV), Exodus 4:5 ("'This,' said the LORD, 'is so that they may believe that the LORD. . . has appeared to you,'" NIV), Exodus 14:31 ("the people feared the LORD and put their trust in him and in Moses his servant," NIV), Numbers 14:11 ("How long will they refuse to believe in me, in spite of all the miraculous signs?" NIV), and Numbers 20:12 ("But the LORD said to Moses and Aaron, 'Because you did not trust in me enough to honor me as holy in the sight of the Israelites, you will not bring this community into the land I give them'" NIV). Thus, instead of viewing the Pentateuch as emphasizing the keeping of priestly law codes, Schmitt's study has taken a long stride toward demonstrating that the Pentateuch really intended to teach "faith" in God and his promises.[17]

But that thesis only raises another issue: is there evidence for a "faith" versus "law" tension in the Torah? All too frequently the Torah has been divided into two major genres: (1) Genesis (i.e., the promise given to the patriarchs) and (2) Exodus-Deuteronomy (i.e., the Sinaitic legal and cultic provisions). Usually, the promises are linked to the faith-theme while the law is seen as a system of works and obedience. However, the "faith-theme" does not simply occur in the narratives about Abraham, Isaac, and Jacob; they are central to the life of Moses as well. Or to put it another way, obedience was not only evidenced in the Sinaitic and Mosaic materials of Exodus to Deuteronomy; Abraham was called to the same obedience, even though he too experienced the centrality of faith and belief, as can be seen in the classical text of Genesis 26:5—"I [God] will bless you [Isaac] . . . because Abraham obeyed me and kept my requirements, my commands, my decrees and my laws" (NIV). Accordingly, it is difficult to place the Torah in two opposing camps, one favoring faith and belief in the promise of God, the other favoring works and obedience. The very terms used for Abraham's obedience were the ones that would later come to denote the whole Mosaic law.

Nevertheless, lingering doubts still persist: perhaps the narrative of Numbers 20:1–13 illustrates that Moses and the Sinaitic legislation did, in spite of our protestations here, represent the counter theme to the faith-theme. Sailhamer, and to a lesser degree Schmitt, argue that the sin of Moses and Aaron in Numbers 20:1–13 was the sin of unbelief.[18] The action of these two men focuses on the negative side of faith and, as a result, stands in bold relief against the faith of Abraham. Explains Sailhamer,

> The narrative strategy of the Pentateuch contrasts Abraham, who kept the law, and Moses, whose faith was weakened under the law. This suggests a conscious effort on the part of the author of the Pentateuch, to distinguish between a life of faith before the law *(ante legum)* and a lack of faith under the law *(sub lege)*. This is accomplished by showing that the life of God's people before the giving of the law was characterized by faith and trust in God, but after the giving of the law their lives were characterized by faithlessness and failure.[19]

The problem with this rather remarkable analysis of a very difficult exegetical and theological issue is that it places the fault with the divinely communicated law itself, rather than with the people. On numerous occasions in the future, the fault would be laid at the feet of the people rather than with either the human or divine lawgiver, or the provisions of the law (e.g., "because they broke my covenant" [Jer 31:32, NIV]; "[b]ut God found fault with the people" [Heb 8:7, NIV]). Moreover, throughout their lives Moses and Aaron were just as much models of faith as was

Abraham. The charge God made against these two leaders was not that they had now turned their backs on God and no longer trusted him as they once did. Rather, they were rebuked for failing to trust God enough to set him forth in the eyes of the people (Num 20:12). It was in their roles as leaders that they failed, not in their own private lives of personal belief and trust. What God invoked was the double indemnity rule for teachers and leaders, as set forth so explicitly later on in James 3:1—"Not many of you should presume to be teachers, my brothers, because you know that we who teach will be judged more strictly" (NIV).

The theology of the Torah is the theology of faith, belief, and trust. That part of the Schmitt and Sailhamer argument rests on firm exegetical grounds. Where, then, do obedience, works, and Moses's directions found in the moral, civil, and ceremonial laws fit? All too frequently it has become popular to refer to the Sinaitic legislation as the 613 commandments God gave Moses at Sinai, 365 being prohibitions equal to the number of the solar days in a year and 248 being commands allegedly corresponding to the number of the parts of the human body.[20] But nowhere in the Torah are the commandments or prohibitions arranged in this way. The very suggestion that this is what we are dealing with in the problem of the law is a clue that the orientation is one of later rabbinical exegesis and not one of Torah exposition.

To come back, then, to our question: what role did the law play in the theology of the Torah? And is that theology still relevant for our day? It is clear that the laws (or as we have argued, the directions given by Moses) exhibited the characteristics of universality, consistency, and prescriptivity.[21] And the ways of righteousness and justice were not to be limited to Israel, but were the hallmarks for all the nations of the earth. Jeremiah warned: "And if [all the wicked neighboring nations] learn well the ways of my people and swear by my name . . . then they will be established among my people. But if any nation does not listen, I will completely uproot and destroy it" (Jer 12:16–17, NIV; cf. 18:7–10).

But how is one able to move from the specific, individual, and particularized command to any sort of modern relevancy for that same word? Three methods have been used in the past, but to these three I will add a fourth.[22]

The Method of Analogy

Analogy presupposes that there is some sort of expressed, or unexpressed, comparison between Israel's laws and the modern world or the Church.

But if the analogy were all that apparent, there would be little room for dispute. Unfortunately, the analogies tend to be more the wish that is parent to the thought, rather than being clearly found in the text. Usually the analogy is located just where Scripture has not drawn it, between Israel and the Church. In this model, what was spoken to the nation Israel is now equated with that which God is addressing to the Church, for Israel has become the Church in this model.

The Method of Middle Axioms

A middle axiom is generally thought to be a principle that is somewhere between a general abstraction (e.g., "justice") and a specific, concrete action. However, in addition to lacking any demonstration that these middle axioms are biblically derived, they tend to end up being altogether too general—so general that they would fit almost any and every situation. Moreover, this method never brings us back to any practical application or to a particular decision.

The Method of General Equity

Many of the earlier confessions of faith, along with the Westminster Confession of Faith, distinguished among the moral, ceremonial, and judicial laws of God.[23] The moral law was taken as those principles that reflected the character of God: here was the backbone for all biblical law. The word equity, in this method, meant that the law could apply to more cases than the particular one it addressed in the concrete and particular circumstances of its scriptural context. Thus, each law exhibited a general moral principle behind it, but it had a number of areas or cases to which it could be applied just as well as to the concrete case recorded by Moses. The point was that the law applied just as well to a number of cases for which it did not expressly provide. This application, however, was not so much an appeal to reason as it was an appeal to the informing theology of the moral law that lay behind each expression of the law. Neither should it be understood to mean that it was a cross-cultural application of case laws minus the cultural expressions. It was a search for the moral law that each law exhibited and that pointed back to both the character of God and the revelation of the moral law that lay behind that law.

This method is surely to be preferred over everything that we have encountered thus far. Nevertheless, even after we had discovered the moral law that lay behind this law, it could not tell us how to proceed from there. More was needed.

The Method of the Ladder of Abstraction

The use of general equity in the preceding method is similar to that used in legal precedents and law courts today. Previous decisions are gathered as one seeks to press the general equity of an older, but different, situation to a modern but unexplored situation. Thus, the lawyer or judge reconstructs the rationale of the earlier case, which serves as the main reason for deciding the previous case (the *ratio decidendi*). This principle in turn is applied to the new case, which demands a search for the moral point or the purpose behind the earlier precedent. Naturally, not all the facts and details of the previous case are relevant nor need they be appealed to at this point.

From this *ratio* we can begin to build our "Ladder of Abstraction." In this method, it is necessary to picture two ladders slanted in toward each other at the top, but anchored at their bases some distance apart. The base of each ladder represents a concrete, particularistic setting, the one the cultural context of the Torah and the other the particular and concrete needs of the contemporary culture in which the reader is located. The point at which the two ladders meet at the top is the general principle, the moral law, or the abstract teaching that lies behind both the ancient context and the modern situation. The interpreter must be able to move from the ancient specific situation through the OT institutional or personal forms to which that specific situation adheres up to the general principle that embraces both the specific and institutional or personal forms in which that principle has been manifested.

It is the identification of the general or moral principle that allows us to take full advantage of the insights of general equity. This general principle also provides us with the authoritative grounds for extending the principle far beyond the limits of application observed in the Torah.[24] Of course, one must be careful in moving from the general principle or the moral precept that lies behind the particular illustration given in the OT to the "consequent sense" named in the contemporary situation. If the application to the modern situation is separate and different from that found in both the general principle and its OT particular setting, it is difficult, if not impossible, to see how such an extension of the thought could have been intended by the writer of Scripture or how it could be authoritatively taught in the Church. Therefore, the consequent extension must apply in the *same sense* to any and each of an indefinite number of contemporary particularizations.

The application of the consequent sense of the universal or general principle to the same, or similar, modern situations can be illustrated in several NT usages. For example, Jesus used Hosea 6:6, "I [the Lord] desire mercy, not sacrifice" (NIV), in Matthew 9:10–13 to justify his eating with publicans and sinners and to justify his disciples's action in eating grain on the Sabbath (cf. Matt 12:1–7). This, however, was not an example of a double sense (or *sensus plenior*), for the principle remained the same, not separate and different, throughout. Each of these texts, the one in Hosea and the two in Matthew, set forth what was necessary for acceptance with God, while erring mortals focused merely on the physical externals of the situation at hand.[25]

Conclusion

Torah, we conclude, is not a collection of prohibitions, rigid strictures, and observances. It is the narrative of the blessing and promise of God. That divine promise-plan freely offered God's gracious gifts to the whole world, first through a man and his family, and then through the nation of Israel.

Accompanying this main theme of blessing/promise were directions as to how, then, believers in the promise should act, live, and comport themselves. These directions mapped out a path, not a rigid system of hoops that one had to jump through in order to initiate or to maintain one's status within the body of the redeemed.

If contemporary believers have any doubts as to the enduring usefulness of Torah, they need only to consult Jesus' estimate on this matter (Matt 5:19): "Anyone who breaks one of the least of these commandments and teaches others to do the same will be called least in the kingdom of heaven" (NIV). In fact, these laws would remain in effect (or be fulfilled) until heaven and earth passed away—an event that was not precipitated by the first advent! Likewise, the apostle Paul considered the law "good" (Rom 7:12–13) and "spiritual" (Rom 7:14); in fact, it was written "for us" (1 Cor 9:8–10). In no way had "faith" nullified the law: "Not at all!" he remonstrated. "Rather, we uphold the law" (Rom 3:31, NIV). Thus, "The law is good, if one uses it properly" (1 Tim 1:8, NIV).[26]

The apostle Paul's summation is fully applicable to Torah: the usefulness and contemporary application of the OT is still profitable for doctrine, instruction, rebuke, correction, and training in righteousness (2 Tim 3:16–17). And that estimate is fully operative in the ancient Torah. In response to the cries of modernity for contemporary relevance, this essay has outlined how one may pursue a fair reading of that text.

NOTES

1. J. T. Burtchaell, "Is the Torah Obsolete for Christians?" in *Justice and the Holy: Essays in Honor of Walter Harrelson*, ed. D. A. Knight & P. J. Paris (Atlanta: Scholars Press, 1989) 113–27.

2. Burtchaell, ibid. 113.

3. See, for example, D. J. A. Clines, *The Theme of the Pentateuch*, JSOTSup 10 (Sheffield: JSOT, 1978); H. Seebass, "The Relationship of Torah and Promise in the Redactionary Composition of the Pentateuch," *HBT* 7 (1985) 99–111; and W. C. Kaiser, Jr., "God's Promise Plan and His Gracious Law," *JETS* 33 (1990) 289–302; idem, "Promise," *Holman Bible Dictionary*, ed. T. C. Butler (Nashville: Holman, 1991) 1140–41.

4. Gen 12:2, 7; 13:15, 16; 15:4–5, 13, 16, 18; 16:10; 17:2, 4–7, 10, 13, 16, 19–20; 21:12–13, 18; 22:16–17; 24:7; 26:3–4, 24; 28:1–14; 32:12; 35:11–12; 46:3–4.

5. See the convenient tables of Scripture references in Clines, *The Theme*, 33–34, 36–43.

6. C. Westermann, "The Way of Promise through the Old Testament," in *The Old Testament and Christian Faith*, ed. B. W. Anderson (New York: Harper & Row, 1963) 208–9.

7. W. Zimmerli, "Promise and Fulfillment," in *Essays on Old Testament Hermeneutics*, ed. C. Westermann, 2nd ed. (Richmond: John Knox, 1969) 90–98; I. Blythin, "The Patriarchs and the Promise," *SJT* 21 (1968) 72.

8. A. Alt, "The God of the Fathers," in *Essays on OT History and Religion* (Garden City, NJ: Doubleday, 1968) 82–84.

9. M. Noth, *A History of Pentateuchal Traditions* (Englewood Cliffs, NJ: Prentice-Hall, 1972) 54–58, 79–115, 147–56.

10. G. von Rad, *Old Testament Theology*, 2 vols. (London: Oliver & Boyd, 1962) 1:168–75.

11. G. von Rad, *The Problem of the Hexateuch and Other Essays* (New York: McGraw-Hill, 1966) 1–26.

12. For a summary of these views, see H. B. Huffmon, "The Exodus, Sinai, and the Credo," *CBQ* 27 (1965) 102–3 nn. 6–10.

13. For example, Joshua 24 refers to statutes, ordinances, and witnesses (vv. 22, 27) and oaths of acceptance (vv. 16, 21). So argues J. A. Thompson, "The Cultic Credo and the Sinai Tradition," *The Reformed Theological Review* 27 (1968) 53–64.

14. P. V. Premsagar, "Theology of Promise in the Patriarchal Narratives," *Indian Journal of Theology* 23 (1974) 121.

15. I have been especially stimulated by my colleague J. H. Sailhamer's article, "The Mosaic Law and the Theology of the Pentateuch," *WTJ* 53 (1991) 241–61.

16. H.C. Schmitt, "Redaktion des Pentateuch im Geiste der Prophetie," *VT* 32 (1982) 170–89.

17. Cf. also Deut 1:32; 9:23. I have argued in detail that the object and method of salvation were the same in the OT as they were in the NT in W. C. Kaiser, Jr., *Toward Rediscovering the Old Testament* (Grand Rapids: Zondervan, 1987) 121–28 (note esp. the lengthy exegesis of Gen 15:1–16). This argument was extended in my article, "Salvation and Atonement: Forgiveness and Saving Faith in the Tenak," in *To the Jew First: The Place of Jewish Evangelism in the On-Going Mission of the Church*, ed. J. I. Packer (forthcoming).

18. Sailhamer, "The Mosaic Law" 254–60; Schmitt, "Redaktion des Pentateuch," as cited by Sailhamer, "The Mosaic Law," 254–60.

19. Sailhamer, ibid., 260.

20. This statement is attributed to Rabbi Simlai (*b. Mak.* 23b). For a history of this system and a list of the 365 prohibitions, see A. H. Rabinowitz, "Commandments, the 613," *EncJud* 5:760–83.

21. For the developments of these characteristics, see W. C. Kaiser, Jr., *Toward Old Testament Ethics* (Grand Rapids: Zondervan, 1983) 24–29.

22. For further details on the line of argumentation used here, see W. C. Kaiser, Jr., "The Weightier and Lighter Matters of the Law: Moses, Jesus and Paul," in *Current Issues in Biblical and Patristic Interpretation: Studies in Honor of Merrill C. Tenney Presented by His Former Students*, ed. G. F. Hawthorne (Grand Rapids: Eerdmans, 1975) 176–92; idem, "God's Promise Plan and His Gracious Law," *JETS* 33 (1990) 289–302; idem, "A Single Biblical Ethic in Business," in *Biblical Principles and Business: The Foundations*, ed. R. C. Chewning (Colorado Springs: NavPress, 1989) 76–88.

23. It is very fashionable these days to make the observation that this tripartite division of the law was unknown both in the Bible and in early rabbinic literature. The most recent voice is that of my former student, D. A. Dorsey, "The Law of Moses and the Christian: A Compromise," *JETS* 34 (1991) 321–34, esp. 329–30. For my rebuttal, see "God's Promise-Plan and His Gracious Law," 290–91.

24. I have been greatly aided and influenced by various unpublished papers of Michael Schluter, which he so kindly shared with me, esp. "Can Israel's Law and Historical Experience Be Applied to Britain Today?" Cf. also his "Guidelines for Applying the Law to Social Polity Today." Naturally, the form my argument has taken is my own responsibility and not that of Mr. Schluter. For a diagram and a further discussion of this point, see Kaiser, *Toward Rediscovering the Old Testament*, 164–66.

25. For further discussion of this essential point, one prominent among Roman Catholic scholars but hardly discussed by evangelicals, see W. C. Kaiser, Jr., "A Response to [the] Author's Intention and Biblical Interpretation," in *Hermeneutics, Inerrancy and the Bible*, ed. E. D. Radmacher & R. D. Preus (Grand Rapids: Zondervan, 1984) 439–47.

26. One of the best analyses of the issues involved in this famous *crux interpretum* is J. P. Braswell, "'The Blessing of Abraham' versus 'The Curse of the Law': Another Look at Gal. 3:10–13," *WTJ* 53 (1991) 73–91.

II
THE
OLD TESTAMENT

The Prophets

7

IMAGES OF YAHWEH: GOD IN THE PROPHETS

John D. W. Watts[1]

The task of this essay is a daunting one—to present the view of God in the prophetic books. Indeed, at first glance, it seems an impossible task since the prophets invoke all kinds of "images" of Yahweh. They speak of him—to name only a few examples—as husband, parent, planter, and forester. To offer readers a comprehensive catalogue of prophetic images of God would surely require an unacceptably long essay—and severely tax reader interest!

My thesis, however, is that the prophetic images of Yahweh all ultimately grow out of two "root metaphors"—Yahweh as King and Yahweh as the Divine Spirit. This essay, therefore, seeks to support that thesis by examining the use of these root metaphors in the various settings in which they occur. From that examination will emerge a well-rounded picture of "God in the Prophets."

The Royal Image: Yahweh is King[2]

The first major way that the prophetic books thought of God was as the King of Heaven. Mettinger has described this way of thinking of God in his study of the names of God.[3] The idea of "king" can well cover the three major forms with which Mettinger deals: "the battling deity, the regnant deity, and God as redeemer, savior, and creator." It is this "root metaphor" that accounts for most of the other ways that God is presented in the prophets. In much the same way that Canaanite mythology presents the gods, the prophets think of Yahweh as king.[4] But, unlike the Canaanite myths, they reserve the idea of deity for Yahweh alone.

The picture of Yahweh as king probably developed in Jerusalem during the monarchy,[5] but it was also latent in earlier images of God.[6] In the prophets, it became the dominant image of God.[7] They portray the reign of Yahweh (they usually call him by this name but seem never to speculate about its origin) in a great variety of settings: the battlefield, his throne room, his temple, and in his relation to the earth, to Canaan, to Israel, and to the individual worshiper.

Isaiah 6 describes the scene of Yahweh in the setting of the heavenly court.[8] "The Lord [is] seated on a throne, high and exalted" (NIV). His majesty is reflected by the robe whose train filled the room. High as he was, above him moved seraphs with six wings. The wings were kept busy covering their faces, their feet, and flying.[9] They sang, "Holy, holy, holy is [Yahweh] of hosts. / The whole earth is full of his glory" (RSV). Their singing added to the glory as doorposts and thresholds quivered and smoke filled the room.

In such scenes, it is common for the courtiers present to be drawn into the discussion of the decisions to be made. In Isaiah 6:11, the prophet asks, "How long, O Lord?" (RSV). Similarly, in 1 Kings 22:20–22 the spirits around the throne are invited to suggest ways to accomplish the fate decreed. In Job 1 the Adversary is asked his estimate of Job. In Isaiah 40:3–6 voices rise in the assembly to do God's bidding, but someone (is it the prophet?) protests that humanity is not worth it (vv. 6–7). He is answered by a member of the assembly.

Other personalities appear in the heavenly court of King Yahweh. In Isaiah 6:5–8 the prophet experiences the glory.[10] He must be cleansed by a burning coal in order to do so. Then he fills a role that is often a part of these scenes. The king needs a messenger to do a task, take a message, or interpret something. So, in vv. 9–13, the prophet is given a message and a task. Similarly, in 1 Kings 22:22–23 a lying spirit is sent to the prophets, while in Job 1:12 the Adversary is dispatched to test Job. Also, Amos 3:7

says, "Surely the Sovereign LORD does nothing without revealing his plan to his servants the prophets" (NIV), suggesting that all genuine prophetic speech originates in this way. Zechariah 1:9 describes a messenger sent from God to interpret Zechariah's visions to him. A similar person meets Ezekiel (40:3) to conduct him through his vision of the new temple. In Genesis 3:24 cherubim are sent to do guard duty at the entrance to Eden.

Typically, scenes in the heavenly court involve some announcement of God's future plans. The scene in Isaiah 6, for example, allows God to announce his decision concerning the fate of Israel. In 1 Kings 22:20 he announces the fate of Ahab, while in Job 1 the fate of Job is in question. Isaiah 40:1–2 announces the reversal of Jerusalem's fate; the messenger in Zechariah's visions communicates the new decisions that Yahweh has reached concerning Israel. The same is true of Ezekiel's visions. These examples are enough to fill out the picture.[11] They may well provide the best way to think of God as he speaks in so many passages in Isaiah and the other prophets: as heavenly king, he decrees the future fate of those addressed.

The king also appears in the setting of the temple in Jerusalem. The opening verses of Isaiah 6 clearly illustrate the close connection between the thought of God in the Heavenly Court and of God in Jerusalem's temple. The vision begins with two references to the temple that have led many interpreters to think that the vision of the heavenly court occurred in the temple in Jerusalem.

Throughout the prophets, Yahweh is pictured as the host to worshipers—all who come. The so-called Zion Theology which is so evident in the Psalms, is used here. Yahweh is portrayed especially in his relation to Zion, rather than to Sinai or even to Canaan. He is particularly related to the temple and to David's family as the royal patrons of the temple. But the prophetic picture is more than that. The wonderful scene in Isaiah 2:2–4 (cf. Micah 4:1–5) portrays the reconstitution of the temple of the future without a king and without a sacrificial cult but open to worshipers from all nations and peoples. The scene emphasizes their close relation to a picture of Yahweh who wants to be known by his identification with the new temple. His *tôrâ* will be taught there, and there pilgrim peoples from everywhere will take training in just international relations. There, too, Yahweh will settle their conflicts with each other.

Isaiah 66 makes clear that this new temple is understood to be the temple that Zerubbabel began to build and that Ezra completed. Yet both the concluding chapters of Isaiah and the Book of Malachi show that the prophets knew of the fierce resistance by the Jerusalem priests to his new vision and its fulfillment.[12] The setting of Isaiah 1:10–28, on the other hand, is within the first (i.e., Solomonic) temple. It portrays Yahweh's judgment against the corruptions of the temple, its priests, and its worshipers in the eighth century B.C. Thus, the book of Isaiah is anchored on both ends to a message that is closely related to the temple and to a view of Yahweh's presence in his temple and his rule over his temple.

Ezekiel's entire vision turns on the sense of Yahweh's presence and the temple. His inaugural vision makes clear that Yahweh's throne is not bound to the temple. The crucial vision in the center (Ezek 10–11) portrays the exit of the Glory from the temple before its destruction. And the closing vision (Ezek 40–48) is concerned, as Isaiah's is, with the shape and function of the new temple, especially as a place where Yahweh's presence can be experienced. In this temple Yahweh alone is king. Those who would acknowledge his kingship come there to do so.

The Book of the Twelve Prophets (i.e., the so-called minor prophets) is also concerned with the temple, even though the theme is not as central as it is in either Isaiah or Ezekiel. Micah's vision (4:1–5) parallels that in Isaiah, but while Isaiah's vision appears toward the book's beginning (Isa 2:2–4), Micah's comes at the center of the Book of the Twelve. Similarly, Zechariah 8 forecasts good things for the temple's future. Vv. 1–2 promise that Yahweh will return to Zion and that it will again be called "The Holy Mountain." Vv. 20–22 also promise a day of such influence for the new temple that people will come from everywhere to worship there. And even Malachi, in the context of fifth-century Judean spiritual apathy, speaks of such a day, albeit with all the problems it brings (Mal 3:1–5).

In sum, Yahweh is seen as the presiding host at his temple in Jerusalem. This is true both of Solomon's temple (Isa 6; Ezek 11) and also of the second temple to come (Isa 2:1–4; 65–66; Mic 4:1–5; 6–7; Ezek 40–48; Hag 2:6–9, 20–23; Zech 1:14–17; 2:10–13; 8:1–3, 7–23; cf. Mic 7:11–12, 16–20; Zech 14). In the New Testament, the Revelation will take this background a step further in its description of the heavenly temple (Rev 21–22).

The King Goes to War

From the temple, from Zion, Yahweh moves out to war (Amos 1:2). Indeed, besides the heavenly court and the Jerusalem temple, a battlefield is the next setting in which the prophets present the divine king. The battlefields and occasions of battle vary from context to context. In some, King Yahweh is himself engaged in combat, in others he directs the actions of his combatants. In still others he uses weather or forces of nature to decide the battle.

Yahweh is known in early biblical writings as a fighter. The Song of the Sea (Exod 15:3) says of him, "Yahweh is a warrior" (NIV). Numbers 21:14 quotes from an early collection of poems called "the Book of the Wars of Yahweh." Though Genesis records few violent encounters, ch. 14 details how Abram rescues his nephew from five invading kings. The account does not speak of Yahweh's participation in the battle, but, significantly, in a subsequent vision to Abram, God affirms "I am your shield" (Gen 15:1). The remark might suggest that Yahweh's protection lay behind Abram's great victory in the preceding chapter.

Yahweh's prowess in battle begins to emerge more fully in the narrative about his personal intervention between Pharaoh's army and the Israelites (Exod 14). The victory is celebrated in Exodus 15. As the Israelites approach Canaan, they face more and more battles. The situation in Canaan appears different from that described in Genesis. With Genesis, the cities mentioned are like open market towns, but in Numbers references to walled cities appear everywhere. The actual invasion involves battles against the East Bank nations of Ammon (i.e., the Amorites, Num 21) and Moab (Num 22–25). Israel also fights the Midianites in Numbers 31. For our purposes what is important is that Yahweh is closely involved in all of these battles.

In the Former Prophets (i.e., Joshua to 2 Kings) Yahweh also goes to war. On the West Bank of the Jordan, Joshua records battles against kings of various important cities (Josh 6–12). Yahweh is involved in the many defensive battles that the book of Judges records. Yahweh defends Israel in battles against a host of hostile peoples: the Moabites, Ammonites, and Amalekites (Judg 3); the Canaanites of Hazor (Judg 4); Midian and the Philistines (Judg 5); and the Ammonites (Judg 11). In Judges 11, the Philistines reappear, this time as a threat to Israel's very survival as a nation, a threat that dominates the wars of 1 Samuel. Again, Yahweh participates in all these battles. Further, David's wars against the Philistines, Moab, Zobah, Damascus, Hamath, Edom, Amon, and Amalek, as well as his friendship with the Sidonians, bring the united kingdom to its dominant position in the ancient world. Again, the books of Samuel credit Yahweh with winning the victory in all these battles.

But the role of Yahweh the warrior seems to change when Solomon succeeds David as king. Solomon makes an alliance with Egypt, secularizes his military, and depends more on diplomacy than on military might to achieve and hold his empire (1 Kgs 2–11). The days of the wars of Yahweh appear to be at an end. After Solomon's death, Israel's northern tribes renounce all loyalty to his successor, Rehoboam, and form their own country, "Israel." Their rebellion leaves Rehoboam as king over "Judah," the country's southern section. Significantly, the history of the divided kingdom is filled with wars among nations like Syria, Moab, Edom, as well as Israel and Judah, but Yahweh is not described as being involved. One exception is the account in 2 Kings 6 relating to the prophet Elisha and the Syrian army (vv. 5–23). There the biblical writer dramatically underscores how "the hills [were] full of horses and chariots of fire all around Elisha" (v. 17, NIV). Yahweh's protective fire ensures Syria's certain defeat.

The Latter Prophets change this picture, however. They portray Yahweh as being involved with wars in Canaan against virtually all the small nations. Of course, by the prophetic period, one stands at the other end of the historical process from the invasions through which Israel won Canaan in the first place. Instead, Israel is being pushed out of Canaan into exile or is hoping to return some of its people to their old homeland. Yet, in the prophets, God still appears regularly on the battlefields that relate to Canaan, and in all of these Yahweh is the major combatant.[13]

Yahweh takes on all the aggressor nations of the eighth to the sixth centuries B.C. He announces, indeed directs, the invasions by the Assyrians in the eighth century B.C. according to Isaiah's reports of the events (Isa 5:26–30; 7:18–20; 10:5). Originally, the Assyrians were Yahweh's instrument of wrath against Israel. But Yahweh has his own problems with his allies of this period, says Isaiah, and is forced to bring them to judgment, too (Isa 10:5–19, 26–27; cf. 14:25; Nahum; Ezek 31; Zech 10:11). Prophecies also detail his combat against the other major aggressor nation, Babylon (Isa 13; 21:1–12), in a context that implies they are directed against the Babylon of Merodach-Baladan of the eighth century B.C.[14] Later, Jeremiah 50–51:58 is clearly directed against the Babylon of Nebuchadnezzar, who wrought havoc on Jerusalem.

Yahweh also fights with the peoples of Canaan in battles against each other and Israel (Isa 9:11–12; Amos 1–2; 3:9–15; 6:11–14; Mic 1:3–7, 15–16; 2:1–5, 12–13). Indeed, these so-called foreign prophecies form a major feature of most of the Latter Prophets. Amos 1–2 is a compact collection of this sort, while larger collections appear in Isaiah (13–23), Jeremiah (46–51), and Ezekiel (25–35). Ezekiel follows up his collection with a chapter against the "the mountains of Israel" after the fashion of Amos 2.

The bulk of the other prophecies, however, concern the small nations in and around Canaan that were once part of David's larger empire. They had continued in various forms to exist throughout the divided monarchy. But under the Assyrian and Babylonian rulers, they had all been reduced to the status of provinces or disappeared altogether as identifiable units. Just why the prophets should make so much of them is not clear at first glance. In any case, they reflect Yahweh's royal responsibility and concern for Canaan, its peoples, and its neighbors. He exercises that concern by battling the Philistines (Amos 1:6–8; Isa 14:28–32; Jer 47; Ezek 25:15–17), Moab (Amos 2:1–3; Isa 15–16; Jer 48; Ezek 25:8–11), Edom (Amos 1:11–12; Jer 49:7–22; Ezek 25:12–14), Aram (i.e., Damascus; Amos 1:3–5; Isa 17; Jer 49:23–27), Tyre (Amos 1:9–10; Isa 23; Ezek 26–28), Sidon (Ezek 28:20–26), and Ammon (Amos 1:13–15; Jer 49:1–6; Ezek 25:1–7).

There are also prophecies against nations who, as neighboring nations, had a great deal of contact and influence in Israel over the centuries: Egypt (Isa 18, 19; Jer 46; Ezek 30–32), Arabia (Isa 21:13–17; Jer 49:28–33), and Elam (Jer 49:34–39). In addition, within the unique literary format of the "foreign prophecies," there are even prophecies against Judah (Amos 2:4–5) and Israel (Amos 2:6–16; Ezek 36).

The process of redefining these nations as provinces of empires progressed through the Assyrian and Babylonian periods but was finally achieved under the Persians. This provided a kind of *pax Persica* in which rivalries were reduced but not eliminated, as Ezra and Nehemiah show. But the nationalistic spirit that had incited countless earlier conflicts had been removed. Only the Hasmonean era (2nd–1st century B.C.) would revive this spirit for Judah. In sum, these "foreign prophecies" have reintroduced the concept of Holy War, of Yahweh as present and active on the battlefield. They, thus, bring the period of the Israelite monarchy to an end with much the same theme as it had begun with David's triumphs.

Finally, to round out the picture we must mention several other battlefields in the Latter Prophets on which Yahweh is active and dominant. He fights battles to protect Zion and to repay her enemies for the violence they did to her (Isa 29:1–12; 31:4–5; Joel 3:16–17, 21; Obad 16–17; Zeph 3:14–17; Zech 9:1–8, 9–17; 12:1–13; 14:2–21).[15] He comes from Paran to rescue his people and his anointed one (Hab 3). He leads Israel and Judah in a renewed invasion of Canaan (Isa 11:12–16) and incites internal disorder even in Egypt (Isa 19:1–17). Further, particular mention should be made of the battles related to the Day of the Lord (Amos 5:18–20; Isa 13:1–22; 14:21–22; 22:5–25; 26:21; Mic 5:10–15; Joel 2:1–11; 3:9–15; Obad 15–18; Zephaniah). The connection between the understanding of Yahweh as king and his role as warrior is particularly clear in these texts.

Some prophecies refer to the battles that occurred in the process of creation and that might be construed to be continuing as a pattern for the last battles of history (Isa 24:18b–20;[16] 25:6–8; 26:19–27:1; 34:1–15).

In Isaiah 51:9–10, the call is for the "arm of Yahweh" to awake

> as in days gone by,
>> as in generations of old.
> Was it not you [Yahweh] who cut Rahab to pieces,
>> who pierced that monster through?
> Was it not you who dried up the sea
> . . .
>> so that the redeemed might cross over? (NIV)

In Isaiah 27:1 one reads:

> In that day
>> the LORD will punish with his sword,
> his fierce, great and powerful sword,
>> Leviathan the gliding serpent,
> Leviathan the coiling serpent;
>> he will slay the monster of the sea. (NIV)

Most important, the prophets picture Yahweh bringing armies and empires against Israel and Judah as punishment for their centuries of sin and rebellion. Isaiah 5 and 10 speak of Assyria in this light, Ezekiel 38–39 of the mysterious Gog in a similar fashion. In all these battles Yahweh fights directly as a warrior in the field, as a commander who directs others in battle, or as commander of the forces of nature in earthquake or drought. He also uses psychological warfare. Whatever the forces used, Yahweh as a warrior seeks to destroy the enemy.[17]

The King's Other Images

Given the greatness of King Yahweh, one is not surprised to find other prophetic images of him in settings other than those discussed above. A survey of these other images will further enhance our view of "God in the Prophets." In the setting of heavens and earth, for example, Yahweh appears as the Creator and Sustainer of the universe (Isa 40:21–22, 25–26). In this cosmic role, he sits enthroned above the "circle of the earth" and "stretches out the heavens" (v. 22). He is the one who created the stars, who calls each of them by its personal name, and who keeps them in their heavenly places (v. 26). In the setting of Canaan, Yahweh is understood as owner of the land, the landlord to whom its residents are accountable. In Canaan, Yahweh is covenant Lord and partner for Israel. This often puts him in position to judge Israel and Judah for their infidelity to the covenant. The early portions of Isaiah and Micah 6 portray such judgment scenes.

In Canaan, Yahweh is Israel's husband (Hos 1, 3; Ezek 23), parent (Isa 1:2–3), and foster parent Hos (11:1–4). Ezekiel's allegorical biography of Jerusalem (Ezek 16) describes him as both foster parent and husband. Elsewhere, the prophets picture him as a planter in Canaan with Israel the seedling that he planted. In Isaiah 5, he has planted Israel as a vineyard, in Ezekiel 17 as a vine. In these pictures Yahweh works within the normal social process where he is king, too. Within that process, there are no great armies to move, but there are social forces to correct, to strengthen, to judge, and to redeem. According to Ezekiel 15, though Israel is a vine, it has failed to bear God-pleasing fruit. Though vines are wood, their wood is useless compared to that of trees and, hence, is only good for fuel. In like manner, says Ezekiel, God will consume Jerusalem and Judah for their unfaithfulness to his covenant. On the other hand, in Canaan Yahweh is also seen as the savior of his people. They hope that he, with his usual military precision and procedures, will protect them from their enemies and return them to the land (Isa 11:10–16).

When the setting is Zion, Yahweh appears as king in Zion (Isa 1:9–24; 4:1–6; 12:1–6). In these passages, the king is intent on cleaning up his capital and restoring it to be a worthy city with righteousness and justice evident in it. In Zion, Yahweh also appears as the personal patron of the Davidic line. Isaiah shows him advising Ahaz in a distressing situation (Isa 7:1–14) and displays in beautiful language the throne names of the descendant of the line of David who deserves to be anointed king (9:1–6). Along that same line, Isaiah 11:1–22 describes the king that Yahweh wants to have on the throne and exactly how God would support such a king. Significantly, all these portraits are in the book that, according to chapter 6, intends to show the end of the Davidic dynasty in Jerusalem. The implication is that, despite his harsh judgment of the Davidic line, Yahweh's commitment to its continuation and greatness remains unchanged.

It is also in Zion that Yahweh appears as the shepherd of his people. *Shepherd* is a usual term for king both in the Bible and in the ancient world. Isaiah 40:11 offers perhaps the most beautiful expression of this motif:

> He tends his flock like a shepherd:
> > He gathers the lambs in his arms
> and carries them close to his heart;
> > he gently leads those that have young. (NIV)

When Zephaniah brings his book to an end he proclaims: "Yahweh, the King of Israel, is with you" (Zeph 3:15b, NIV). Then he goes on to picture Yahweh's work in terms of a shepherd: "I will rescue the lame / and gather those who have been scattered" (Zeph 3:19, NIV). Similarly, Zechariah 10–13 repeatedly refers to kings as shepherds. In the closing section, which describes their destruction, the prophet portrays God as the one who will take over the shepherds' responsibilities:

> They will call on my name
>   and I will answer them;
> I will say, "They are my people,"
>   and they will say, "[Yahweh] is our God." (Zech 13:9, NIV)

So, other images of Yahweh develop from the root metaphor of Yahweh as king on his heavenly throne, in his temple, and on various battlefields. As cosmic king he is the Creator and Sustainer of the universe, the one who is able to keep it running because he made it. He is also the landlord of Canaan who has entered into a special relationship with his tenant, Israel, a relationship centered on the covenant. Finally, from covenant roots spring other metaphors—Yahweh as husband, parent, foster parent, planter of vineyard and vine, king reigning in Zion, and shepherd of all his people.

Yahweh as the Divine Spirit

The second prophetic "root metaphor" is of Yahweh as the Divine Spirit. This metaphor seems to offer the one exception to the general prophetic pattern of viewing God as king, for it presents Yahweh as the Personal Spirit in sacred tryst with a single worshiper. Jeremiah's so-called confessions—his personal outpourings of suffering and despair—portray this kind of personal relationship. Jeremiah tries to fulfill his prophetic calling but runs smack into walls of persecution and public ridicule for his preaching. To continue ministering is only possible through repeated periods of prayer and anguish spent with God (e.g., Jer 10:23–25; 12:1–13; 15:15–21; 17:12–18; 20:7–13, 14–20).

The closing section of Isaiah offers a second example of this image. Isaiah 55 opens with an invitation to any and everyone to come and participate in Yahweh's feast (v. 1). Strikingly, this invitation and the following content reflect a radical change in the nature of the temple and of temple worship. The section specifically pictures salvation and personal fellowship with Yahweh as open to people that Israel in the past tended to exclude—non-Israelites, eunuchs, and the very ill (Isa 56:3–8). Yahweh will accept sacrifices and offerings from all of them at his temple, but the temple's central purpose will be as "a house of prayer for all nations" (56:7, NIV). Further, Isaiah 57:13b says: "The [one] who makes me his refuge / will inherit the land / and possess my holy mountain" (NIV). In other words, in God's eyes, voluntary dependence on the Lord is more important than having Israelite blood. Finally, Isaiah 57:15 offers an almost startling description of how Almighty God wants to live intimately with ordinary people:

> For this is what the high and lofty One says—
>   he who lives forever, whose name is holy:
> "I live in a high and holy place,
>   but also with him who is contrite and lowly in spirit,
> to revive the spirit of the lowly
>   and to revive the heart of the contrite." (NIV)

Isaiah 58:5–14 goes on to describe the worship that such persons will bring as a fast—the very kind of fast that meets Yahweh's specifications. Even more radically, Yahweh covenants with such persons that "[m]y Spirit, who is on you, and my words that I have put in your mouth will not depart from your mouth . . . forever" (59:21, NIV). Isaiah 61:1 also gives witness of such an indwelling spirit of Yahweh:

> The Spirit of [Yahweh of Hosts] is on me,
>   because [Yahweh] has anointed me
> to preach good news to the poor. (NIV)

Similarly, Micah 6:6–8 speaks of the same kind of person:

> With what shall I come before [Yahweh]?
>   . . .
> He has showed you, O man, what is good.
>   And what does [Yahweh] require of you?
> To act justly and to love mercy
>   and to walk humbly with your God. (NIV)

To this stunning affirmation Micah 7:7 provides a fitting reply:

> As for me, I will keep watch for [Yahweh],
>   I wait in hope for God my Savior;
>   my God will hear me. (NIV)

Finally, two other evidences support our claim that the prophets view Yahweh as a personal spirit who seeks close relationship with people. First, one sees this relationship in prayers in the prophets, whether prayers given by the prophets or reported by them (e.g., those of Jonah [Jonah 2:2–9], Hezekiah [Isa 38:10–20], and Jeremiah [Jer 32:16–25]). Each of these demonstrates a personal spirituality that is remarkable.[18] Second, this relationship is evident in the accounts of the calls of the prophets. Despite their diversity, these reports of God's commissioning conversations with prophets all share the same understanding of the nearness of the spirit of God to each prophet. Whether as Amos' first vision (Amos 7:1–3), Hosea's marital trouble (Hos 1:2–9; 3:1–3), Jeremiah's story (Jer 1:4–10), or Ezekiel's "send-off" (Ezek 2:1–3:11), all these demonstrate the sense, so compelling and convincing, of the nearness and reality of Yahweh's Spirit.[19]

Conclusion

Images of God proliferate in the prophets—husband, parent, planter, forester, host, and so on. But the thesis of this essay is that they are all the outgrowth of two root metaphors, Yahweh as King and Yahweh as the Divine Spirit near to everyone who seeks and prays to him. Yahweh is king in heaven, over all the world, in Canaan, in Zion, and wants to be so in Israel. He is near and available to anyone who seeks him. These ideas summarize Yahweh as the prophets see and portray him.

NOTES

1. To David Hubbard, dear friend, colleague, fellow editor, my president at Fuller, leader for evangelical Christians, conciliator, model of compassion, stirring and eloquent preacher. Congratulations.
2. The scholarly discussion involves the works of Mowinckel (1922), Eissfeldt (1928), Alt (1953), Gray (1956, 1961), Schmidt (1961), Lipiński (1965), Gray (1979), Dietrich (1980), Mettinger (1985), Jörg Jeremias (1987). See a review by Cazelles (1960). (See Mettinger's bibliography.) When we deal with prophetic literature, the original relation to Canaanite mythology lies far in the background. But the themes and "root metaphor," as Mettinger calls it, are still very much alive, as the new book edited by M. Hengel and A. M. Schwemer (*Königsherrschaft Gottes und himmlischer Kult* [Tübingen: J. C. B. Mohr, 1991]) shows.

3. T. N. D. Mettinger, *In Search of God: The Meaning and Message of the Everlasting Names* (Philadelphia: Fortress, 1988).

4. Ibid.

5. See J. D. W. Watts, *Basic Patterns in Old Testament Religion* (Pasadena, CA: Jameson, 1971) ch. 3, "The Monarchic Pattern."

6. Albright and Cross related the traces of it in the earliest Hebrew epic poetry to the Canaanite views of the Divine Council. P. D. Miller (*The Divine Warrior in Early Israel* [Cambridge, MA: Harvard University Press, 1973]) has summarized the views of that school of thought.

7. The interesting thing here is that prophetic books dating from the exilic and post-exilic period should revive with such vigor a basic motif of early Israel's epic poetry. The topics of salvation, judgment, and divine kingship provide the theological basis for their theology just as it had for the earlier age.

8. Similar descriptions may be found in 1 Kings 22:19–22 and Job 1:6–12; 2:1–7. See D. M. Flemming, *The Divine Council as Type Scene in the Hebrew Bible* (Ph.D. diss., Southern Baptist Theological Seminary, Louisville, 1989).

9. 1 Kings 22:19 speaks of "the host of heaven standing around him on his right and on his left" (NIV). Also present in the court room is a spirit. Job 1 tells of "the sons of God" who came to "present themselves before Yahweh." The "Adversary" (*haśśātān*) was among them.

10. Cf. 1 Kgs 2:19; Ezek 1:4–28.

11. Since H. Wheeler Robinson's article ("The Council of Yahweh," *JTS* 45 [1944] 151–7) and the many studies relating the ancient Israelite poems to Ugaritic mythology, a growing understanding of the role of the Divine Assembly may be traced. The interesting point here is the use of this in the prophets as well as in the Psalms.

12. See the notes in my *Isaiah 34–66*, WBC 25 (Dallas: Word, 1987) 337–66.

13. The pictures drawn in Israel's early poetry have been thoroughly researched, particularly as they parallel the pictures in Ugaritic myths; cf. H. Fredriksson, *Jahwe als Krieger* (Lund: Gleerup, 1945); G. von Rad, *Der heilige Krieg im alten Israel* (Göttingen: Vandenhoeck & Ruprecht, 1962); Miller, *The Divine Warrior in Early Israel.*

14. See Isaiah 39 and my comments in *Isaiah 1–33*, WBC 24 (Dallas: Word, 1985) 184–200, 266–75.

15. Isaiah 36–37 (cf. 2 Kgs 18:17–19:37) offers a prototype in narrative form of Yahweh's defense of Zion.

16. Many commentators would include Isaiah 24:21–23, but I have contended (*Isaiah 1–33*, 325) that the "powers in the height" should be translated "the army of the highlands" and understood as a group of armies in Canaan.

17. While recognizing the three settings discussed above (i.e., throne, temple, and battlefield), one should not expect them to be too neatly separated from one another. In fact, the prophets understood them to be closely interrelated, i.e., all part of the picture of Yahweh as king. Though a prophet focuses on one setting, the others are assumed to lie in the background. So, Yahweh as king comes from his heavenly throne to do battle or to be present in his temple. Or Yahweh decrees from his throne the rebuilding of his temple, etc.

18. See R. E. Clements, *In Spirit and in Truth* (Atlanta: John Knox, 1985) 113–46.

19. For more on this idea, see S. Terrien, *The Elusive Presence* (San Francisco: Harper & Row, 1978) 236–61.

8

IMAGES OF ISRAEL: THE PEOPLE OF GOD IN THE PROPHETS

Leslie C. Allen

The mission of the classical prophets clusters around political crisis. Their period, stretching from the eighth century to at least the fifth century B.C., embraced the dangerous eras of Assyrian and Babylonian domination, eras that brought increasing loss of national independence and eventual exile. The period extended to the Persian era, when a significant number of the exiles returned and achieved an uneasy survival. These prophets refused to see national misfortune from a purely political perspective. They were religious idealists who insisted that a higher agenda was being played out in the setbacks, reprieves, and downfall of two nations that shared a common theological tradition, Israel and Judah. They saw themselves as interpreters of crisis in terms of the ongoing will of Yahweh, the God of these twin nations.

Israel's Receipt of Covenant Grace

The prophets maintained that the present could not be understood apart from the past. Drawing on extant hymnic and narrative traditions, they worked with the concept of a partnership between Yahweh and his people, a relationship that extended back into distant history. We may loosely speak of this as a covenant relationship. In so doing we are steering a middle course between two extremes: on the one hand, the comprehensive employment of the term "covenant" by Walther Eichrodt in his *Theology of the Old Testament,* for whom it became "a cipher/symbol for all the 'good' tendencies of Israelite faith,"[1] and, on the other, the narrower usage of the Old Testament itself, which reflects a basically northern tradition that infiltrated south and came to dominate Judean religious thinking. The prophetic books use a network of terms, formulas, and motifs that point to a relationship that may be conveniently summed up in terms of covenant.

The classical prophets saw their national contemporaries as heirs of a basic encounter that was still decisive for them. This insight was evidently derived from popular theology fostered by the local sanctuaries. Accordingly, the references to this encounter are often allusive, sufficient to recall longer lessons learned at the shrines. Thus, Hosea could declare in God's name to citizens of the northern kingdom:

When Israel was a child, I loved him,
   and out of Egypt I called my son. (Hos 11:1)[2]

Like grapes in the wilderness,
   I found Israel.
Like the first fruit on the fig tree, in its first season,
   I saw your ancestors. (9:10)

Yet I have been the LORD your God
   ever since the land of Egypt;
you know no God but me,
   and besides me there is no savior.
It was I who fed you in the wilderness,
   in the land of drought. (13:4–5)

We notice an oscillation between "your ancestors" and "you." There is a significant flexibility between the past and present, as the prophet recalls the archetypal period of the exodus and wilderness wanderings, and characterizes it as the time when Israel became Yahweh's significant other, and vice versa.

Hosea's contemporary, Amos, also addressed the present generation of God's people as current heirs of a living tradition:

> Yes I destroyed the Amorite
>   before them. . .
> Also I brought you up
>   out of the land of Egypt,
> and led you forty years in the wilderness,
>   to possess the land of the Amorite. (Amos 2:9–11)
>
> You only have I known
> of all the families of the earth. (3:2)

Micah, too, spoke of this salvation in contemporary terms (Mic 6:4–5). The naturalness with which this is done suggests that these prophets were doing nothing new. They appear to have taken over a theological extrapolation current in cultic circles of which we may find a later illustration in Psalm 81:6–16 (Heb. 7–17). Each generation in turn became the "you" whom Yahweh had saved. The old, old story of God's saving work became ever new. It did not merely lie in Israel's past but was a perennial window upon the purposes of God for succeeding generations.

In similar fashion Isaiah spoke of Yahweh's settlement of the people in the land:

> Let me sing for my beloved
>   my love-song concerning his vineyard:
> My beloved had a vineyard
>   on a very fertile hill.
> He dug it and cleared it of stones,
>   and planted it with choice vines . . . . (Isa 5:1–2)

The prophet starts low key, claiming to be speaking as "best man" on behalf of his bridegroom friend. The "love-song" employs language with romantic associations (cf. Cant 2:15; 4:16; 8:12). Only as he proceeds does it become clear that he is speaking a parable about God's relationship with his people. Again, past and present are fused in his representation of Yahweh's loving care.

Jeremiah looked back to the formative wilderness period with the same perspective of contemporization:

> I remember the devotion of your youth,
>   your love as a bride,
> how you followed me in the wilderness,
>   in a land not sown.

Israel was holy to the LORD,
the first fruits of his harvest. (Jer 2:1–3)

In principle the present generation was one with its ancestors, sharing both in their short-lived loyalty to God and in their basic position of privilege before him. The Deuteronomistic History (Joshua-Kings), which in Jewish tradition belongs to the prophetic canon and whose final edition was produced in the exilic period, also finds the basis of God's covenant with Israel in his saving deeds, from the time of the patriarchs till the occupation of the land (Josh 24:2–13).

Israel's Covenant Obligation

The earlier prophets tend to have sets of key terms that they use to summarize the moral obligations of the bond between God and his people. In their employment of such terms we find examples of the principle of obligation that pervades the prophetic literature. Hosea's terms are "steadfast love" (*hesed*) and "knowledge" (*da'at*). The different ways in which he uses them show that they cover a range of meaning. This range may be illustrated as a cone-shaped structure of relationship and response:

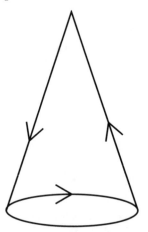

Where "knowledge" is concerned, Yahweh entered into a knowledge of Israel. In turn, Israel came to know Yahweh. This latter knowledge was not merely a vertical relationship, but was worked out in a horizontal development of communal living. It was Yahweh who initiated this wide-ranging relationship: "I knew [NRSV "fed"] you in the wilderness" (Hos 13:5).[3] Accordingly, Israel's perspective can be described as "you know no God but me" (13:4). It was the duty of the sanctuaries, through the priests who served there, to perpetuate this "knowledge" (4:6), which was not only relational in terms of an exclusive commitment to him (cf. 5:3), but also cognitive, an appreciation of his saving acts and the social obligations he had laid on his saved people. These latter objects of knowledge comprise a "holy tradition" that "constituted the heart of Israel's identity as a community."[4] The obligations are summarized as "the law *[tôrâ]* of your God" (4:6; 8:1) and, indeed, also as "the covenant" (8:1). The "knowledge of God" in 4:1 (cf. 6:6) is defined by the decalogue-like listing of 4:2.

As for "steadfast love," it too seems to embrace Israel from a divine source. Israel was meant to respond in both love of God and love of fellow Israelites. The term "steadfast love" is not used so comprehensively as "know" and "knowledge," but it is clear that when it is employed of Israel's response to Yahweh in 6:4 (NRSV "love"), it takes its cue from God's prior attitude to them. The references to God's initial "love" (*ʾōhaḇehû, ʾahaḇâ*) in 11:1, 4 so suggest. This vertical response on Israel's part was meant to flow down into a channel of human interrelationship, as the use of "steadfast love" in 4:1 (NRSV "loyalty") and 6:6 shows. In general one may compare the triple use of the term "love" (*agápē, agapáō*) in two NT passages, 1 John 2:19–3:18 and 4:7–5:5. They refer not only to (1) love bestowed by God, but also to (2) love directed to God and to (3) love within the community of faith, which shows that "God's love abide[s] in" those who love. Moreover, the second and third elements are fused in that "love of God" is defined as to "obey his commandments." The similar coverage in Hosea and John is mutually illuminating. Covenant love and covenant obligation are inextricably linked. Spirituality is embodied in a positive way of life that is a corollary of faith.

Amos's pair of terms is "justice" and "righteousness," which are used together in Amos 5:7, 24 and 6:12. "Righteousness" (*ṣedāqâ*) has been defined as "the quality of life displayed by those who live up to the norms inherent in a given relationship" and "the rightness that belongs to those who fulfill their responsibilities which their relationship to others creates."[5] "Justice" (*mišpāt*) is an institutional outworking of this quality through the lawcourts. It must be remembered that recourse to judicial processes was straightforward in ancient Israel. The elders who sat in the town gateway (5:10, 12) could expeditiously take on the role of judges to deal with complaints brought to them. Amos does not tie such social order into an overt theological network as Hosea does, but the association of injustice with "transgressions" and "sins" in 5:12 is suggestive. Clearly, for him too, there was a direct link between the will of Yahweh and right relationships within the community.

Isaiah used the same pair of terms as Amos. He presented them more obviously as God's relational expectations for Judean society: "and he expected justice. . . , / righteousness. . . ." (Isa 5:7). These ideals were once characteristic of Jerusalem (1:21; cf. 10:2). The messianic figure of 9:7 (Heb. 6) would restore them to Israel. In turn, the Deuteronomistic History presupposes the detailed covenant obligations of Deuteronomy. Its account of the period of Joshua presents an approximation to the ideal of what Israel ought ever to have been, prepared to live within the constraints of the covenant and to be faithful to Yahweh (Josh 24:14–24; Judg 2:7). There is, then, a clear and consistent testimony that high standards of spiritual commitment and social welfare were set before Israel in its role as covenant partner. Yahweh provided a "good way" (Jer 6:16) along which his people were to travel. How did Israel match up to such ideals?

Israel's Irresponsibility

The prophetic contexts in which the sets of general terms for covenant obligation are used are persistently negative in tone:

> There is no . . . loyalty [hesed],
>   and no knowledge of God in the land. (Hos 4:1)
> But you have turned justice into poison
>   and the fruit of righteousness into wormwood. (Amos 6:12)
>
> He expected justice, but saw bloodshed;
>   righteousness, but heard a cry! (Isa 5:7)

Hosea went on to list a litany of social sins that illustrated the lack of any horizontal outworking of the vertical relationship between Yahweh and his people (4:2). Amos was complaining that the verdicts of Israel's judges, which should have been the outcome of righteousness, left a bad taste in the mouth and caused grievous harm. In explaining his parable, Isaiah expressed the bitter disappointment of the Lord of the covenant. He used word play, to which the Hebrew ear was emotionally sensitive, contrasting $mi\check{s}p\bar{a}t$ ("justice") with $mi\check{s}p\bar{a}h$ ("bloodshed"), and $s^e\underline{d}\bar{a}q\hat{a}$ ("righteousness") with $s^{ec}\bar{a}q\hat{a}$ ("cry [for help])." Judah produced fakes, which were the opposite of the real thing.

In prophetic descriptions of the people's irresponsibility, references to Yahweh's saving grace are often used to accentuate their irresponsible reactions, as a nasty surprise. On God's behalf Hosea declares, if the textual tradition of the LXX is correct: "The more I called them, the more they went from me." (Hos 11:2). After detailing Israel's offenses in Amos 2:6–8, Amos gives a list of Yahweh's benefits in vv 9–12, in order to provide a stark contrast between human ingratitude and divine grace. In his parable of the vineyard, Isaiah, too, describes God's frustration at Judah's response to all his efforts:

> What more was there to do for my vineyard
>   that I have not done in it?
> When I expected it to yield grapes,
>   why did it yield wild grapes? (Isa 5:4)

In turn Micah asks in God's name what on earth went wrong: "O my people, what have I done to you? / In what have I wearied you?" (Mic 6:3). The questions, which are posed before a survey of Yahweh's "saving acts" in the past, are satirical and amount to an implicit accusation of his people. The fault was theirs, not his. Their sacred history should have forged strong bonds of appreciation and commitment.

Micah proceeds to put an exasperated protest on Israel's lips. Addressing the prophet, the community avows its commitment to God—in purely religious terms. They were prepared to go to any lengths in their worship, whatever it cost in self-denial: "With what shall I come before the LORD, / and bow myself before God on high?" (Mic 6:6–7). The prophet's reply shows that they had missed the point. Not worship but way of life was the litmus test of a healthy relationship with God:

> He has told you, O mortal, what is good;
>   and what does the LORD require of you
> but to do justice, and to love kindness [*hesed*],
>   and to walk humbly with your God? (6:8)

The old covenant ideals still held good: "justice" that remembered other people had rights, "steadfast love" that took its cue from God's own love, and lives lived in obedience to the Lord of the covenant.

Micah's contrasting of worship and way of life reappears as a standard element in other prophets. An organic unity between behavior and true worship is assumed. They could not function as alternatives but only as twin requirements. Worship offered without a compatible way of life was unacceptable to Yahweh. Isaiah rejected Judah's offering of sacrificial worship and even prayer (Isa 1:11–15). As Yahweh looked at hands outstretched in earnest prayer, he could see only the bloodstains of social injustice upon them. What was required was a moral equivalent of the ritual washing that had preceded the so-called worship:

> Wash yourselves; make yourselves clean;
>   remove the evil of your doings from before my eyes;
> cease to do evil,
>   learn to do good;
> seek justice, rescue the oppressed;
>   defend the orphan, plead for the widow. (1:16–17)

Isaiah, like Micah, was not rejecting worship in principle. His problem was not with worship but with the worshipers and their defective lifestyle. This is evident from his introduction to the oracle, in which he disparagingly calls Jerusalem, thronged with pilgrims, "Sodom" and "Gomorrah" (1:10). There seems to be an implicit reference to the entrance liturgy by which pilgrims before their worship were reminded of the moral qualifications they had to meet (see Pss 15; 24:3–6; cf. the priority in Matt 5:23–24). It was because the priests had not maintained such moral security checks that the prophet had to reject their ensuing worship as lopsided.[6]

Similarly, Hosea declared on Yahweh's behalf: "I desire steadfast love and not sacrifice, / the knowledge of God rather than [or "without"] burnt offerings" (Hos 6:6). Ideally, God looked for a dual response. However, since worship had to be grounded in moral integrity, Hosea said that Israel's version of worship that evidently here accompanied their avowals of vv 1–3 was unwelcome. Amos, likewise, declared that Israelite worshipers were *personae non gratae* to Yahweh (Amos 5:21–23). Their unreal worship of sacrifice, hymns, and music would not do. Yahweh's prior requirement was ethical in nature: "But let justice roll down like waters, / and righteousness like an everflowing stream" (5:24). Earlier in Amos 5 the cultic formula "Seek me and live" was reinterpreted in non-cultic terms. Yahweh was no longer to be found at the local sanctuaries, which had ceased to be beacons of ethical challenge. Rather,

> Seek good and not evil,
>   that you may live;
> and so the LORD, the God of hosts, will be with you,
>   just as you have said.
> Hate evil and love good,
>   and establish justice in the gate. (5:14–15)

Israel's obligation of moral obedience was a precondition of Yahweh's cultic presence in blessing. The focal point of his will was to be found in the quality of their communal life. Worship had become an easy option that professed to honor God, while the worshipers dishonored him in the rest of their lives. As Isaiah protested in God's name,

> [This] people draw[s] near with their mouths
>   and honor[s] me with their lips,
> while their hearts are far from me,
>   and their worship of me is a human
>   commandment learned by rote. (Isa 29:13)

"Lips" are contrasted with "hearts," which represent human wills that decide for God and follow his directives.[7] The worshipers are described in the Hebrew as "this people," which Isaiah sometimes uses as a deliberate substitute for "my people." The replacement is impersonal and has a ring of distaste.[8]

Jeremiah was insistent that the aura of sanctity and inviolability that traditionally surrounded the Jerusalem temple was no umbrella for immorality. Yahweh declared through him: "Has this house, which is called by my name, become a den of robbers in your sight?" (Jer 7:11).The prophet went on to subordinate Israel's sacrificial traditions to its ethical mandate (7:22–23; cf. Amos 5:25). In his denunciation of unacceptable worship, Jeremiah included the cultic sins of bringing incense to Baal and going "after other gods that you have not known" (v 9). It was a charge he often leveled (e.g., 2:6–32). In this accusation of utter disloyalty he was updating charges Hosea had brought against northern Israelites, of contaminating Yahwism with Canaanite theology and practices (e.g., Hos 7:14; 9:10; 11:2).

Ezekiel, too, blended social criticism with cultic denunciation of this type. His priestly background made him especially sensitive to pagan practices performed in the temple area (Ezek 8:5–16). He saw the whole history of Israel, from before the exodus until the exile, as permeated by paganized worship, which violated the very basis of Israel's relationship with Yahweh (Ezek 20; cf. Exod 20:2–3). The Deuteronomistic History, which sought to explain why the exile had occurred (cf. 1 Kgs 9:8), found the answer in Israel's basic disloyalty to Yahweh, which had triggered such drastic punishment at his hands (v 9). It presents a history of Israel's persistent failure to live up to the obligations of the covenant (see 2 Kgs 18:12; 21:14–15).

A lack of integrity pervades the accusations found in the prophetic literature. It testifies that inconsistencies abounded, whether between

God's gracious revelation and Israel's moral ingratitude, or between the left hand that offered worship and the right hand that engaged in wrongdoing, or even between professions of religious loyalty offered both to Yahweh and to pagan deities. Yahweh had no option but to counter such a lack of integrity with actions that spoke louder than prophetic words of accusation.

Israel's Rejection at Yahweh's Hands

What could be represented as an eventual fact in the Deuteronomistic History was already a clear prospect for the pre-exilic prophets. All the foregoing prophetic references to covenant grace and obligations and Israel's failure to meet them are prolegomena to the prophets' explanation of the political crises that overwhelmed first the northern kingdom and then the southern. Diagnosis prepares for a grim prognosis: God's people were heading for certain disaster. That disaster would come via foreign invasion, loss of political control, and national destruction, but for those who had eyes to see, in their shadow Yahweh himself was stalking. Amos tolled the bell for Israel's demise:

> Fallen no more to rise
>   is the maiden Israel;
> forsaken on her land,
>   with no one to raise her up. (Amos 5:2)

> The end has come upon my people Israel;
>   I will never again pass them by. (8:2)

He also predicted defeat for Israel's supposedly invincible army (2:13–16; cf. 6:13). He subtly wove the tradition of Israel's initial possession of the land into this sinister picture by portraying it in terms of divine destruction (2:9). Woe betide any who stood in Yahweh's way—even Israel! He provocatively set side by side Israel's election and liability:

> You only have I known
>   of all the families of the earth;
> therefore I will punish you
>   for all your iniquities. (3:2)

As Theodore H. Robinson commented, "His special relationship to his people meant not privilege to do wrong, but responsibility to do right."[9]

Latent in Amos's logic was a tradition of accountability that Israel had flouted. His negative deduction firmly demolished the complacent optimism of popular theology (cf. 5:14).

He went so far as to deny any special value for Israel in the exodus:

> Are you not like the Ethiopians to me,
>   O people of Israel? says the LORD.
> Did I not bring Israel up from the land of Egypt,
>   and the Philistines from Caphtor and the Arameans from Kir? (9:7)

It is not immediately clear how far we are to take these shocking questions. Their negativism stands in tension with the affirmation of Amos 2:10 ("I brought you up out of the land of Egypt"). Presumably, because Israel had become "a sinful kingdom" (9:8), its self-excommunication from God's saving purposes is meant.[10] Israel had demoted itself to the level of Israel's enemies who had experienced Yahweh's providential direction in his role as Lord of the nations.

Amos led the way in a prophetic program of reversing accepted beliefs about God's relation to his people. This is especially evident in his reinterpretation of the concept of the "day of Yahweh," which was evidently a positive element in popular theology. We may extrapolate from Amos's new definition and from later prophetic usage that it connoted a future divine incursion into the world, which was to bring about salvation and blessing for Israel and affliction for other nations. Indeed, it may be that his denunciation of surrounding nations in 1:3–2:3 was an elaboration of the negative side of this coming intervention, which he himself used for different ends.[11]

Then, as in 2:6–13 Amos extended the negativity of God's intervention to Israel's coming experience, so in 5:18–20 he explicitly reinterpreted their own expectations along such negative lines:

> Alas for you who desire the day of the LORD!
>   . . .
> It is darkness, not light;
>   as if someone fled from a lion,
>   and was met by a bear . . . .

Israel's hopes are denounced as false security that future events would belie: feeling safe, they would suddenly be exposed to danger. Instead of light, which connotes salvation (cf. Ps 27:1), there would come the darkness of disaster and death (cf. Ps 88:6 [Heb. 7]).

Amos inaugurated a prophetic tradition that became a regular motif of classical prophecy. Isaiah envisioned the day of Yahweh as a time when a storm of divine visitation would sweep down the land bridge between Asia and Africa, through Lebanon, Bashan, and southward, engulfing Judah in its destructive path (Isa 2:12–19). Similarly, Zephaniah depicted it as a worldwide *dies irae*, from which Judah could not claim automatic exemption (Zeph 1:2–2:4). Ezekiel incorporated the tradition into his insistence that Judah would fully and finally fall to the Babylonians (Ezek 7:1–23; cf. 13:5). Looking back, Obadiah interpreted its fate in 587 B.C. as indeed the outworking of the day of Yahweh (Obad 8–14; cf. v 15 and Lam 2:22).

Hosea announced the reversal of Israel's covenant traditions in the naming of his children at God's behest. Lo-ruhamah or "Not pitied" was his daughter's name. An interpretive comment links it with the refusal of further forgiveness for the northern kingdom (Hos 1:6).[12] Even more unequivocally, Hosea's second son is named Lo-ammi or "Not my people." The naming is explained in a public interpretive oracle that may be rendered: "you are not my people and I am not your I AM" (1:9). The usual English rendering, including that of NRSV, follows a textual tradition that has little ancient support, by closing with "and I am not your God," which has probably suffered assimilation to "You are my God" in 2:23 (Heb. 25). It is more likely that an echo of the play on the name "Yahweh" in Exodus 3:12–15 is intended: he is positively present with his people, the one who is there for them.[13] Such was the normal corollary of being the people of God, but now that relationship was to be terminated. Now Israel would be God's ex-people.

The prophetic literature speaks with one voice in predicting national dissolution as the inevitable consequence of radical infidelity. It firmly distances itself from a Micawber-like prophesying that credulously misapplied divine goodwill (cf. Mic 2:6; 3:11; Jer 6:13–14; 29:24–32; Ezek 13). Nevertheless, God's last word was not one of disaster but of hope.

Promises of Israel's Renewal

The Deuteronomistic History surveys Israel's past history from the ruinous standpoint of the exile. With regard to any positive prospects, it only expresses the most tentative of expectations. It prays for favorable treatment of the exiles at the hands of their captors (1 Kgs 8:50) and finds some fulfillment in King Jehoiachin's change of fortune (2 Kgs

25:27–30), which might also prove to be a faint resurgence of the prom-ise vested in the Davidic covenant (2 Sam 7:16; 2 Kgs 8:19; cf. Ps 89:49). The theological cycle of disobedience, punishment, and deliverance in Judges (Judg 2:11–18; 3:7–9; 10:6–16) and the History's interest in re-pentance (Judg 10:10; 1 Sam 7:3; 12:10; 1 Kgs 8:33–53) may be evidence that the epic was designed to provoke repentance and confession of sins, in the hope that Yahweh would be moved to deliver even from exile.[14]

The books of the classical prophets have a much more certain hope. They attest a stark polarity of judgment and salvation for Israel. Modern readers are liable to ease this literary juxtaposition by toning down the judgment, as if it were a hiccup, a slight setback in the relationship with Yahweh. However, as David Hubbard has well said of Amos 8:2, "The *end* . . . is the succinct summary of Israel's fate, as sure and final as the ring-ing down of a theater curtain or the final frames of a motion picture."[15] Ezekiel is to be respected when he describes the theological turning of the tide from judgment to salvation as veritable life after death (Ezek 37:1–14). By a miracle of divine grace the people who have no future are granted a future. The literary form of the prophetic revelation is apt to confuse the reader into thinking that the prophets announced disorien-tation and reorientation in the same breath. No audience would have respected so ambivalent a message. Clearly, in historical terms a gap sepa-rates the good news from the bad. Hosea's messages of hope, for instance, must have been given to those whom bitter experience was at last teach-ing the truth of his messages of judgment. The prophetic books are al-bums in which messages have been artistically arranged, often irrespec-tive of their diverse historical settings.[16]

Hosea 1–3 presents a medley of oracles nestling within the prophet's two symbolic experiences of a marriage that failed and a remarriage. Part of the symbolism is a glorious renaming of the children of the marriage. Lo-ruhamah becomes Ruhamah or "Pitied," and Lo-ammi becomes Ammi or "My people" (2:1 [Heb. 3]; cf. 1:10 [2:1]; 2:23 [25]). The new names celebrate election in place of rejection. Hosea's announcement, which is problematic in terms of the actual future of the northern kingdom, was appropriated by Judah in the Judean edition of the book that has come down to us. The new act of God would put the clock back. The gift of the land would be renewed to a devoted Israel: "she shall respond as in the days of her youth, / as at the time when she came out of the land of Egypt" (2:15 [Heb. 17]) But resetting the theological clock was not enough. The human failure that soon marred the old covenant relationship must not be permitted to recur. This time the hon-eymoon would not be a nine days' wonder (cf. Jer 2:2). Instead, the new entry into the land would be "a door of hope" (Hos 2:15 [Heb. 17]). The promise is given that God will endow his covenant partner with gifts of needed virtues; justice, steadfast love, mercy, and faithfulness would be the marks of the new relationship (vv 19–20 [Heb. 21–22]).[17]

Jeremiah, who was in so many ways the heir of Hosea's insights, transmitting them to the southern kingdom, took up the theme of the moral empowerment of God's people. The former divine "husband" would make "a new covenant" with them (Jer 31:31–34).[18] This covenant would be marked by continuity with the past in that the old standards of the *tôrâ* would still be uncompromisingly required, the same entity of "Israel" was to be involved, and the same purpose of achieving a covenant relationship held good. But the people would be transformed, so that one might speak of a renewed people rather than of a new covenant. A new, constant motivation to obey God's covenant standards would be ensured by the internalization of his will. No longer would his people have an external mandate to live up to: "I will put my law within them, and I will write it on their hearts (v 33; cf. 24:7).

The promise addresses a problem that haunts Jeremiah's oracles of judgment—the radical nature of the people's disobedience. It was a phenomenon that Hosea had known before him: "Their deeds do not permit them / to return to their God. / For a spirit of whoredom is within them" (Hos 5:4). In turn, Jeremiah deplored the moral habits into which the people had locked themselves, having become oblivious to his earlier appeals for repentance:

> Can Ethiopians change their skin
> or leopards their spots?
> Then also you can do good
> who are accustomed to do evil. (Jer 13:23)

> The sin of Judah is written with an iron pen; with a diamond point it
> is engraved on the tablet of their hearts. (Jer 17:1)

Only Yahweh could break this impasse, first by wiping the slate clean with forgiveness (Jer 31:34) and then by creatively remodeling defective human nature into an efficient moral instrument. Then the old covenant ideal could be restored: "I will be their God, and they shall be my people" (v 33).

For Ezekiel a similar miracle of the mind had to take place. He, too, was deeply conscious of a radical sinfulness that pervaded the history of God's people, so that the very exodus was overshadowed by their sinning (Ezek 20:4–10). The only remedy lay in a "heart" transplant, which had to accompany the gift of restoration to the land. Their wills of "stone" would be replaced by a new sensitivity to God's will (11:19–20; cf. 18:31; 36:26–27). Both Jeremiah and Ezekiel, then, shared Hosea's concern over human obedience. All three found the answer in an eschatological change wrought by God, so that what his people should do matched what they could do. For Ezekiel, as for Jeremiah, the ideal of covenant peoplehood would then be achieved.

For Second Isaiah, Israel's positive destiny that would follow its exilic doom depended on its status as "servant" or minister and thus representative of Yahweh. Deaf and blind though this servant still was to his call and work (Isa 42:18–25), Yahweh declared that in view of Israel's ancient election to this status he would forgive their sins (44:21–22) and restore them (41:8–10; 44:1–5; 45:4; cf. 48:20). Their divine master would graciously intervene to help the unworthy servant-people and so honor the previous covenant bond.[19]

Israel at the Door of Hope

The prophetic literature sets the exile as the great divide between judgment and salvation. So the narrator in the book of Haggai represents the post-exilic community of faith as "the remnant of the people," heirs of the post-catastrophe promises of God (Hag 1:12, 14; 2:2). Likewise, the prophet Zechariah celebrates the future of "the remnant of this people" (Zech 8:6, 11, 12).[20] The theological claim must be taken seriously: here was inaugurated eschatology.[21] The prophetic notion of a remnant builds a bridge between the outworking of divine judgment and the possibility of salvation. It is associated especially with the Isaianic tradition. Isaiah named his son Shear-jashub, "A remnant shall return" (Isa 7:3), evidently promising King Ahaz of Judah that the armies of Israel and Aram that threatened his throne and capital would be decimated (cf. Amos 5:3, 15).[22] In Isaiah 10:20–23 the name is reinterpreted in terms of a mere remnant of the whole people of God who would spiritually turn back to God. In 11:11, 16, the name and its meaning are applied to the Jewish diaspora who were to return home (cf. 28:5). In 4:3 "the remnant" refers to those who were to live in the new Jerusalem, in an extrapolation from the sparing of Jerusalem as the sole survivor of Sennacherib's ravages in 701 B.C. (1:8–9), via the restored capital of 1:26. In 46:3 the term is used positively of the Jewish exiles. The dynamic quality that the term eventually acquired may be gauged from Micah 4:7, where it stands in synonymous parallelism with "a strong nation."

The return from exile saw, then, the inauguration of eschatology—but not its consummation. An interim period emerged between the past and future tenses of salvation. The people looked back to their remarkable restoration to the land, at least in partial terms, and looked forward to the fullness of God's eschatological promises. Psalm 126, with its pairing of praise and petition, reflects the poignant ambiguity of the post-exilic situation. For such a situation Third Isaiah echoed his prophetic heritage by blending exhortation and promise:

> Maintain justice,
>> and do what is right,
> for soon my salvation will come,
>> and my deliverance be revealed. (Isa 56:1)

There is a conscious borrowing of the covenant ideals of First Isaiah and the eschatological hopes of Second Isaiah.[23] The pre-exilic oracles of judgment were still God's word. In their radical form they belonged firmly to the past. Their very fulfillment in the people's history authenticated them and turned them into a guarantee that the oracles of salvation would also come true. But in the new community created by God, the judgment oracles remained valid as a challenge to moral reformation. Their sober analyses of a past community of faith were a mirror that God's present people still needed to check up on their relationship with God (cf. Zech 1:46; 8:14–17; Isa 58:1–14; 59:1–15; Mal 3:5). By heeding their warnings the people could prepare for and hasten God's coming.

Post-exilic prophets developed the motif of the day of Yahweh. We noticed earlier that Obadiah, in tune with Zephaniah and Ezekiel, historicized it in terms of the Babylonian invasion and destruction of Judah. But what of the international parameters of the motif in earlier prophetic writings? If God's people had been judged, surely the turn of other nations, especially those at whose hands Judah had grievously suffered, could not be far off. So, Obadiah went on to proclaim that for them, too, Yahweh's day would come, in a manifestation from which Judah would now be exempt (Obad 15–17a). Then, with Judah's oppressors off its back, the way would be open for full possession of the promised land, to the glory of God (vv 17b–21). The emphasis on Israel's salvation as a final feature of the day of Yahweh may represent the re-surfacing of a much older element whose reality Amos had necessarily denied for his generation because it was earmarked for judgment.

Joel borrowed the motif of the day of Yahweh, partly to help the community through a certain harrowing experience of their own and partly to develop Obadiah's general teaching about the people's past and future.

He interpreted a severe locust plague, which put Judah's survival in jeopardy in terms of the day of Yahweh, so as to stimulate repentance among the spiritually indifferent. The averting of the plague and consequent promises of blessing opened up afresh the issue of where Judah stood in relation to the day of Yahweh, in its broader sense, and to the whole eschatological agenda that now clustered round it. Obadiah's promise is reiterated that God's people had nothing more to fear from the negative manifestation of "the great and terrible day of the LORD" (Joel 2:31–32 [Heb. 3:4–5]; 3[4]:16). However, its foreign version would be unleashed upon other nations whose victim Judah had been in the late seventh and early sixth centuries (3[4]:2–8, 19).

As for the salvation of Israel, it would include a spiritual remaking that parallels those promised by Jeremiah and Ezekiel. Joel predicted in God's name an outpouring of his prophetic spirit on the whole community (2:28–29 [Heb. 3:1–2]). The promise serves as a fresh cameo of renewal that both echoes Moses' wish in Numbers 11:29 (cf. 12:6), that all Yahweh's people might be prophets, and stems from Joel's own experience. At the outset of his ministry, Joel stood as sole perceiver of the divine will before he persuaded the community to share it. What was needed was for all the people to be Joels in spirit, sharing fully in a prophet-like commitment to the purposes of God.

Malachi also featured the day of Yahweh, but he reverted to its negative aspect. It would be a time of refining judgment for individuals within the community who were not committed to his moral will, while the obedient would be immune (Mal 3:1–5, 16–4:6 [Heb. 3:24]). This note of partial judgment for the returning or returned exiles goes back to Ezekiel (Ezek 20:35–38; 34:17–22; cf. Zeph 2:3). In Third Isaiah the recipients of judgment are contrasted with God's "servants," who are the heirs of the servant-people promises of Second Isaiah (Isa 65:1–15).

This selection of highlights from the prophetic representation of the people of God could well be fleshed out with amplifications and qualifications. But enough ground has been covered to show that the prophetic revelation was grounded in a particular segment of human history, an experience of crisis that cast deep shadows before and after it. Its initial purpose was to give meaning to what otherwise would have been a senseless chaos. Just as Edward Gibbon explained the fall of the Roman Empire in terms of its internal decay, so the fall of first the northern kingdom and then the southern one was predicted as the inevitable result of willful departure from wholesome traditions. But for the prophets the figure of Yahweh loomed over this terrible interplay of cause and effect, as one who had been ignored and misrepresented at the people's peril.[24]

That fact opened up new possibilities, for in God's heart, where grace as well as justice resided, lay eventual "plans for your welfare and not for harm, to give you a future with hope" (Jer 29:11).

God's grace emerged not only in the restoration of his people to their land, but in the provision of further prophets to pick up the pieces in the rickety aftermath of crisis. Through their pastoral messages of both challenge and encouragement the people survived, heirs of the old oracles of judgment as instruments of reformation and heirs also of the old and renewed oracles of salvation that provided morale-raising goals of certain, if elusive, hope.

Implications for Today

In turn, the Church, no stranger to eschatological hope deferred, has received the complete prophetic revelation as part of its canon of Scripture. Of us, as of the post-exilic community, it may be said, "and with them [are] the prophets of God, helping them" (Ezra 5:2). The pre-exilic prophets' role as unwearying exponents of a social conscience has constant relevance for secular as well as Christian circles of relationship. For, when the teaching of Romans 13:1–7 is applied to a democratic community, Christian citizens are obliged to accept responsibility for their society by promoting in it justice and fairness. Any society, since it is made up of heterogeneous groups of fallible beings, suffers from internal strain, which is compounded by external vicissitudes. Injustice, whereby one group is benefited at the expense of another, is perpetuated both wittingly and unwittingly. Christians have a mandate to raise prophetic voices and to support attempts to achieve as great a social equilibrium as possible. We are warned against being spiritual schizophrenics, professing one set of values in our worship and practicing or tolerating a quite different set in daily life.

Overall, pre-exilic prophecy poses a problem for the Christian interpreter because of its radically anti-establishment stand. Not every church is the church of Laodicea (Rev 3:14–17), nor is our society totally corrupt. The post-exilic community of faith already had to face up to this difficulty. It must be remembered that the prophetic canon reached its fullness in post-exilic times. Canonically we look over the shoulders of later readers who had problems enough but basically held a pro-establishment, theologically positive perspective. From them we learn to find both spiritual encouragement and ethical challenge in the prophetic literature. Standing like them in an eschatological interim, we Christians may learn with them how to live in the warm glow and searching light of God-given hope.

NOTES

1. N. K. Gottwald, "W. Eichrodt, Theology of the Old Testament," in *Contemporary Old Testament Theologians*, ed. R. B. Laurin (Valley Forge: Judson, 1970) 25–62, esp. 54.
2. Biblical quotations are taken from the NRSV, unless otherwise indicated.
3. For a defense of the Hebrew text, see F. I. Andersen and D. N. Freedman, *Hosea*, AB 24 (Garden City, NY: Doubleday, 1980) 634–35; D. R. Daniels, *Hosea and Salvation History*, BZAW 191 (Berlin: de Gruyter, 1990) 71.
4. P. D. Hanson, *The People Called: The Growth of Community in the Bible* (San Francisco: Harper & Row, 1986) 159.
5. J. L. Mays, *Amos*, OTL (Philadelphia: Westminster, 1969) 92–93, 108.
6. Cf. H. Wildberger, *Isaiah 1–12* (Minneapolis: Fortress, 1991) 51.
7. Eichrodt explained the prophetic rejection of worship in terms of depersonalization of the divine-human relationship: "[The] prophets put up . . . a passionate resistance against anything that tends to depersonalize this relationship . . . . So far as his will, the core of his personality, is concerned, man . . . declines to recognize the claims of his divine Lord" (*Theology of the Old Testament*, 2 vols. [Philadelphia: Westminster, 1961–67] 1:365).
8. Latinists will appreciate that the Vulgate captures it well with *populus iste* ("this [despicable] people").
9. *Prophecy and the Prophets in Ancient Israel* (New York: Scribner's Sons, 1923) 69.
10. Cf. D. A. Hubbard, *Joel and Amos*, TOTC (Downers Grove: Inter-Varsity, 1989) 234: "[T]heir Exodus contained no uniqueness to protect them from judgment once they had ruptured the covenant."
11. Cf. J. Barton's contention that Amos 1:3–2:3 is grounded in Israel's popular belief that Yahweh acts as guarantor of international conventions of conduct (*Amos's Oracles against the Nations* [Cambridge: Cambridge University Press, 1980] 40–50). Cf. also G. von Rad, *Old Testament Theology*, 2 vols. (New York: Harper & Row, 1962–65) 2:137 n. 14: "The new thing [about Amos 5:18–20] is not that Amos spoke of darkness at the Day of Jahweh, but that he believed that the darkness would also threaten Israel."
12. One would like to link the name with the characterization of Yahweh as "merciful" or "compassionate" (*raḥûm*) in Exod 34:6, but it is rooted in Judean tradition. Certainly readers of the Judean redaction of the book of Hosea (cf. Hos 1:1) would have made such an association.
13. Cf. *NJB* "I do not exist for you" in Hos 1:9.
14. See von Rad, *Old Testament Theology*, 1:342–43, 346; H. W. Wolff, "The Kerygma of the Deuteronomic Historical Work," in *The Vitality of Old Testament Traditions*, ed. W. Brueggemann & H. W. Wolff (Atlanta: John Knox, 1975) 83–100.
15. *Joel and Amos*, 108.
16. This is probably true even in the case of the closely knit passage Hosea 2:2–15 (Heb. 4–17). Cf. H. W. Wolff, *Hosea*, Hermeneia (Philadelphia: Fortress, 1974) 41: "Thus, although vv 16f [EVV 14–15] probably do not form an original rhetorical unit with the previous verses, we certainly have a kerygmatic unit according to the sense of the present literary composition." Cf. also J. F. A. Sawyer, *Prophecy and the Prophets of the Old Testament* (Oxford: Oxford University Press, 1987) 108–9; Daniels, *Hosea and Salvation History*, 95–96.
17. NRSV renders "in righteousness," etc., but the Hebrew preposition *beth* is more

probably to be taken as of price, as with the same verb in 2 Sam 3:14: cf. REB "bestowing righteousness . . .; making you faithful . . . ." The terminological chart in J. D. Newsome, Jr., *The Hebrew Prophets* (Atlanta: John Knox, 1984) 41, shows that, if *ʾᵉmûnâ* ("faithfulness") is equated with *ʾᵉmet* in 4:1, all but one of the terms is used of Israel elsewhere in the book. However, the exception, *raḥᵃmîm* ("mercy") is significant: contextually it echoes the changing of the name of Hosea's daughter. Does it, then, refer to a divine attribute? Not necessarily. Just as Yahweh's steadfast love *(ḥesed)* was to be reflected in Israel's experience, so the implication may be that Yahweh's mercy would be so reflected (cf. the reflection of Yahweh as *raḥûm* ["merciful"] in Ps 111:4, which features in Ps 112:4). The concluding clause "and they shall know the LORD" (Hos 2:20) is suggestive, in the light of the pairing of "steadfast love" and "knowledge" as human entites elsewhere in Hosea. It implies that here, too, "steadfast love"—and so the other virtues—are to be demonstrated by the new Israel. Strictly, the bride-price was paid to the bride's father, but he lacks a counterpart in the marriage allegory of Hosea, and it is Israel that receives the gifts and so, fittingly, their benefit (D. J. A. Clines, "Hosea 2: Structure and Interpretation," in *Studia Biblica 1978: I. Papers on the Old Testament and Related Themes*, JSOTSup 11 [Sheffield: JSOT, 1979] 83–103, esp. 94).

18. See B. W. Anderson's insightful study of the pericope, "The New Covenant and the Old," in *The Old Testament and Christian Faith*, ed. B. W. Anderson (New York: Herder and Herder, 1969) 225–42.

19. The servant-people also feature in the "responses" to the first three Servant Songs at 42:5–9; 49:7–12; 50:10–11; see J. L. McKenzie, *Second Isaiah*, AB 20 (Garden City, NY: Doubleday, 1968) xxxix.

20. C. L. Meyers and E. M. Meyers judge the "remnant" references in Haggai to be "devoid of theological meaning," unlike the instances in Zechariah (*Haggai, Zechariah 1–8*, AB 25B [Garden City, NY: Doubleday, 1987] 417). However, their emphasis on the literary nature of Haggai and Zechariah 1–8 as a composite work (pp. xliv–xlviii) and their chart of correspondences between Haggai and Zechariah 7–8 (p. xlix) strongly suggest that the "remnant" references at beginning and end function as an inclusion in which, holistically at least, the initial references share the theological quality of the final ones. Wolff interprets "remnant" in Haggai 1 as "a term which is applied to the exiles as bearers of the promise" (*Haggai* [Minneapolis: Augsburg, 1988] 51–52). R. Mason has suggested that the positive response of the people to God's word through the prophet constituted them as the "remnant" of prophetic hope ("The Prophets of the Restoration," in *Israel's Prophetic Heritage*, ed. R. Coggins et al.; [Cambridge: Cambridge University Press, 1982] 137–54, esp. 145).

21. Cf. W. A. VanGemeren, *Interpreting the Prophetic Word* (Grand Rapids: Zondervan, 1990), 186–87, 208–9.

22. See R. E. Clements, *Isaiah 1–39*, NCB (Grand Rapids: Eerdmans, 1980) 83.

23. See R. Rendtorff, *The Old Testament: An Introduction* (Philadelphia: Fortress, 1986) 199–200.

24. Cf. P. D. Miller, Jr., *Sin and Judgment in the Prophets: A Stylistic and Theological Analysis*, SBLMS 27 (Chico, CA: Scholars Press, 1982) 132–39.

9

IMAGES FOR TODAY: WORD FROM THE PROPHETS

Carl E. Armerding

The challenge of this article is to bring together images from Israel's prophetic past with images of God's prophetic word for today. It is that challenge to which the life and work of David Allan Hubbard have been a continual response. It is an honor for me, with such a theme, to follow in his train.

Before turning to the work at hand, a word on the assigned task is in order. The first challenge is to work within the canonical and theological rubrics set up by the editors of this book—i.e., to discuss God, the people of God, and a word for today from the prophets—without missing what the prophets are really all about.[1] Since Jeremiah 18:18 identifies the prophets specifically with the Word of Yahweh (*dᵉbar yhwh*), this article must stay close to the concept of revelation. Whatever "images for today" may arise among the prophets of Israel, if the Word of Yahweh through his servants is obscured, the correct images will have been lost with it.

A second challenge is to do the Bible's prophetic literature justice within limited space. The fact is that within the prophetic canon lie two distinct kinds of literature, known from antiquity as the Former Prophets (Joshua– 2 Kings) and the Latter Prophets (the Major and Minor Prophets). Given editorial limitations, I have chosen to draw my primary illustrations from the Latter Prophets themselves, but do not want thereby to suggest that the Former Prophets do not present a theological point of view (or, with equal plausibility, points of view), or that this point of view cannot plausibly be called "prophetic."[2] Third, there is also the challenge of contemporaneity. Unlike the previous two chapters on the prophets, this chapter calls for a concentration on what those ancient texts mean for today.[3] With two previous chapters devoted to images of God and Israel, chiefly in the *then*, we must be satisfied to ask how these images take meaningful shape in the *now*.

The Question of Images

Before beginning, however, we must clarify what the concept of image implies.[4] For "image" the *Concise Oxford Dictionary* offers a range of definitions, beginning with an "artificial imitation of the external form of an object" (e.g., a statue), and moving toward the less physical and more metaphorical meanings. Thus, for example, an "image" can be scientifically precise, like the optical counterpart of a reality viewed in a mirror, or refracted through a lens. By reflection, the mirror in the bathroom gives us a realistic "image" of how we will appear to our family at the breakfast table; by refraction, lenses bring the reality of other "images" closer to us so we may see them clearly (my bifocals do that job!). These metaphors of reflection and refraction surely have something to teach us as we consider the hermeneutic task of understanding the prophetic *dābār*.

On the other hand, by "image" we may mean a metaphor or simile by which an idea or concept is pictured for its contemporaries. The purpose of the image, of course, is to capture the idea or concept, itself, through appeal to the imaginative faculties of the mind, informed as they are from both visual and conceptual directions. Applied simply to the prophetic doctrines of Yahweh, metaphors like the "shepherd tending his flock" (Isa 40:11), or the "cosmic measurer and marker of the heavens" (Isa 40:12), reveal far more to the reader than does scientific or theological prose discourse.

The prophets, then, may best be understood, whether in the then or the now, as they appeal to our imagination. Whether through metaphor or simile, or in the plain-language presentation of ideas and concepts, we find ourselves faced with the truth of Almighty God and his works, as a series of images reflected in the mirror of Scripture, or even refracted through scriptural lenses, inexorably refocusing the realities in the clear undistorted light of God and his Word. In summary, as we move from then to now, the goal must be to see clearly the realities pictured by the prophets, to capture and be captured by the great ideas and concepts that are mediated through prophetic proclamation. At the level of language itself, we will need to hear plain statements in plain language (e.g., "In faithfulness he will bring forth justice," Isa 42:3, NIV) and be confronted by the reality that, despite changes in culture and history, "faithfulness" and "justice" in Isaiah's time have a univocal relationship to the same qualities today.

At the level of indirect language (i.e., simile or metaphor), however, our task will be to consider both explicit and implicit metaphorical language in the prophets. Also, we will have to create our metaphors with which to translate prophetic concerns into contemporary images. Finally, the idea of reflection or refraction may also aid the search. If we think of the prophets as mirrors and lenses, with contemporary images produced by reflection or refraction, the emergence of images of reality without the distortion left by the hermeneutical gap may be the happy result.

Images for Today

Within these boundaries, the theological outline of the book reminds us that our contemporary images must deal (1) with Yahweh, the covenant God of biblical literature, (2) with the Word of Yahweh itself, and, of course, (3) with Israel, the community that receives the Word of Yahweh. How each of these ancient "images" corresponds to, or shapes, an answering reality in our own day is the question with which this survey must wrestle.

As a method, I have chosen to highlight three representative metaphors of Yahweh, (Yahweh as Lord of History; Yahweh as Savior-Healer; Yahweh as Husband-Father) each of which forms a dominant image in one or more of the great literary prophets of Israel. Each image presents a facet of the character of Yahweh, and together they summarize the dominant features of Yahweh as presented to and understood by the Old Testament believing community. Then, from the central metaphors of Yahweh will follow discussion of the subsidiary metaphors that flow from these three dominant images of Yahweh and that illuminate the

prophets' views of the "people of God" and the "Word of God." Although
each section will feature a particular prophet, the themes and imagery of
the entire prophetic corpus has far too much in common to restrict any
given image to a single prophet. Illustrations will be drawn from the rich
imagery of prophecy wherever appropriate.

In one sense, the entire schema—God, Word, People—presents a beautiful reflection of the trinitarian nature of the Christian faith. Yahweh,
the source and controller of life, the God whose covenants represent the
basis for all OT proclamation, is the first person of the Trinity. Yahweh's
Word, as the dynamic expression of the mind of God, corresponds graphically to the presentation of Christ in the NT, and is the Trinity's second
person. The people of God, both in the OT, and especially in the NT, are
called into being by the Spirit of God, and form the locus for the Spirit's
presence as the third person of the Trinity. Together these three, in prophetic preaching and in the reality of history, create a unity, even as the
consideration of metaphors relating to all three will tend to unify the
theology of the OT prophets.[5]

But there is yet another image within prophetic literature that must be
considered, both *then* and *now*. Quite apart from the material of revelation itself (the *dābār*), pointing to God and forming the community, there
is the powerful image of the prophet himself. From antiquity, the prophetic person has fascinated and challenged the reader, with no sign of
that fascination abating. A vast literature on prophetic revelation con-
tends that one must begin with the prophetic person, or personality, for
in no part of Holy Writ is the messenger so much a part of the message.[6]
And although it cannot be given space in this article, a chapter on "images for today" must at least acknowledge that claims for prophetic ministry, and prophetic gift, based largely on OT models, continue throughout the NT period, right into the present, and remain one of the most
powerful contemporary images of prophetic revelation.[7]

Habakkuk: Yahweh as Lord of History

An entire set of prophetic images relates to the power of Yahweh to do
something about the evil and violence that are endemic in the world.
The question is not, initially, one of redemption or restoration; it focuses
rather on whether Yahweh has, or possibly is inclined to use, the power
required to deal with ubiquitous evil and injustice. Philosophically, this
image is related to the problem of evil rather than to the problem of
redemption, which is the focus of a different set of metaphors.

Habakkuk is perhaps the most interesting OT representative to deal with the question. Within the OT, his prophecy is unique in that it contains no preaching but a series of dialogues with God over the central question. A third chapter forms a poetic response, and plumbs the depths of a faithful response to impending evil with an intensity and pathos rarely excelled. The picture of Yahweh is less metaphorical than most, yet appeals strongly to the imagination. Habakkuk's dialogue is an almost desperate appeal to a higher authority, in form not entirely unlike the appeal of the pathetic city rulers of Palestine to Bronze Age Amarna Egyptian Pharaohs,[8] yet in content a model of faithful prayer. Yahweh is appealed to, not in terms of "how" he can control evil, but "why" he does not! "How long, O Yahweh, must I call for help, but you do not listen? Or cry out to you, 'Violence!' but you do not save?" (Hab 1:2, NIV). The questioner, unlike our contemporaries who engage in endless debates over military strength, has little concern for whether Yahweh has the ability to save; this seems to be assumed. The question, rather, is why a sovereign Lord and Ruler of history would not bring about what he is obviously capable of effecting.

Yahweh replies in a series of ongoing dialogues. Habakkuk had asked whether Yahweh would step in and smash the violent society around the prophet in Israel. Yahweh answered, "I am going to do something in your days that you would not believe, even if you were told. I am raising up the Babylonians, that ruthless and impetuous people" (Hab 1:5–6, NIV). They will come and destroy faithless Israel; they will sweep across the earth, and nothing will prevent their advance (Hab 1:5–11)!

If the first question concerned whether Yahweh, as Lord of History, had the will to destroy evil, the second question (1:12–2:1) focuses on whether he can retain his purity and justice while manipulating a variety of evil forces to accomplish his purposes. Can Yahweh, as Lord of History, be both powerful and just? It is the age-old question of theodicy, a question that has troubled believers since the beginning of recorded history.

To this question, Yahweh replies with a challenge to faith (2:2–5) and a series of woe oracles (2:6–20) that graphically pronounce complete and ultimate destruction on the evil in Israel, and indeed on evil itself, but never resolve the philosophical questions raised by the prophetic cry. As is often the case in a biblical response to questions of theodicy, the solution presented builds on two pillars: (1) a longer, eschatological view of history, and (2) the character and permanence of God. Habakkuk 2 is no exception. Verse 14 is the centerpiece, "For the earth will be filled with the knowledge of the glory of [Yahweh], as the waters cover the sea" (NIV), while v. 20 forms a climax, "But [Yahweh] is in his holy temple; let

all the earth be silent before him" (NIV). The administration of justice
will eventually become universal, through Yahweh's continuing presence
as the Lord of History. By contrast, the Babylonian, like the Assyrian before him, has no future and no enduring presence, having "[built] his
realm by unjust gain" (2:9, NIV).

Other prophets, of course, contribute to the image of Yahweh as Lord
of History in a variety of ways, but Habakkuk is unique in the form and
content of his theodicy. About the same time, Jeremiah (25:8) portrays
Yahweh summoning all the peoples of the north, together with "my servant" Nebuchadnezzar of Babylon, to come against Israel for judgment,
after which he, too, pictures (vv. 11–12) an eventual punishment of
Babylon and restoration of Israel. Typical of prophetic references to the
time of fulfillment, Jeremiah's "seventy years" stands in contrast to
Habakkuk's indeterminate "the earth will be filled . . . ."

Isaiah, too, is at the center of this tradition, albeit with even more royal
or governmental language. Chapter 9 is representative, set in a time (ca.
700 B.C.) when the Assyrian hordes are threatening to extinguish the light
of Israel. While the intensity of theodicy found in Habakkuk, and even in
Jeremiah's personal encounters with Yahweh, is missing, the historical
perspective is the same. A day is coming when "there will be no more
gloom" (v. 1, NIV). "The people walking in darkness have seen a great
light" (v. 2, NIV), for the yoke that has burdened them, the bar across
their shoulders (v. 4), has been shattered. All this comes through the
zeal of Yahweh of Armies (v. 7, NIV The Lord Almighty), through the birth
of the child who will be called "Wonderful Counselor, Mighty God, Everlasting Father, Prince of Peace" (v. 6). "Of the increase of his government and peace there will be no end. He will reign on David's throne
and over his kingdom, establishing and upholding it with justice and righteousness from that time on and forever" (v. 7, NIV).

Relationship to Word and Community

Images of Yahweh as Lord of History, and Just Governor, are so typical
of the prophets that many would consider them the central message of
prophecy. Subthemes, such as the Day of Yahweh,[9] the Kingdom of God,
and the Messianic Age, are subsets of the concept. But what is the relationship of this image to the prophetic word and the community of Israel? Again, the response is at the very heart of prophetic imagery. For,
what Yahweh carries out on the stage of history, he does through the
agency of his sovereign Word. The word of God is the governmental edict

that summons Nebuchadnezzar to battle (Jer 25:9), even as it pronounces the curse on that king's violence, greed, and treachery (Hab 2).

In Amos 1, a powerful metaphor of Yahweh as Judge, the word comes in the form of a legal indictment against the nations. Isaiah 55:11 sums it up, "[S]o is my word that goes out from my mouth: it will not return to me empty, but will accomplish what I desire and achieve the purpose for which I sent it" (NIV). The true force of this statement is to be found in the preceding analogy (v. 10), "As the rain and the snow come down from heaven, and do not return to it without watering the earth and making it bud and flourish, so that it yields seed for the sower and bread for the eater, so is my word" (NIV). The governing, correcting, and sending word of Yahweh is both creative and effective, though always related to historical activity rather than magical force, in the sense of the incantation formulae common to the ancient Near East.[10] The word, then, is the agent of Prince (or Governor/King/Judge) Yahweh, and the prophet is the human vehicle through which the word comes.

The image of Yahweh as Lord of History has natural implications for the people of Israel. For Habakkuk, the question of Israel's survival is the key to history. One senses that, for Habakkuk as undoubtedly for other prophets, a conflict exists between the unconditional covenant promises to Israel and the governmental conditions for the survival and prosperity of the nation. The fact remains that Israel, by any standard of justice, has forfeited the right to survive, and Habakkuk is himself caught up in what that may mean. But, for the promises to remain intact, and thus the mission of Israel to emerge triumphant, Israel must survive. To this problem Habakkuk is given no answer, for the answer must await the exilic prophets Jeremiah and Ezekiel. Habakkuk himself must rest his case in God's utter and complete faithfulness, power, and goodness (ch. 3). Israel's future fades into the future glory of Yahweh.

Contemporary Themes

Habakkuk's enigma has its echo in at least three contemporary themes, all of which remain more basic to the enigmas of existence than does any other subset of questions. First, the problems of evil, violence, lawlessness, together with the wrongful employment of power, continue to challenge belief and confront modern thoughtful humanity with the continuing problem of basic goodness and meaning in life. Related to this is the problem of relating goodness to power. Does any overriding standard, or even personal force, exist to determine how and whether power will be used in the service of the good? A third major philosophical problem concerns direction within history. Is history going somewhere, as both Christians and Marxists affirm, or is it merely "a tale told by an idiot, signifying nothing"? A final question is more narrowly focused among believers of all kinds. Assuming that there is a God of justice, can he be approached, and do such exercises as prayer and faith have power to accomplish change in the world?

The image of Yahweh as Lord of History rests on two assumptions, both of which remain as powerful in their appeal today as ever. Properly understood, they remain perhaps the only truly satisfactory solution to the problems of contemporary as well as ancient humanity. The fundamental assumption is that God exists as both Lord and Judge, and that he is both powerful and good. The prophetic proclamation, whether in Habakkuk or elsewhere, assumes rather than argues this point, which may not be good enough for much of modern philosophy. But basic to the question of the argument's utility is the question of its validity. Believers from every page of history continue to affirm this kind of God, and for them such a foundation makes utter good sense.

The second assumption is that history is under the control of God, who is both powerful and good, and that he is directing its affairs according to a timetable that, in the light of eternity, is entirely justifiable. Concomitant to this is the assumption that the struggles of this present evil age can only be understood against the background of the whole span of God-ordained history. The earth will be filled with the knowledge of the glory of Yahweh (Hab 2:14). Little attempt is made by those who speak for God to resolve every personal question, or solve every human riddle. Instead, the believer is called to look ahead to the end, when in light of the whole the parts will become clear.

But what of those who do not believe? Does proclaiming God's existence as Lord, and even his goodness, or his commitment to ultimate justice, make any sense in a world where belief is in short supply? My conviction is that it does, not because modern humanity will easily grasp the force of the logical argument, though a powerful apologetic for belief has always existed. Rather, in a world that is faced with no satisfactory alternative and that continues to show itself ready for "spiritual" solutions the Yahweh of the Bible may represent the only answer that makes any sense at all.

Our purpose is not to develop the apologetic, but simply to say that, properly understood, the image of Yahweh as supreme Lord of History, Governor of the Universe, and Righteous Judge, offers modern humanity an alternative to the nihilistic search for meaning so common to our generation. Simply stated, there may be no other answer, and in the apologetic of Scripture such verities are often proclaimed rather than argued.

Isaiah: Yahweh as Savior, Healer, Restorer, Cleanser, Branch, Root, Stump, Suffering Servant

An entire set of prophetic images of Yahweh picture the healing or restoration of a broken, wounded, fallen, or captive Israel. In these metaphors, Yahweh comes as the Agent of Salvation, the Great Physician/Healer, the One who Brings Back Captives, the Giver of New Life, or the Root/Branch/Stump of renewed life. In many ways, this set of images, with its focus on "salvation," can itself claim to be central for OT theology, and certainly for the prophet Isaiah, whose name comes from the same root.[11] A major subimage within this group is the well-known Suffering Servant of Isaiah 41–53, whose mission to Israel, and in Israel, is clearly one of vicarious healing (Isa 53:4–6). It is significant that in this, as in related metaphors of Yahweh, the root cause of the nation's woes is their transgression or rebellion against the covenant standard. The prevailing aspect of this group of images will differ according to the individual passage, but what unifies the group is the concern for restoration of that which is broken, dead, or dying.

For example, Isaiah of Jerusalem begins his prophecy with an indictment, moving quickly through the metaphor of rebellious children (1:2–4) to that of an injured body (vv. 5–6):

> "Your whole head is injured,
>   your whole heart afflicted.
> From the sole of your foot to the top of your head
>   there is no soundness—only wounds
>   and welts and open sores,
> not cleansed or bandaged or soothed with oil." (NIV)

The figure quickly shifts to other, equally poignant metaphors (a lone hut in a field of melons, v. 8) or descriptions of the terrifying reality ("your country is desolate, your cities burned with fire"). But time and time again the figure will return to an image or language of salvation or healing. A little later in the same prophecy (5:1–7), the metaphor changes to a vineyard where the fruit is bad, though the image of Yahweh in this extended metaphor is limited to destroying the vineyard. Normally, however, Yahweh is seen as the Cleanser of the stained garment (1:18), Purger of the dross (1:25), the Branch of renewed life in the dead tree (4:2–6), the Fiery Consumer of the thorns (10:17), or supremely the God who becomes Salvation for his beleaguered people (12:2–6).

As with Yahweh as Lord of History, the image of Yahweh as Savior cannot be limited to a single prophet. A particularly memorable passage in Hosea (14:4 [Heb. 5]) specifically employs Hebrew healing terminology (the verb *rāpā*), together with the language of love (the verb *ʾāhab*), to express Yahweh's promise for the last days when Ephraim will be restored and will again "blossom like a lily" or "send down his roots . . . like a cedar of Lebanon" (v 5, NIV). Hosea's use of the metaphor overlaps with his central metaphor, Yahweh as Lover, but demonstrates the universal biblical truth that Yahweh's salvation is based squarely on his love. Expressions of tenderness combine with metaphors of new life and restored purity to convey a strong impression of Yahweh as caring for, comforting, restoring, and delivering his beloved people. Even the abandoned vineyard (Isa 5) is only given up after all possible measures have been taken to achieve its restoration (cf. v. 4, "What more could have been done. . . ?" NIV). In many ways the high point of prophetic salvation language continues to be Isaiah's Servant figure, in which the ultimate tragedy of God's abandonment of the righteous sufferer to become "an offering for sin" (*ʾāšām*, "guilt offering," Isa 53:10) leads to the complete restoration and universal comfort of the people of Yahweh.

Relationship to Word, Community

Images of the Word of Yahweh have a certain similarity within each group of metaphors. As seen above, the word is that which is active and dynamic and brings about salvation in the same manner as it directs history. For Isaiah, a particularly significant image of the word comes in the call of the prophet (ch. 6). Here, as with the nation itself, cleansing is needed prior to service or restoration, and the cleansing comes from the very throne of God, through the agency of a burning coal, applied to the lips (the source of the word) of the prophet (Isa 6:6). Like the people, the prophet is cleared of guilt and his sin is atoned for (v. 7). Thus having effected salvation (cleansing, atonement), the word is now free to run its judging and saving course throughout the land, cutting away the deadwood, laying waste the evil cities, until naught but "the holy seed will be the stump in the land" (v. 13, NIV).

The connection of word with messenger is, thus, given another dimension. The word of Yahweh must first have been in the messenger; only then can it effectively run its course and do its work. The messenger is then a vital part of the salvation process ("How beautiful on the mountains are the feet of those who bring good news," 52:7, NIV). The Servant figure (who may be the prophet) is endowed by Yahweh with "an instructed tongue, to know the word that sustains the weary" (Isa 50:4, NIV). His own ears have been opened and he is not rebellious (50:5), unlike those who have ears that do not hear and a heart that does not understand (Isa 6:10).

Images of the community follow the metaphor. If Yahweh is Savior, Healer, Comforter, and Redeemer, the community represents the restored city, the wounded but healed body, the comforted sufferer, or the renewed stump. All of these figures point to a day when the nation Israel would be given fresh hope, following a period of purging and cleansing, as the light of Yahweh's Word runs its course. The "holy seed" becomes the "stump," a figure that, like many others in the prophets, points to the prophetic doctrine of a restored "remnant."

Contemporary Themes

In many ways the theme of salvation or healing is closest to New Testament theology, with its emphasis on sin and salvation in Christ. Healing itself is very much a part of the gospel accounts, though the common vocabulary employed *(iáomai, therapeúō)* is generally quite distinct from the NT usage of the verb "to save" *(sōzō)*. But, whether in the NT or the OT, both images may be grouped together on the basis of the common employment of related metaphors. Each of these, together with other figures of redemption and restoration, speak of the gracious restoration, cleansing, comforting, healing, and renewal of the people of God.

What this has to do with contemporary humanity should be obvious. It doesn't take much imagination, reading this kind of prophecy, to identify the condition of Israel with the condition prevailing in our own time. The continuing ravages of war, the human suffering created by failed economic systems, the widespread effects of greed, continued imbalances between the rich and the poor—all these point to a society for which the metaphors of sickness, disease, brokenness, captivity, and isolation are all appropriate.

On the other hand, the restoration of such a society, often connected with utopian economic or social schemes, has increasingly become a chimera. Attempts at continent-wide common markets, vast aid, and self-help programs, together with World Health Organization programs to wipe out disease and provide clean water, seem to do little to alleviate the suffering of a humanity too complex to work simply, and too fragmented to work cooperatively. Nationalism, ethnic and religious rivalries, economic disparities, and just plain greed all work to destroy almost as quickly as the builders can build. Is there an answer?

Isaiah's vision remains, in these circumstances, both clear and appealing. With their vision of a restored millennial community (though see also Isa 11:6–9) accomplished by the "zeal of Yahweh of Hosts" (Isa 9:7; 37:32), the so-called Second and Third Isaiahs particularly build on the image. Never did humanity have more need for some reason to believe that those who build houses will live in them, or that those who plant vineyards will drink of their fruit (Isa 65:21). Frustration with progress has become endemic, as economic disasters follow hard after one another and whole continents are ravaged by the AIDS epidemic.

But, as with the vision of Yahweh as Lord of History, the real question comes at the point of credibility. It is one thing to speak of a "balm in Gilead" with "healing for the wound of my people" (Jer 8:22, NIV), but another to find it. In the cry for universal reconciliation and restoration, the questioner is reminded of another, later, visionary, who, carried into the heavens from his exile on Patmos, was captivated by the hidden promise of a word from God sealed up in the forbidden scroll (Rev 5–13). John the Divine[12] instinctively knew that somewhere in the mysteries of the universe there was salvation, and after seeing the Great Throne in heaven, and him who sat upon it, John knew who had the key. But the mystery of redemption of humanity was locked away in a sealed scroll, and it was quickly apparent that "no one in heaven or on earth or under the earth could open the scroll or even look inside it" (NIV).

I am convinced that John's plight is a parable of modern, thoughtful, concerned humankind. And just as God provided a solution through the Lion of the tribe of Judah, who "has triumphed [and] is able to open the scroll and its seven seals," (NIV) so modern society will continue to weep for the lost vision of true healing and restoration, until one is revealed who can break the deadlock and release salvation. But what kind of figure can possibly meet this crying need?

There is one prophetic figure in whom all the imagery of healing and salvation is gathered together, who answers fully the cry of a broken world in our own day. The Suffering Servant of Isaiah's oracles, the true Wounded Healer, is not only John's "Lion who is a Lamb," but one who, having borne the sins of many, and is able fully to enter into the tragedy of the human condition, can offer salvation. Perhaps no other prophetic image, or no other prophetic figure, has such potential to satisfy the quest of our broken world and bring about the healing for which we all long.

Hosea: Yahweh as Lover, Husband, Father

Another powerful set of images, picked up later in the NT's vision of God, pictures Yahweh as a faithful, but rejected Husband, or secondarily as a Father whose children have forgotten him. Though the richness of biblical metaphor for God as Mother is sometimes overlooked,[13] the most powerful images of Yahweh in prophetic witness are of Husband and Father. This, of course, is to be expected, for the corresponding metaphor of the people of God is a much-loved bride or a beloved son. While such images recur in a variety of contexts, the classic picture of Yahweh as Husband or Lover is in Hosea, where images of Yahweh as Father also emerge. In a day when covenant-love is both rare and misunderstood, such a metaphor of Yahweh remains one of the most powerful pictures of God available.

Hosea's spurned lover is a familiar biblical image. The prophet himself takes on the role, called to "Go, take to yourself an adulterous wife and children of unfaithfulness" (Hos 1:2, NIV).[14] The purpose is clear from the outset: the land is guilty of the vilest adultery, and the prophet will serve as an object lesson. Children are born of this union, each with a symbolic name indicating that God has broken his covenant with Israel and Judah. But suddenly the image changes. It is discovered that the first-born son, Jezreel, whose name means "God scatters," can also signify "God sows"! The people who have become "no people" are again to become the people of God. The broken covenant, the bill of divorce, will be set aside, and the union of husband and wife is restored.

In a powerful extension of the metaphor, Hosea 2 outlines the cost of the restoration, both to the aggrieved husband (Yahweh) and to his un-faithful spouse (Israel). For him the cost is literally to go out and woo his wife again, speaking tenderly to her heart, and turning her tears (the Valley of Achor, 2:15) into a door of hope. The new betrothal will be "in righteousness and justice, in love and compassion" (2:19, NIV), and from the renewed union the whole land will regain its fruitfulness (2:21–22).

For the people, too, the cost is high. Reconciliation of this kind does not come without getting to the root of the problem. For Israel, the problem was misplaced love (2:5–8), and years of attributing to other lovers the good gifts of Yahweh's covenant faithfulness. A period of enforced separation from the blessings, an image re-enforced in chapter 3 and fulfilled in the exile, will bring the errant wife back to her senses. The point of the whole image is this: if Israel had only remembered the true source of her life in the land, she would have kept to her first love. In Babylon, she will be forced to remember, and, in the language of another powerful image, the prodigal son, she "comes to her senses."

Her husband, on the other hand, has never forgotten, and can never forget.[15] This ability of the divine lover never to forget his first love recurs in a variety of images throughout the prophets and serves as a foundation for any theology of Yahweh's utter faithfulness to his covenant-love.[16] The point is expanded in a variety of prophetic metaphors, all of which convey, in the most tender language of human experience, the unforgettable love of a mother for her child (Isa 49:14–16), a father for his son (Hos 11:1–4), and, of course, the oft-repeated love of the husband Yahweh for his unfaithful wife (cf. Jer 3:6–20; Ezek 23).

Even the strongest biblical injunctions abhorring divorce (e.g., Mal 2:10–16) are based on this "covenant-loyalty" of Yahweh, following the lines of the basic metaphor. Yahweh hates divorce (Mal 2:16), not because he is unaware of human frailty and the limitations of relationships, but because "breaking faith" (Mal 2:14–16) is completely and diametrically opposed to everything for which Yahweh stands. If, then, there is a biblical metaphor that comes closest to the heart of describing Yahweh in his relationships, this is it. No other prophetic metaphor so powerfully calls forth a response from a world starved for meaningful relationships, or defines for secular as well as Christian humankind the nature of true love.

Relationship to Word, Community

In the first metaphor (Lord of History) the Word of Yahweh is a word of "power," and in the second (Savior, Healer) it is a word of "healing/salvation." Here the focus has shifted; the Word of Yahweh is now a word of "love." Biblical terminology for love, as well as a biblical theology of love, finds its basic semantic range in the images of the metaphor we have considered. Not only the prophets, but the entire OT and NT concept of the love of God builds on this fundamental and powerful image of Yahweh as covenant-lover.

Covenant-love, the fleshing out of Yahweh's covenant commitment to his people, is tough love. It is a "love which will not let me go," to quote the language of one hymn writer.[17] The loving word of Yahweh is, above all, a faithful word. For the community, Israel, the metaphor is foundational to its existence as a covenant people. From the days of oppression in Egypt, when the text graphically reminds the reader that "[God] remembered his covenant" (Exod 2:24, NIV), there is never a time when God's faithful care for his people is not connected with his covenant promises. And it is virtually impossible to consider the covenant faithfulness of Yahweh throughout the OT without soon being carried back to some form of the basic metaphor of love. Husband, Father, Mother, Lover: Yahweh is all of these, and in each image the accent is on the utter faithfulness, loyalty, and love of Yahweh himself.

Contemporary Themes

It is not difficult to discover a multitude of ways in which this theme responds to contemporary concerns. At the start, we are reminded of the stark contrast between this kind of tough, uncompromising, compelling love, and the shallow, ephemeral, and transient picture of that which passes for love on the modern screen or in the pages of the Harlequin romance. In a world where "love" is the theme of every pop song, we may be tempted to feel that our society "loves too much." In light of the contrast between the covenant-love of Yahweh and modern romantic love, it could be argued that we love far too little, and in our loving we may miss the essential point of what true love is.

Although covenant-love is represented as a steely "will to love," far from the romantic love that finds its essence in feelings, covenant-love actually incorporates the best of both. The difference is that covenant-love—the love that is Yahweh—can and will endure long after the feelings that provoked it and that it provokes have dissipated. Surely, in all of literature there is hardly a more poignant reminder of human tenderness and longing than that painted by Hosea 2 of the aggrieved husband speaking tenderly to his errant and wandering wife, determined that he cannot and will not let her go until the full bloom of their love is restored.

A second contemporary theme, powerfully informed by this metaphor of Yahweh and his people, deals with the nature of forgiveness and restoration when relationships are broken. Brokenness is all around us, whether in international relationships, strife among various interest groups or ethnic communities, or the common but epidemic occurrence of divorce. The image of Yahweh, based as it is on tough love and redemptive action, recognizes that reconciliation comes only at great cost. In our own day, when reconciliation often turns out to be a mere papering over of differences, the model of reconciliation pictured in the image of Yahweh as aggrieved Lover, and illustrated supremely in the cross of Jesus Christ, is a model that should stand as a powerful apologetic for the gospel.

Finally, in a day when many people, both within and without the Church, think of God as a harmless old gentleman, a wrathful judge, or a legalistic pedant, the image of Yahweh presented in these passages is a forceful alternative. The love of God, not in some abstract form, but in the particularity of the drama of redemption played out through Scripture, and pictured in the metaphor we have considered, has the potential to break through the jaundiced, cynical skepticism of our modern age, an age that, however skeptical, can still be moved by the power of sacrificial, tender, and faithful love.

Conclusion

The essay above has merely sampled the rich imagery of prophetic metaphor and has looked at prophetic theology through only one lens. Other metaphors come immediately to mind, but the purpose of the essay is to illustrate method, as well as to capture a few dominant themes with contemporary relevance. If through this lens, prophetic preaching can break out of the distortions of so much that passes for truth and value in the world around us, my purpose in writing will have been more than satisfied.

NOTES

1. This book follows a certain theological structure, the shape of which mirrors both the structure of the Hebrew canon (Torah, Prophets, Writings) and a set of rubrics (God, the people of God, the Word of God) not unfamiliar to OT theologians. Although neither of these volumes uses these rubrics exactly, see for example, Th. C. Vriezen, *An Outline of Old Testament Theology,* 2nd ed. (Oxford: Basil Blackwell, 1970); or W. Eichrodt, *Theology of the Old Testament,* 2 vols. (London: SCM Press, 1961/1967), esp. vol. 2.

2. Concerning the possible origin of the Former Prophets within prophetic circles and its characteristic theological viewpoint(s), see the standard introductions to the so-called Deuteronomic History (e.g., T. E. Fretheim, *Deuteronomic History* [Nashville: Abingdon, 1983]). The continuing diversity of opinion concerning the exact shape and provenance of such a work should not obscure the general

agreement that Joshua through 2 Kings represents a unified, didactic historical account, reflecting the theological concerns both of the Book of Deuteronomy and of the reforming prophets from Amos onward to the exile. Even "stories of the prophets" within the Latter Prophets (e.g., narrative sections of Jeremiah) are clearly part of the didactic art of the books themselves and have stimulated a significant body of secondary literature in recent years.

3. Concerning the alleged dichotomy between "what the text meant" (its descriptive sense) and "what it means" (its prescriptive sense), see K. Stendahl, "Biblical Theology, Contemporary" *IDB* 1:418–32. Stendahl's rigorous and (in my view) ultimately unworkable distinctions have evoked considerable response; cf. the summary in G. Hasel, *Old Testament Theology: Basic Issues in the Current Debate*, rev. ed. (Grand Rapids: Eerdmans, 1975) 35–38. One need not fully identify with the purely descriptive aim of some biblical theologians, while still maintaining that a text may be studied as a unity, but from the separate poles of antiquity and contemporaneity.

4. In one sense, of course, the prophets opposed anything to do with images, at least in the sense of the creature trying to capture the glory of Uncreated Splendor through representations from the created order itself. Among the writing prophets, the sarcasm of the so-called Second Isaiah (40:18–20; 41:7, 22–24; 42:17; 44:9–20; 46:5–7; 48:5) represents the high point of prophetic denunciation of "images," achieved ironically by means of some of the most powerful literary images in biblical revelation. But it is not of such images that we are to think.

5. Sadly, for the moment we must omit consideration of a contrasting set of metaphors, all of which form a backdrop to the great central images of Yahweh, his true Word, and his faithful community. So, the prophets scathingly portray the folly of false gods, the idols of the nations. Additional images also present a counterfeit word, in the deceiving words uttered by false prophets, diviners, and magicians. Communities in rebellion, the exact antithesis of the community of the Spirit, welcome, and seem to thrive on, such words. These communities know not God, and in so far as they represent covenant Israel, their rebellion is a major reason for the crisis in covenant love at the heart of the prophetic critique.

6. Two notable examples must suffice. J. Lindblom, *Prophecy in Ancient Israel* (Oxford: Basil Blackwell, 1962), devotes almost half of his volume to the phenomenon of the prophet. A. Heschel, *The Prophets* (New York: Harper & Row, 1962), divides the outline differently but is equally fascinated by the person of the prophet.

7. Cf. Lindblom's comment (*Prophecy in Ancient Israel*, 26) concerning the wealthy, noblewoman St. Birgitta of Sweden (14th cent. A.D.), whose visions and words from Yahweh influenced popes and kings alike: "I am inclined to add that, among all the representatives of the prophetic type outside Israel, there are few who have so great an affinity with the prophets of the Old Testament as Birgitta . . . ."

8. A series of desperate appeals from city-state rulers in Palestine from the mid-fourteenth century B.C. were uncovered in 1887 at Tell el-Amarna on the middle Nile in Egypt. In sharp contrast to the response of Yahweh, the Pharaohs of the late XVIIIth Dynasty, Amenophis III and IV (Akhenaton), seem unable to exercise any effective control over their vassals. The scene is pathetic, not majestic.

9. See especially Amos 5:18–20, Joel, and the later prophets. Scholars have long searched for a historical or theological background to the concept. See W. A. VanGemeren's survey of the scholarly work of Mowinckel, Fensham, Weiss, and von Rad (*Interpreting the Prophetic Word* [Grand Rapids: Zondervan, 1990] 214).

10. Texts of this sort, though common in Egypt (cf. J. B. Pritchard, ed., *Ancient Near Eastern Texts* [Princeton, NJ: Princeton University Press, 1955] 326–30) and Mesopotamia, have generally not been preserved in Palestine. The pillar and oath between Jacob and Laban (Gen 31:45–54) may represent such a magical formula within Israelite history. For a review of the extensive literature on the relationship between Hebrew *dābār* and the concept of "word" in a magical sense, see J. Bergman and H. Lutzmann, "dabar," *TDOT* 3:84–94 and R. B. Edwards, "Word," ISBE 4.1104–5.

11. Studies of both OT and NT words for salvation abound; cf. especially J. F. A. Sawyer, *Semantics in Biblical Research: New Methods of Defining Hebrew Words for Salvation*, SBT 2/24 (London: SCM Press, 1972), together with studies of the word groups *yāšǎʿ* in Hebrew and *sōtēr/sōzō* in Greek. The question of the relationship of divine salvation and healing has been covered extensively in the secondary literature, but for the purpose of this chapter the association of healing and broader deliverance metaphors in prophetic literature is sufficient.

12. Or "John the Theologian" (Gk. *theológos*), the title of the author of Revelation in Greek.

13. E.g., Isaiah 49:15 ("Can a mother forget the baby at her breast . . . ? I will not forget you," NIV) or Isaiah 66:13 ("As a mother comforts her child, so I will comfort you," NIV).

14. Commentators continue to disagree over whether Gomer bat Diblaim is an adulterer *before* the marriage or becomes such later. Most arguments depend more on the implications for the analogy than on clear grammatical analysis of the ambiguous (*ʾēšet zǝnûnîm*).

15. A central theme of Scripture is that "God remembers" his covenant, e.g., Exod 2:24. The prophet Zechariah ("Yahweh remembers") is himself a reminder to the people that they, too, are called to remember the covenant.

16. This article is not the place to explore covenant terminology like the common biblical term, *ḥesed*, which re-enforces the metaphor being considered. For *ḥesed*, in addition to various word-study books, see N. Glueck, *Hesed in the Bible* (Cincinnati: Hebrew Union College Press, 1967) and K. D. Sakenfeld, *The Meaning of Hesed in the Hebrew Bible: A New Inquiry* (Missoula: Scholars Press), 1978.

17. In the hymn of that name by George Matheson. The hymn-writer, whose blindness led his fiancée to break the engagement, is but one of millions who have understood the permanence of divine covenant-faithfulness against a background of human disappointment.

II
THE OLD
TESTAMENT

The Writings

10

IMAGES OF YAHWEH: GOD IN THE WRITINGS

Roland E. Murphy

The charge of hubris is inescapable. How can one write about the God of the Writings, or for that matter, of the theological potential of those books?[1] One is reminded of the Louvain volume entitled "the biblical idea of God," or one of the articles contained therein, "God among the wise men of Israel," by A. Barucq.[2] And recently there appeared *The God of the Sages: The Portrayal of God in the Book of Proverbs*, by Lennart Boström.[3] Although the latter title appears more manageable, there remains an enormous extent of material and time covered in the Book of Proverbs: wisdom sayings from the pre-exilic period in most of Proverbs 10–31, but lengthy post-exilic exhortations in Proverbs 1–9. These precedents may sound like an excuse for covering such a large expanse in this essay. But the extent is appropriate in a *Festschrift* for David Hubbard, who combines in his person manifold talents featured by the sages, historians, storytellers, and psalmists of the Ketubim.

As a classification, the Ketubim are not on a par with the Law and the Prophets (tôrâ and nᵉbî'îm), which complete the three-stepped canon with which we are familiar.[4] But how truncated the Hebrew Bible (or Tanakh) would appear to be without the Ketubim—without Psalms or

Job, for instance. And we may consider another rather astonishing fact. When the Jewish community began to associate certain scrolls (*m^egillôt*) with certain feasts at the beginning of the medieval period, it was from among the Ketubim that the choice was made. They are, in the liturgical order of feasts: Song of Songs for the Sabbath of the Passover; Ruth for Shavuoth; Lamentations for the Ninth of Ab (the destruction of Jerusalem), Qoheleth (i.e., Ecclesiastes) for the Sabbath of Succoth, and Esther for Purim. As one might expect, the only questionable entry here is Qoheleth, which the Sephardic (i.e., Mediterranean) Jews did not read on any feast but which the Ashkenazic [i.e., Northern European] Jews read on Succoth. Another minor but popular classification, which seems to be derived from Christian liturgical practice, is "wisdom literature" (i.e., Proverbs, Job, Ecclesiastes, and, among the Apocrypha, Sirach and the Wisdom of Solomon).

Finally, our knowledge of the post-exilic period is sketchy at best. The Ketubim are a precious source for knowledge of a period that has been described as *in gurgite vasto* ("a vast abyss"). We would really know little about the restoration of Judah without Ezra and Nehemiah and the stunning recapitulation of Israel's history by the Chronicler. And our knowledge of apocalyptic would be stunted without the Book of Daniel. Thus, although the Ketubim might appear to be an afterthought, an addition into which disparate writings were eventually swept, they constitute a rich source for our knowledge of Israel. While dating remains somewhat uncertain, it is reasonable to claim that only parts of Proverbs 10–31 and many Psalms are clearly pre-exilic (i.e., before 587 B.C.).

We are at a loss to explain the formation of the Ketubim within the canon.[5] There is something trim and neat about the Law and the Prophets (Earlier and Later), but the Writings represent the final stage in the murky process of canonization, when "the other books of our ancestors" (as the Greek translator of Sirach describes the Ketubim in his prologue) were being assembled and finally approved. Although the issue of authorship is not an important historical factor in the formation of these books, it might be noted that David is represented because half of the psalter is attributed to him, and Solomon is represented by Proverbs, Ecclesiastes, and the Song of Solomon. In addition, a major portion is given over to these two kings by the Chronicler (1 Chr 10:1–29:30; 2 Chr 1:1–9:31). All this may be merely a coincidence. We will treat this literature in the broad categories of history, wisdom, *m^egillôt*, apocalyptic, and prayer.

History

The "Chronicler" can serve here as a code name for the author(s) of 1–2 Chronicles and Ezra–Nehemiah.[6] The concerns of the book stand out clearly. It begins its "history" with no less than Adam and in nine chapters descends by way of genealogy to the death of Saul in 10:1–14 ("so Saul died for his unfaithfulness," 10:13, NRSV). Even in the genealogical lists it is obvious where the interests of the Chronicler lay: ch. 3–4 give the descendants of David and Judah, ch. 6 those of Levi. Thus, temple and worship are the concerns of the author (and surely of the post-exilic community as well). David established the cultic personnel (and the Levites are conspicuous here), and Solomon built the temple. Furthermore, when the division of the united monarchy takes place under Rehoboam, attention is thenceforth given entirely to the kingdom of Judah, while the northern kingdom of Israel is treated only when pertinent to Judean history and the Chronicler's own theology. The Chronicler is a stout defender of what he sees as the Lord's justice. God must inexorably punish the infidelity of kings and people, down to the destruction of Jerusalem and the exile of 587 B.C. (cf. 2 Chr 6:36–39; 33:10–11, 12–13; 36:21).

Many other sources besides the books of Samuel and Kings were utilized by the Chronicler (e.g., 1 Chr 29:29), but he had his own story to tell. The Davidic dynasty, the temple, and the cult (featuring especially the Levites and various personnel) are the main characters. History is ruled by a sense of divine retribution: prosperity for those who are faithful, doom for the unfaithful. But it is not without theological significance that the final verses (2 Chr 36:22–23) with their orientation to a better future, are repeated at the beginning of Ezra (1:1–3). Once again the Lord sets about delivering the people: "The LORD stirred up the spirit of King Cyrus" (NRSV).

The Books of Ezra and Nehemiah describe the period of the restoration in broad strokes. There are several waves of returnees: those led by Sheshbazzar (Ezra 1:8); those led by Zerubbabel and Joshua (3:8, the time of the prophets Haggai and Zechariah who urge the rebuilding of the temple). Almost 100 years later, Ezra leads another group back and establishes the Mosaic law among the community. Nehemiah, a cupbearer for King Artaxerxes II, returns twice to Judah (cf. Neh 13:6–7), and he ensures the rebuilding of the walls of Jerusalem. The history of this period is murky because the historical sequence of the two main personalities, Ezra and Nehemiah, is difficult to determine. Nonetheless, the Chronicler presents a vivid picture of these fragile days that were marked by so much opposition from the neighbors of Judah.

After this historical work there are only the slimmest gleanings to be had from the Bible concerning the rest of the Persian period (see Esther and Judith). After the death of Alexander the Great, Judah existed under the domination of the Egyptian Ptolemies (3rd cent. B.C.) until the Seleucids of Antioch took over Palestine and precipitated the Maccabean revolt (2nd cent. B.C.). It was during this post-exilic period that the high priest became the virtual ruler of the Jewish community, despite the foreign yoke. Meanwhile, the Jews of the diaspora (i.e., those living outside Palestine) became significant in their own right (e.g., the influential community at Alexandria in Egypt).

The brief historical sketch provided by the work of the Chronicler needs to be kept in mind as background to the Ketubim. Early on, the last of the prophets appear (Haggai and Zechariah about 520; Malachi about 70 years later), but for the Writings we are confronted with a wide variety of compositions that have enriched the Hebrew Bible. Even if their ancestry can be traced in varying degrees to the pre-exilic period, many psalms and proverbs (and perhaps Job and individual poems in the Song of Songs) owe their preservation to the mood of the time. Theological questions adumbrated in previous generations, such as the nature of monotheism, retribution (Job), the mystery of God (Qoheleth), relation to non-Jews (Ruth, Esther), and a fixed liturgy (now without the Ark of the Covenant, but with a sparkling array of psalms), come to the fore.

Wisdom Literature

One of the most brilliant achievements of the Israelite community was the dynamic involved in the wisdom literature.[7] The teaching of the sages in the pre-exilic period was far more open and subtle than many moderns are willing to grant. They recognized the complexity of reality and the mystery of God (e.g., Prov 21:30–31). But lessons were to be inculcated and youngsters were to be trained, without being weighed down with details and distinctions that they would soon discover for themselves. The firm teaching about the fear of the Lord (Prov 1:7, "The fear of the LORD is the beginning of knowledge," NRSV) and the inevitable results of virtuous and evil (read: wise and foolish) conduct dominates the introduction to the Book of Proverbs (chs. 1–9) and is liberally sprinkled throughout the sayings in Proverbs 10–31.

Divine retribution is seen as following the traditional distinction between good and evil actions. It is a doctrine already preached in Deuteronomy and in the Deuteronomistic History (Joshua–2 Kings). The lessons of history perhaps made it easier to take shelter in generalizations. But the wisdom literature made a point of dealing with human experience and reality, and pious generalizations fell afoul of the vicissitudes of experience. Hence, the author of the Book of Job takes issue in a masterly way—yet without providing a simple "answer"—with the incomplete and often oversimplified view of the older sages.[8]

While this writer does not really solve the mystery of divine retribution, his work is in direct tension with the traditional doctrine of the sages. And it does more than this; it raises one of the fundamental questions of human life: does one serve (love) God for oneself or for God (the question Satan directs to the Lord in 1:9)? This is a powerful introduction to the debate that takes place between Job and his three friends. Although all of them are non-Israelites, they all reason on the premises of traditional wisdom doctrine. The friends defend orthodoxy, while Job defends his own integrity (of which the events of chs. 1–2 have convinced the reader).

In ch. 31 Job lays down the gauntlet to the Almighty, and it is here that one might expect the intervention of God, which does not occur until ch. 28. The intervening chapters are taken up with the poetic exhortations of Elihu, who attempts to bolster the argumentation of the friends. But the speeches of the Lord in chs. 38–41, ostensibly debating with Job, are puzzling. They present the divine power and wisdom in magnificent poetry, but Job did not need such a lesson as this. He was well aware of divine might. Hence he receives no "answer" of any theological kind. But he is satisfied by the theophany of the Lord: his eyes have seen the one whom he had known only by hearsay (42:5). In a sense, that is his answer; his vision has brought him more deeply into the mystery of God's ways.

The twelve chapters of Ecclesiastes have enjoyed a remarkable history.[9] Qoheleth (his "name" in Hebrew whose meaning remains a mystery) clearly sets down in writing ideas that do not sit well with the accepted theological orthodoxy. He is not content to say that the law of retribution does not always function. He simply denies that anyone can make sense out of what God is doing (3:11; 8:17; 11:5). His approach to life is that of a sage (in fact, the author of the epilogue termed him a *hākām* ["wise one"] in 12:9). He admitted that his search for wisdom ended in failure—it was beyond him (7:23). Along with his dour observations about reality (all is *hebel*, or "vanity") are his exhortations to "eat and drink" (e.g., 2:24; 5:18). One is to enjoy life as much as possible, precisely because of the non-life that awaits the Israelite in Sheol. However, this exhortation is not the message. The message is that life is vain and absurd; the best one can do is to enjoy whatever the mysterious God may give.

The various "contradictions" that are featured in this book have also stamped the history of its interpretation. Early on, the fathers of the church assigned the "difficult" passages to knaves with whom "Solomon" was dealing. These "voices" within the book can be seen in the effort of modern scholars to find several hands at work in the twelve chapters—some representing orthodoxy, as opposed to Qoheleth's alleged unorthodoxy. However, it seems best to explain the book as the work of one man, a complex thinker to be sure. It is too facile to attribute certain lines to another writer. Traditional Jewish and Christian interpretations went their own ways in the general characterization of the book. As exemplified in the commentary of Jerome, the work could be read as an ascetical treatise (the joys of this world are paltry and unsatisfying). Such a view is evident from the quotation of Qoheleth (1:2) in the opening lines of the spiritual classic, *The Imitation of Christ.* Jewish tradition emphasized 12:13, "Fear God, and keep his commandments" (NRSV).

The wisdom movement continued in Israel beyond the three books just mentioned. Indeed, some have classified the Joseph story (G. von Rad) and the Succession Narrative (R. N. Whybray) as wisdom writing, but one would like a stricter definition of wisdom than they give.[10] There are, however, two apocrypha books that are unmistakably preoccupied with wisdom: Sirach (Ecclesiasticus, as it is also called)[11] and the Wisdom of Solomon.[12]

Finally, there is the mysterious figure of personified Wisdom that flits in and out of the wisdom literature.[13] Wisdom is clearly personified as a woman in Proverbs (see 1:20–33; 8:1–36; 9:1–6). She appears as a prophet, as one who threatens but also cajoles and, most importantly, offers life, which was the greatest acquisition promised to all who pursued Wisdom. In Proverbs 8, there is a mysterious description of her origins from God before creation; apparently, she even cooperates with God as "master worker" (the meaning of ʾāmôn in 8:30 is problematic) in the act of creation. In Sirach she is again personified and identified with the Torah (Sir 24:23). She is described as taking up her residence in Zion at the Lord's bidding, and she ministers to God in "the holy tent" (24:8–10). Finally, in chs. 7–9 of the Wisdom of Solomon, Lady Wisdom emerges as practically divine ("breath of the power of God, and a pure emanation of the glory of the Almighty . . . a reflection of eternal light, a spotless mirror of the working of God, and an image of his goodness," Wis 7:25–26, NRSV). Von Rad once wrote of personified wisdom in Proverbs 8: "So wisdom is truly the form in which Jahweh makes himself present and in which he wishes to be sought by man. 'Whoso finds me, finds life' (Prov viii. 35). Only Jahweh can speak in this way."[14] Wisdom seems best understood as a mysterious communication from God—in nature and in the Torah (Sir 24:23) and ultimately in Jesus Christ (according to Paul in 1 Corinthians 1:24, "Christ the power of God and the wisdom of God," NRSV).

The Mᵉgillôt

Although Ecclesiastes is treated above among the wisdom books, it will be remembered that it was read on the Sabbath of Succoth. Since this was traditionally a time of rejoicing at the harvest, the choice of Qoheleth is understandable. Several times he urges joy and pleasure (2:10, 24; 3:12, 22; 5:17; 8:15; 9:7–9; 11:7–10). Thus, the use of this book at the joyous feast of Tabernacles is quite selective.

The Song of Songs was associated by the Jewish community with Passover.[15] It was interpreted in allegorical fashion in the Targum as a history of the Lord's dealings with the chosen people from the days of Egypt (hence the association of the book with the feast of Passover) through the monarchies down to the final eschatological period. It is a remarkable fact that both Jewish and Christian exegesis agreed on a similar approach to the work: for Jews it spoke of the love of the Lord for Israel and for Christians it reflected the love of God (Christ) for the church and the individual soul. Hence, from the days of Origen on (ca. A.D. 200), the "spiritual" interpretation flourished at the hands of Gregory the Great, Bernard of Clairvaux, and John of the Cross up to our own day. However, if this traditional interpretation is not to be simply dismissed, it must also be recognized as incomplete. The songs that make up the Canticle (as it is also called) deal directly in the literal sense with love between a man and a woman. There is general agreement that these are exchanges of love between two characters (there is only one man, not two, vying for the love of the woman). The poems express all the typical attitudes of love: desire, admiration, appeals for a rendezvous, descriptions of the beloved, boasts, and even teases. An alert reading of the Song is called for, since there are sudden switches of speakers and locales. The language and the images are often highly unusual for Western taste ("Your nose is like a tower of Lebanon," 7:4), but the Song has also given us the immortal line, "love is strong as death" (8:6, NRSV).

The Book of Ruth may be classified as a novella or short story, and one of the most beautiful in its genre.[16] The main action, concerning the bereaved Naomi and Ruth, the Moabite widow, takes place in Bethlehem when the two women return from their luckless days in Moab. The gallantry and generosity of Boaz are met by the cunning and boldness of

Ruth. When an unnamed kinsman yields his right of redemption to Boaz (perhaps a Levirate marriage? cf. Deut 25:5–10), the wedding can take place. The son born to them is proclaimed as "born to Naomi" (4:17) and named Obed, the father of Jesse, who was the father of David. This genealogical appendage orients the story toward David's Moabite forebears, and also explains its position in the sequence of the Greek Bible (or LXX), just before the Books of Samuel. The rural flavor of the story, with the harvest at the center of ch. 2, makes Ruth a fitting choice for the feast of Weeks (or Pentecost), which was associated with the barley harvest. In this story of divine providence, the God of Ruth is portrayed as the God who is intensely involved with ordinary people, even Moabites.

The Book of Lamentations constitutes a genre distinct from the laments of the psalter; it contains prayers concerning the fall of Jerusalem in 587 B.C.[17] They are written in acrostic style: the verses begin with successive letters of the Hebrew alphabet (except for ch. 5, which has 22 lines, the number of letters in the alphabet). They excel in pathos and feeling, as a poet speaks, or a personified Jerusalem speaks or is spoken to. Chapter 3 differs from the rest because of the use of the first person singular, wherein a representative seems to speak in the name of the community. The attribution to Jeremiah may have been prompted by an inexact interpretation of 2 Chronicles 35:25. The image of God implicit in these chapters can be summed up by Exodus 34:6–7, "a God merciful and gracious . . . keeping steadfast love for the thousandth generation" (NRSV).

The last of the *megillôt*, Esther, is of course the reading for the feast of Purim ("lots"; cf. 3:7; 9:24–26).[18] As it stands it deals with the reversal of lots that were supposed to determine the slaughter of the Jewish people by the Persians under Xerxes I ("Ahasuerus," 485–64 B.C.) and the wicked Haman. Instead, the Jews are saved by the intercession of Esther, and the feast of "lots" came to be observed as a joyous occasion. The genre of the book has remained a puzzle: novella (with echoes of the Exodus deliverance)? a historicized wisdom tale? The most that can be certainly maintained is that it bears all the marks of fiction: the unlikely events (e.g., the extreme ages of Mordecai and Esther; a royal grant to slaughter a people after a year's notice, etc.). But the story is artfully contrived and features several motifs: concealment (that Esther is a Jew; that Mordecai once saved the king's life, etc.) and especially antitheses and reversals (the opposition between Mordecai the Saulide and Haman the Agagite; Haman's suffering the manner of death he planned for Mordecai; Haman feasts while Mordecai fasts, etc.). The motif of delay is obvious in 5:3–8: Esther postpones the dinner invitation for the King and Haman to the following day, when Haman will experience his undoing. The delaying tactic is balanced by certain chapters that run at a very fast tempo (esp. chs. 5–6).

The art of the narrative has not been sufficient to overcome objections from some quarters. It is true that God is not mentioned once, although there seems to be a veiled allusion in 4:14. However, the apocryphal additions (from the LXX) have many references in Queen Esther's prayer (LXX 14:1–19). The book is a story of the strange ways of divine Providence.

Apocalyptic

The word apocalypse means "revelation" and usually designates revelation of a specific kind: often by a vision, through the intervention of a heavenly mediator or angel.[19] The one who receives the "revelation" is hidden under a pseudonym, such as that of an ancient person (e.g., Enoch, Ezra, Baruch, and, in the present case, Daniel). The message usually deals with the end time, when the good will be rewarded and the evil punished in a next life. The apocalypses were not without reference to their own period of history; thus in Daniel the battle between good and evil is against the background of the persecution of the Jewish people by Antiochus Epiphanes (d. 163 B.C.).

The Book of Daniel is easily divided into stories (ch. 1–6) and visions (basically four: chs. 7, 8, 9, and 10–12). The stories describe how the Lord delivered Daniel and others when they risked their lives out of fidelity to the law. These tales probably circulated for many years before they were prefaced to the visions. They are pertinent to Jewish life in the Diaspora and during the Maccabean times, for they proclaim that God will protect those who remain faithful to the Torah. In ch. 3 (in the LXX) are to be found some additions: the prayer of Azariah and the song of the Three Young Men. These and the story of Susanna and also of Bel and the Dragon (also found in the LXX, and not in the Hebrew text) fit into the "story" character of the first chapters. The visions in ch. 7–12 are separate from the earlier stories and are genuine examples of apocalyptic literature. They are unified in their thrust concerning the hostile kingdom of Antiochus Epiphanes. But the full message is that the eschatological kingdom of God will be given to the "holy people of the Most High" (Dan 7:27, NIV). Despite the tribulations of the faithful, God remains in control of history. In the eschaton, the climax of all history, Daniel's "people shall be delivered" (Dan 12:1, NRSV).

Prayers

"Prayers" (*t*ʰ*hillîm*) is the title for the book of Psalms. They have proved their worth as prayers throughout history. But the scholarship of this century has given us solid insights into the kind of prayers they are, that is, both liturgical and highly literary. Their liturgical character means that they were composed in the first instance for worship in the temple. They were not simply outstanding poems that came to be used as prayers. One can see clearly that the psalmist is often a kind of master of ceremonies, summoning a community to sing God's praises in the temple (e.g., Pss 33, 47, 49, 96–100).

The second "discovery" of twentieth-century scholarship was to abandon history for literary analysis that determined the various genres (hymn, lament, etc.) that structured the psalms. This lesson could and should have been learned earlier. It was long recognized that David could not be the author of the half of the psalter attributed to him. The superscriptions of the psalms are ancient Jewish tradition, found already in the LXX, but they are not a true index of authorship, any more than Solomon for wisdom literature or Moses for the Pentateuch. The meanings of most of the technical terms in the superscriptions (e.g., Shiggaion, Ps 7; Jeduthun, Ps 62) are simply unknown to us. The ancient tradition attempted to pinpoint the specific setting of psalms in the life of David (e.g., Ps 51, after the sin with Bathsheba). Today we realize that we cannot be that specific about the historical origin of any psalm. But this in turn is a gain for all, since the psalm remains open-ended and not tied to a particular event. Its meaning is more generally applicable to ourselves because the setting is broader (i.e., we identify with its joy, sorrow, complaint, etc.).

The literary analysis of the various types of psalms is the normal approach since the fundamental studies of H. Gunkel and S. Mowinckel.[20] These have been modified to a certain extent by later scholars such as C. Westermann and W. Brueggemann, but the analysis of Gunkel remains basic.[21] The hymns or songs of praise call upon two themes to celebrate: the Lord's action in Israel's history and in creation. Songs of thanksgiving (or declarative songs of praise according to C. Westermann) acknowledge the Lord as the rescuer of the individual or of the community, and they issue a praise for the deliverance. The lament, both individual and collective, is an appeal for deliverance from some evil (enemies, sickness, suffering, sin, etc.). It is accompanied by motifs about why the Lord should intervene and affirmations of trust and confidence in his ability to do so. These are the three basic genres, but other classifications have been based upon content (e.g., Zion psalms, royal psalms, and wisdom psalms).

There has been a recent trend to recognize wholeness and context in biblical books. The question is, Should we interpret a proverb separately from the context of an immediate chapter? Sometimes, it must be admitted, the finding of a context for a proverb is a subtle undertaking. The psalter can be viewed in the same way: is it really just to treat the psalms separately, or have they an added level of meaning by reason of the context in which they are found?[22] For example, what weight is to be given to Psalm 1, which introduces the entire psalter and emphasizes meditating on the law of the Lord day and night? It recommends that the reader choose good over evil; the two ways of good and evil are copiously exemplified in the rest of the psalter. Granted that the psalter (and Proverbs as well) is the result of assembling various collections, can one detect certain inner connections among them (and also with the rest of the OT) that are important for interpretation?[23]

There is the old saw, *lex orandi, lex credendi*: prayer reveals what a person believes. This is fully verified in the 150 psalms that were composed over some centuries of Israel's existence. Yet there are not many explicit treatises on the "theology of the psalms."[24] We may conclude that while the psalms throw light on both God and people, they actually tell us more about human beings. We will single out certain of many aspects that could be featured.

Paradoxically, it is the humanity presented in the psalms that deserves first notice, because it is in the heights and depths of human experience that the Lord is met. As Martin Luther put it so well,

> What is the greatest thing in the Psalter but this earnest speaking amid the storm winds of every kind? Where does one find finer words of joy than in the psalms of praise and thanksgiving? There you look into the hearts of all the saints . . . . On the other hand, where do you find deeper, more sorrowful, more pitiful words of sadness than in the psalms of lamentation? There again you look into the hearts of all the saints, as into death, yes, as into hell itself . . . . When they speak of fear and hope they use such words that no painter could so depict for you fear or hope, and no Cicero or other orator so portray them. And that they speak these words to God and with God, this I repeat, is the best thing of all. This gives the words double earnestness and life.[25]

The average Bible reader tends to take monotheism in the OT for granted. It is astonishing how many read words like "Who is like you, O LORD, among the gods?" (Exod 15:11, NRSV; cf. Pss 86:8; 97:9; 135:5), without any question arising as to whether or not they mirror monotheism. The fact is that biblical monotheism was practical, not theoretical, at the beginning. The Decalogue witnesses to this in the very first commandment, presupposing that other gods do exist ("no other gods before me," Exod 20:3, NRSV) but that the Lord alone is to be worshiped. "He is to be revered above all gods" (Ps 96:3, NRSV), and "all gods bow down before him" (Ps 97:7, NRSV). The background to this is the concept of the heavenly court of the Lord. The members of this court are the "heavenly beings" (Ps 29:1, NRSV with a footnote that the Hebrew is "sons of gods"). It would be some time before the more or less theoretical monotheism of Deutero-Isaiah (40:18, 25; 41:23, 29) would lead to claims such as those in Pss 115:4–8 and 135:15–18.

Moderns tend to conceptualize creation as making something out of nothing, and they can call upon the unusual use of the word *bārā'* (Gen 1:1, "create"; cf. Pss 89:12, 47; 104:30; 148:5). Only God is used as the subject of the verb, and there is never anything indicated out of which something is made. But this static and abstract notion of creation is not clearly indicated in the Bible. The psalms in a particular way express the truth in the mythological language of Israel's neighbors. The activity of God in creation was something to be relished and savored. It was greater than the conflict of Baal with Yamm (Sea), which was known from Ugaritic lore (cf. Ps 89:9, NRSV, "you rule the raging of the sea"; also Pss 69:7; 93:3). Chaos was personified in monsters, like Leviathan (Ps 104:26) or Rahab (Ps 89:10), whom the Lord had tamed. This is a different insight into what is so majestically and serenely described in Genesis 1!

The creation of human beings is seen as a true marvel, something almost too stupendous to think about (Ps 8). Yet with it is combined repeated emphasis on human transience. Humans are compared to mere breath (*hebel*; cf. Pss 39:4–5; 62:9), or to the grass that withers (Pss 90:5–61; 103:15–16). Life is precarious. Humans live because the breath of God (*rûah* or *nišmâ*) is in them; this is the divine breath mentioned elsewhere (Gen 2:7; Ps 104:29–30). Without it there remained only death and Sheol (Eccl 12:7). Those who died were thought to go to Sheol, a place of non-life, localized in the belly of the earth. For the psalmists, the worst aspect of this was the absence of the Lord: "For in death there is no remembrance of you, in Sheol who can give you praise?" (Ps 6:5, NRSV; cf. 88:3–6). It was not that Sheol was beyond God's reach (cf. Amos 9:2; Ps 139:8) but that no loving contact with the Lord occured there. One merely existed in Sheol, for it was the great leveler of all, the virtuous as well as the wicked (Job 3).

More than this, Sheol—so often paralleled with Death (*māwet* or *môt*)—was conceived as a dynamic power. Sheol/Death was not something static that awaited every human being; it was felt to be an evil that pursued every living person. Its power was manifest in all the various evils that humans experience: sickness, persecution, sin—all the ugly aspects of the frail human condition. That is why the psalmist can say, "You brought up my soul from Sheol!" (Ps 30:3). In a sense, this is a metaphorical use of the term. The psalmist was not dead nor was there any resuscitation; but the personal condition of the psalmist was as good as dead. The hand (Ps 89:48) or power of Sheol had grasped him even while living. The experience of non-life (sickness, etc.) is the experience of Sheol.

This understanding of life and death demonstrates that immortality, or living with God in the next life, was not an issue throughout most of the OT. One's immortality was in one's good name, in one's posterity through whom one lived on. Yet it is a striking fact that the psalter has been the prayerbook par excellence for Christians who do believe in a personal immortality, perhaps because death is confronted, not brushed aside or watered down, in the psalms. Life is also present, even if it is only the life of the here and now. But this life included the presence of God. Perhaps these are the reasons that the psalms have provided a voice for all kinds of people. Christoph Barth has observed:

> H. Gunkel says of the individual psalms of lamentation that they are "the place where the religion of the psalms comes into conflict with death." In a less well-known comment, O. Noordmans says of this conflict that the psalms are the greatest of all the wonders of the world; for without giving any clear knowledge of the nature of death, "they have helped one generation after another to pass through death."[26]

Epilogue: The Theological Potential of the "Writings"

The God of the Ketubim is not very different from the God of the Torah and the Prophets. The Books in the "Writings" echo many aspects of the past tradition. The history of the Chronicler is as sacred as the history recorded in the earliest books. The book of Lamentations records a depth of feeling over Jerusalem's fall that can be detected in the tender words of God in Hosea and Deutero-Isaiah. The importance of Torah is matched by Ezra, a new Moses who interprets the Law for the restored community. The temple of Solomon is rebuilt in 520–15 B.C., and the liturgy inaugurated here is continued, enriched by a steady stream of psalms. As the Book of Daniel confronts a new persecution, so also the Book of Esther hints at the pogroms to which the community was subject at the hands of new conquerors who replaced the Assyrians and Babylonians of old. The wisdom movement was considerably enlivened as it reached down through Job and Ecclesiastes to Sirach and the Wisdom of Solomon.

Perhaps it is in the wisdom literature that we can see one striking development that goes beyond what we meet in earlier parts of the canon. It is the mystery of God. This is not to say that God is without mystery in the rest of the OT. The words in Isaiah 55:8 (NRSV) ring true, "For my thoughts are not your thoughts." But the intensity of the mystery from the point of view of frail humanity is brought out more severely in the books of Job and Ecclesiastes and in the laments of the psalter. That faith-filled admission of Qoheleth comes back to haunt all human confidence: "I looked at all the work of God: no one can find out what is done under the sun. Therefore humans search hard, but no one can find out; and even if the wise man says he knows, he cannot find out" (Eccl 8:17, author's translation).

NOTES

1. The Writings (*Ketûbîm*) is the third main section of the Hebrew Bible besides the Law and the Prophets. For bibliography on the Writings see R. E. Murphy, "The Writings," in *The Biblical Heritage in Modern Catholic Scholarship*, ed. J. J. Collins & J. D. Crossan (Wilmington: Glazier, 1986); R. Rendtorff, "The Writings," in *The Old Testament: An Introduction* (Philadelphia: Fortress, 1986) 245–88; B. S. Childs, "The Writings," in *Introduction to the Old Testament as Scripture* (Philadelphia: Fortress, 1979) 501–655.

2. *La notion biblique de Dieu*, BETL 41, ed. J. Coppens (Gembloux: Duculot, 1976). The article by Barucq (169–89) is "Dieu chez les sages d'Israël."

3. ConBOT 29 (Stockholm: Almquist & Wiksell, 1990).

4. On the importance of the three-stepped canon see R. E. Murphy, "Old Testament/ Tanakh—Canon and Interpretation," in *Hebrew Bible or Old Testament? Studying the Bible in Judaism and Christianity*, ed. R. Brooks & J. J. Collins (Notre Dame: University of Notre Dame Press, 1990) 11–29.

5. Cf. S. Leiman, *The Canonization of Hebrew Scriptures* (Hamden, CT: Archon, 1976).

6. On these books see H. G. M. Williamson, *1 & 2 Chronicles*, NCB (Grand Rapids: Eerdmans, 1982); idem, *Ezra, Nehemiah*, WBC 16 (Waco: Word, 1988). There is considerable recent discussion about authorship that can be dispensed with here for lack of space; see the summary discussion by R. North in *NJBC*, 23:3, pp. 362–63.

7. On the wisdom literature in general see G. von Rad, *Wisdom in Israel* (Nashville:

Abingdon, 1970); R. E. Murphy, *The Tree of Life: An Exploration of Biblical Wisdom Literature*, ABRL (New York: Doubleday, 1990).

8. See D. J. A. Clines, *Job 1–20*, WBC 17 (Dallas: Word, 1989); J. G. Janzen, *Job*, Interpretation (Atlanta: Knox, 1985).

9. For the interpretation of Qoheleth see M. V. Fox, *Qoheleth and His Contradictions*, BLS 18 (Sheffield: Almond, 1989); N. Lohfink, *Kohelet*, NEchtB (Würzburg: Echter, 1980); R. E. Murphy, *Ecclesiastes*, WBC, (Dallas: Word, 1992).

10. Cf. G. von Rad, "The Joseph Narrative and Ancient Wisdom," in *Studies in Ancient Israelite Wisdom*, ed. J. L. Crenshaw (New York: Ktav, 1976); R. N. Whybray, *The Succession Narrative*, SBT 9 (Naperville: Allenson, 1968). The Succession Narrative consists of 2 Samuel 9–20 + 1 Kings 1–2.

11. Cf. P. W. Skehan and A. Di Lella, *The Wisdom of Ben Sira*, AB 39 (New York: Doubleday, 1987). The fifty-one chapters of Sirach (as referred to by chapter and verse in the enumeration of the NRSV) are a mine of wisdom sayings and poems that remind one of Proverbs. Ben Sira turns out to be a serene sage who could invite his audience to his "house of instruction" (51:23). He was a traditionalist, unruffled by the upsetting views recorded in Job and Ecclesiastes, writing about 180 B.C., just before the outbreak of the Maccabean revolution.

12. For a succinct commentary see A. G. Wright, "Wisdom," *NJBC*, 33:1–59 pp. 501–22, and the discussion by M. Gilbert, "Sagesse de Solomon," *DBSup*, II: 58–119. The Wisdom Solomon is unique in that it was originally written in Greek and probably by an Alexandrian Jew of the diaspora. It is an interesting mixture of Greek thought (see the four cardinal virtues mentioned as the fruit of wisdom in 8:7) and Hebrew wisdom (especially the midrashic history of the Egyptian plagues in chs. 11–19).

13. For a more detailed treatment of Lady Wisdom see C. Camp, *Wisdom and the Feminine in the Book of Proverbs*, BLS 11 (Sheffield: Almond, 1985); the "short essay" by C. Fontaine in *HBC*, 501–3; R. E. Murphy, "Lady Wisdom," in *The Tree of Life*, 33–49.

14. Cf. G. von Rad, *Old Testament Theology*, 2 vols. (New York: Harper & Row, 1962) 1:444.

15. On the Canticle see M. V. Fox, *The Song of Songs and the Egyptian Love Songs* (Madison: University of Wisconsin Press); R. E. Murphy, *The Song of Songs*, ed. S. D. McBride Hermeneia (Minneapolis: Fortress, 1990).

16. Cf. E. F. Campbell, Jr., *Ruth*, AB 7 (Garden City: Doubleday, 1975); J. Sasson, *Ruth* (Baltimore: Johns Hopkins University Press, 1979); R. L. Hubbard, Jr., *The Book of Ruth*, NICOT (Grand Rapids: Eerdmans, 1988).

17. Cf. D. R. Hillers, *Lamentations*, AB 7A (Garden City: Doubleday, 1972); H.-J. Kraus, *Klagelieder (Threni)*, BKAT 20 (Neukirchen: Erziehungsvereins, 1958); Claus Westermann, *Die Klagelieder: Forschungsgeschichte und Auslegung* (Neukirchen-Vluyn: Neukirchener, 1990).

18. C. Moore, *Esther* AB 7B (Garden City: Doubleday, 1982); R. E. Murphy, *Wisdom Literature* FOTL 13 (Grand Rapids: Eerdmans, 1981) 152–70; M.V. Fox, *Character and Ideology in the Book of Esther* (Columbia, SC: University of South Carolina, 1991).

19. Cf. J. J. Collins, *The Apocalyptic Imagination* (New York: Crossroad, 1984); idem, *Daniel*, FOTL 20 (Grand Rapids: Eerdmans, 1984).

20. H. Gunkel and J. Begrich, *Einleitung in die Psalmen* (Göttingen: Vandenhoeck & Ruprecht, 1933); S. Mowinckel, *The Psalms in Israel's Worship* (Nashville: Abingdon, 1967).

21. C. Westermann, *Praise and Lament in the Psalms* (Atlanta: Knox, 1981); W.

Brueggemann, *The Message of the Psalms* (Minneapolis: Augsburg, 1984). The latter applies the categories of P. Ricoeur to classification: orientation, disorientation, and new orientation.

22. See, for example, G. Wilson, *The Editing of the Hebrew Psalter* (Chico, CA: Scholars Press, 1985); J. Mays, "The Place of the Torah Psalms in the Psalter," *JBL* 106 (1987) 3–12.

23. See James Kugel, "Topics in the History of the Spirituality of the Psalms," in *Jewish Spirituality from the Bible through the Middle Ages*, ed. A. Green, World Spirituality 13 (New York: Crossroad, 1988) 113–44, esp. 136. Kugel calls attention to "Scripturalization" of the psalms: "For as the psalms became Scripture, they did so with an interpretive strategy attached: they were not to be interpreted as a self-standing book of prayers or praises, any more than Proverbs was meant to be a self-standing collection of wise sayings. Both were adjuncts to the rest of Scripture, to be read in the light of other books . . . . No categorical statement will do here, but there is an apparent tension between the Psalms-as-texts-for-teaching (i.e., from God to man) and the Psalms-as-texts-for-worship (i.e., from man to God); the more they are familiar in the former role, the less suitable it seems, they appeared in the latter."

24. The most famous is perhaps H.-J. Kraus, *Theology of the Psalms* (Minneapolis: Augsburg, 1986). The main divisions of his volume demonstrate the usual topics that are treated: the God of Israel, the covenanted people of God, sanctuary and worship, the king, hostile powers, and the individual before God. See also J. Day, *Psalms*, OTG (Sheffield: JSOT Press, 1990).

25. M. Luther, *Word and Sacrament, I, Luther's Works*, ed. E. T. Bachmann (Philadelphia: Fortress, 1960) 35:255–56.

26. C. Barth, *Introduction to the Psalms* (New York: Charles Scribner's Sons, 1966) 49.

11

IMAGES OF ISRAEL: THE PEOPLE OF GOD IN THE WRITINGS

John Goldingay

The Writings do not form a literary and theological unity to the extent that the Torah, the Former Prophets, and the Latter Prophets do, but among them they suggest a variety of "images of Israel." This essay surveys the most important of these images.

Israel as a Worshiping Congregation

Israelite worship moves between the triad of prayer and teaching in the family or in other small groups, the priestly round of sacramental worship in the temple, and the entire community's celebration of great pilgrim festivals—Passover, Pentecost, and Tabernacles. In the Writings, the individual lament psalms likely presuppose family or small-group worship as the context in which people prayed for healing or restoration.[1] The regular round of temple worship is a focus in the narrative of Chronicles (e.g., Hezekiah's restoration of the temple and its worship, 2 Chr 29; 31). The festivals are celebrated by the whole people together (e.g., 2 Chr 30; Neh 8:13–18), partly to safeguard the orthodoxy of their observance. The community worship offered at local shrines is deprecated, perhaps mainly because of its syncretistic associations (e.g., 2 Chr 31:1–3).

The worship of the Psalms has commonly been thought to have three facets.[2] It involves praise in response to who God is and how God works, lament and plea in the context of God's not being and acting in the way Israel would expect, and public testimony when God turns back and once more acts in faithfulness and power. It is in such worship that Israel thus discovers, expresses, and grows in its faith.

The praise of the Psalms belongs especially "in the congregation of the committed (*ḥᵃsîdîm*)" (Ps 149:1), and perhaps specifically in the context of the great pilgrim festivals. These recall different acts of God on Israel's behalf; they also celebrate God's kingship and grace as creator and rejoice in the gifts of creation. This praise involves both unrestrained exuberant honoring of Yahweh as king and bowed prostration before the creator who deigns to be "our God" (see Ps 95). In Israel's worship, ritual form, orthodox belief, awed reverence, and joyful hope appear together as essential features of Israel's relationship with God, without any sense of tension (e.g., Ps 22; 147:11; 1 Chr 15:25–28; 2 Chr 30:13–27; Ezra 3). Such worship is world-creating. Against the perceptible world it sets one that is characterized by justice, truth, and meaning because it belongs to Yahweh. It declares this world more real and powerful than the perceptible world and invites its participants to live in it as the more real of the two worlds, and thereby to make the perceptible world more like the real world.[3]

The lament of the Psalms belongs in two contexts: gatherings of the community as a whole for prayer during crises such as famine and defeat, and gatherings of smaller groups to pray with individuals in their personal crises. The book of Lamentations also models the communal prayer that lays hold on Yahweh in the experience of disaster; acknowledgment of sin is sometimes a feature of it (cf. Dan 9; Ezra 9; Neh 1; 9). The temple is especially a place of prayer. As a place where Yahweh dwells, it is also a place toward which people pray, particularly when their failure in relation to God has brought them defeat, deprivation, loss, and exile. In such contexts, self-humbling, prayer, seeking of God's face, and turning from wrong ways will meet with a response from the God who will hear, forgive, vindicate, and heal (2 Chr 6:18–40; 7:12–16; also the intercession of 30:18–20; Dan 6:11–12).

The testimony given in the Psalms issues from the acts of deliverance that bring such crises to an end. The normal pattern of Israel's life with Yahweh comprises calling on Yahweh, experiencing Yahweh's deliverance, and glorifying Yahweh as their deliverer as they fulfill the promises made in the midst of their prayer (Ps 50:14–15; cf. 65:1–3). The deliverance of the individual also draws the congregation as a whole into the grateful confession that glorifies Yahweh (Ps 22:22–27). Thus, one makes one's confession "in the company of the upright, in the assembly" (Ps 111:1). Material offerings accompany and give costly support to praise, plea, and testimony. Joyful communal feasting is a natural concomitant when people make offerings of animals and crops to Yahweh. One of the joys of the powerless when restored from affliction is to rejoin the feasting of the worshiping congregation (Ps 22:26).

Israel as One People

Chronicles is fond of noting that worship and other activities involve "all Israel." It emphasizes that Israel never wholly lost the form in which it began, the twelve-tribe unit. All the tribes are thus equal, but some are more equal than others: the entire story of Israel's origins led to the choice of Judah. That might glorify Judah, but it might also warn it to be careful lest it fall, as Ephraim had fallen (Ps 78:9–11; cf. the argument of Rom 11:20–21). Judah cannot take its position for granted. All Israel had lived a life of recurrent rebellion and had experienced God's grace (Ps 78:12–66). This might also hint that the merciful God has not yet finished even with Ephraim.

Chronicles omits the story of the northern kingdom after its separation from Jerusalem, implying that it is not part of Israel's story. It also regards cooperation with the northern kingdom as a dangerous enterprise (2 Chr 20:35–37). But people in the north retain the potential to return to a relationship with Jerusalem and thus a proper relationship with Yahweh (2 Chr 11:13–17; 15:9–15; 30:1–27). The story of Israel's origins in 1 Chronicles 1–9 gives an honored place to exploits of northern tribes; the story of the establishment of the monarchy and the worship of Jerusalem is told to show that these belong as much to the north as to the south, and the subsequent story shows that the division between north and south was never absolute.[4]

Israel's oneness also extends through the generations. Chronicles has a strong concern to link Israel's ancestors, the First Temple community, and the Second Temple community, not least via the pattern, the place, and the equipment of its worship. The belief that the worship of Jerusalem inherits the varied traditions of Israel further buttresses the conviction that it stands as Israel's one cultic resource. Horeb (2 Chr 5:10), Shiloh (1 Chr 9:5), Gibeon (1 Chr 9:35–44; 16:37–42), and Moriah (2 Chr 3:1) all come together on Mount Zion. The tabernacle and its altar (1 Chr 21:29–22:1; 2 Chr 1:4–6) and the covenant chest (1 Chr 13; 2 Chr 6:41) find their place in the temple. Zadokites, Levites, and prophets all take part in its ministry. Communities that might value varying traditions are invited to see all as fulfilled in Jerusalem; they can and must make it their center.

Israel as an entirety stands within God's historical purpose. The history of Israel often threatens to break down, but never actually does so. God's grace in the past is a basis on which to trust in such grace for the future, though the fragility of the community's sense of linkage with the past is hinted in Ezra 3. The story emphasizes continuity with Moses, with David, and with the period immediately before the exile (vv. 2, 10, 12). It also records the weeping that accompanied joy as the people celebrating the occasion sensed discontinuity with the past as well as continuity (vv. 12–13).

Israel is Abraham's offspring, Jacob's children (Ps 105:6–11, 42). As such they have been protected, provided for, increased, and released (vv. 12–41), and therefore are called to obedience (v. 45). The trouble is that, besides being one in God's giving over the generations, Israel is one in its own waywardness over the generations—a oneness in disloyalty, insubordination, and blasphemy in the face of God's giving (of promise, deliverance, rule of life, provision, territory, preservation). In its prayer (e.g., Neh 9) Israel implicitly pleads for the divine consistency of grace to keep overcoming the human consistency of sin, so that the pattern of grace, sin, loss, and restoration may never falter at the third stage. Explicitly it asks God not to make the ancestors' failures a basis for later judgment (Ps 79:8). It affirms that one generation is not punished for an earlier generation's sin; if it turns back to God from waywardness it can be forgiven and healed (2 Chr 7:14). It also affirms that retribution is not an inexorable principle. Each generation stands before God with an open future, responsible for its own destiny.[5]

Israel as a Community that Cares

The idea of seeking and valuing solitariness is alien to the OT. Even in their individual prayers and praises people speak from within a rich community heritage and as members of the community.[6] The individual's hurt arises not least from being rejected and alone, "scorned by the people" and attacked by a "group of evildoers," people who belong to the same community and fellowship (Ps 22:6, 16; 25:16; 55:12–14; 102:6–7). The individual abjures membership in a community of evildoers, in preference for membership in the community that worships Yahweh (Ps 26:5, 12). Survival (and even triumph) issues in part from seeing oneself in the triple context (1) of a cloud of witnesses who have proved God in the past, (2) of a supporting, worshiping community before which the sufferer testifies to God's responsiveness in the present, and (3) of another "people" who will still confess Yahweh on the basis of such testimony in the future (Pss 22:3–5, 22–25, 30–31; 35:27; 42:4). The interdependence of individual and community is important to the individual, but also to the community itself. It shares in the blessing of the individual's experience of deliverance as it joins in the response of praise (Ps 30:4; 31:23–24; 32:11; 40:9).

The community is one that cares. Its vision is that all should have enough—indeed plenty—and that none should cry out in distress (Ps 144:12–15). It declares a blessing on people who do care about the powerless, feeble, and insignificant rather than despising them (Ps 41). Its vision is for a community that weeps with the weepers and rejoices with the joyful (Pss 34:3; 35:13–14). It knows that moral considerations determine whether someone can dwell on God's hill or join the circle of those who seek Yahweh's face (Pss 15; 24). Joyful praise is appropriate to the just or upright because the words and deeds of the one they praise are characterized by justice and uprightness (Ps 33:1–5). Thus, "properly conceived, the temple is a place of electrifying holiness that cannot tolerate injustice." The cultic and the ethical are "two sides of the same experience."[7]

Sometimes the vision just referred to meets no realization. Elimelech's community experienced famine, loss, and displacement (Ruth 1), though his family's story also illustrates the way the community can care for its weak (Ruth 2). The weepers can have their pain exacerbated rather than relieved by the response of their community (Pss 42:3, 9–10; 43:1–2). Worse than that, the community (or elements within it) is often characterized as wicked, recalcitrant, godless, mischievous, greedy, murderous, thieving, adulterous, oppressive, arrogant, scoffing, trusting in worldly resources, deceitful, and foolishly self-deceived (Pss 1; 5; 35; 36; 50; 52; 55). It knows conflict within as well as without. Power within it lies with the perjurious, the wealthy, and the taunting, who stand over against the righteous, the godly, the committed (to God and to others), the covenant-keeping and torah-delighting, who are powerless, fearful, fleeing, vengeful, vulnerable, groaning, with God's promise all they have to trust in. In another sense the wicked belong only formally to the community. The real Israel is the community of the just (Ps 1:5). Widow, alien, and orphan compose the people of Yahweh (Ps 94:5–6).

In part the expectation that Israel should behave as a community is based on a vision of Israel as a family of brothers and sisters. This image is implicit in the genealogies that are a prominent feature of the Writings, though these also likely reflect the power struggles and identity crises of the Second temple community. They indicate that, like any family, Israel has its family arguments. The image is explicit when all Israel's "kindred" join in great festive events (1 Chr 12:40; 13:2). It is the basis for prophetic appeal and rebuke (2 Chr 11:4; 28:9–15), but in such situations straight talking within the family can lead to matters being sorted out, and even issue in worship (Neh 5).

Israel as a National State

In the Writings Israel is a state when the story opens; shrine and monarchy are of more dangerously unequivocal and mythical significance than is the case in the Torah and the Prophets. As a nation Israel is a territorial entity, by the inalienable gift of Yahweh (Pss 135:12; 136:21–22; 1 Chr 28:8). When people do not enjoy the land as their ancestors had (Neh 9:36–37), the affirmation that it is their secure possession is the more important. On the other hand, Daniel, Ezra, Nehemiah, and Esther witness to the possibility of full life and political success in continuing dispersion.

As a nation Israel has a capital, the location of its shrine, but also in its own right a place of fortified strength, material prosperity, and architectural splendor. The restoring of its walls and population is calculated both to bring its disgrace to an end and to improve its security (Ps 122:3; Neh 2:17; 7:1–4; 11:1–2). Jerusalem is the center of the nation's life. To Israel's rest in its country there corresponds Yahweh's rest in Zion after wandering (Ps 132; 1 Chr 28:2; 2 Chr 6:41). Indeed, the country is Yahweh's place of rest first; only as a consequence of this can it become Israel's place of rest (Ps 95:11).[8]

As a nation Israel has a leadership structure. Israel is both a theocracy, a kingdom over which Yahweh reigns, and a monarchy, a kingdom over which a human ruler reigns. The Davidic kings sit on Yahweh's throne reigning over Israel on Yahweh's behalf; Yahweh's kingdom lies in their power and will always do so (1 Chr 17:13–14; 28:5; 29:23; 2 Chr 9:8; 13:5,

8). David is made king in fulfillment of Yahweh's word concerning Israel (1 Chr 11:10). He is important for Israel's sake rather than vice versa (1 Chr 14:2). By Yahweh's power he experiences victory over his enemies (Ps 18:46–48), but like the rest of Israel he moves between weakness, fear, abandonment, and grief, and joy, confidence, strength, and acceptance (Pss 5; 6). The difficulty is that all leadership, which theoretically exists for the sake of those it leads, easily comes to be important in its own right. Psalms and Chronicles witness to a growing gap between people and king and a shrinking gap between king and God (Ps 45:6). In theory, worship of the one true God relativizes all other powers. "But what happens if one earthly norm becomes excluded from the relativization of all that is mundane?"[9]

Chronicles expresses no explicit hope regarding the future of the suspended monarchy. This silence has been variously interpreted. Since Daniel is more overtly concerned for the future and its visions give a prominent place both to earthly kings and to Yahweh's kingship, when it expresses no hope concerning Israel's own monarchy, its silence is less equivocal. In Daniel 7 sovereignty is taken from four animals and given to a human-like figure; the animals stand for human kings, but the entity that apparently corresponds to the human-like figure is not another king but "holy ones on high" or "holy people on high," who in some sense represent Israel.[10]

Israel as a Warring Army

As a nation Israel is also a body involved in political relations with other nations over which it is destined to exercise authority. Its existence is lived like that of other nations in its world, and it often comes into conflict with local peoples (some ethnically or religiously related) and with more distant imperial powers that might be military or political threats (see Pss 46; 83; Ezra 4–5; Neh 2; 6). It prays as a political entity under pressure from enemies without as well as from enemies within (e.g., Pss 53; 54; 59).

Functioning as an army follows from being a nation. When Israel is under attack, Yahweh is the shield around Israel protecting it, or the stronghold or fortress hiding it, or the one whose aide surrounds it with his military camp, or the savior who arises in its midst to rescue it at the critical moment (Ps 2:12; 5:11–12; 34; 46; 125:2; 144:2). In success the booty of battle belongs to God, so David's victories provide the resources for building the temple. The actual temple-builder is to be not the bloodstained warrior (like sexual intercourse, war involves ritual stain) but his son whose name marks him as a man of rest and in whose reign Israel will experience quiet and peace (1 Chr 22:8–9). Yahweh the warrior teaches Israel to fight (Ps 144:1) and uses Judah and Ephraim as baton and helmet (Ps 60:7). But war is destined to cease because Yahweh's purpose to subject the nations is destined to be achieved (Ps 46). The Writings' contrary attitudes toward war are familiar in the modern world: it is better to be at peace than at war, but it is better to be dead than red; and it is necessary to fight with relish when that seems the only way to achieve your destiny.

While the offensiveness of David's census (1 Chr 21) may lie in its implicit trust in human military resources, foresight over fortification, resources, and defense is affirmed where these combine with urgent prayer, trust in Yahweh, and action "in Yahweh's name" as Yahweh's representatives (2 Chr 13–15). The most splendid—even baroque—embodiment of these attitudes appears in the story of Jehoshaphat's battle with peoples from the east (2 Chr 20).[11] The people seek Yahweh, fast, and lament; through a Levite, Yahweh urges them not to fear, reminds them that the battle belongs to God, and gives them their battle instructions (which amount to an invitation to watch Yahweh act); the people bow down to worship and the Levites stand up to praise; Jehoshaphat appoints a choir, which sings while Yahweh sets an ambush involving the hostile armies' self-destruction. The story ends with booty, worship, astonishment on the part of the nations, and a period of quiet rest. Psalm 149 provides a lyric for this remarkable holding together of worship and warmaking, Psalm 18 a testimony to deliverance of this kind, and Psalm 47 a witness to the expectation that the nations will indeed come to acknowledge that God subdued peoples under Israel. The view that Chronicles' attitude is superseded by Jesus has not generally been held by Christians. Oliver Cromwell's troops and many others have sung Psalms before battle,[12] and levitical chaplains still accompany the armies of "Christian" nations.

Israel as a Flock under Yahweh's Protection

Israel is a flock provided for, rested, pastured, led, watered, refreshed, protected, and reassured by its shepherd (e.g., Pss 23; 95:7). The more general theme of Israel as a people under Yahweh's protection finds paradoxical expression in Esther. The story vividly portrays the reality of the world's pressure on Israel's very existence, and of Israel's miraculous survival and triumph. It provides the strongest scriptural assertion of the significance of ethnic Israel, one with which Christian theology has often failed to come to terms.[13] It is the one book in the Hebrew Bible that resists Christian supersessionism absolutely, as Luther saw, and it is one that the holocaust of Hitler might take from the periphery of the canon to its center.[14] Jews once more lament the way the nations seek to destroy them, but the response to their lament comes not (explicitly) through an act of God but through an act of a woman,[15] and one who had concealed her Jewishness. The result is not the exaltation and reverential fear of Yahweh by a people, but the exaltation of Mordecai and the abject fear of the Jews by a people.

Israel as Yahweh's Chosen Possession

All peoples owe allegiance to Yahweh as creator and lord, but Israel is Yahweh's particular inalienable possession, Yahweh's valued personal property (Pss 33:12; 106:5; 135:4; cf. 28:9; 74:2; 78:62, 71; 94:5, 14; 106:40).[16] If Israel is merely the part of the world over which Yahweh more overtly exercises sovereign rights at the moment, that in itself makes Yahweh's acts in Israel significant for other peoples. They are designed to enable the whole world to acknowledge the way Israel's God can save, and to do so with joy because this God also governs and guides all peoples (Pss 47; 66; 67). Israel's was not a missionary faith, but it was a faith that made universal claims.[17]

To put the point more centripetally, the peoples of the world are expected to gather together to worship in Jerusalem, declaring the praise of Yahweh as the one who hears and liberates the doomed and stripped captives (Ps 102:15–22). All the peoples of the earth in their apparent glory but actual fragility will pay attention and come to worship Yahweh as their sovereign (Ps 22:27–29). The story of Ruth encapsulates that purpose in a vignette, while Chronicles also notes the place of foreigners in the story and worship of Israel (1 Chr 2; 2 Chr 6:32–33; 30:25; cf. Ezra 1:1–11; 6:1–5). "What can one say about the self-consciousness of a provincial cultic community tolerated by the Persian Empire which yet portrays history from Adam onwards as taking place all for her own sake?"[18]

To say that Yahweh chose Israel is, thus, not to say that other peoples are rejected. Within Israel Yahweh especially chose Levi, Judah, and David for particular purposes (Ps 78:68, 70; 1 Chr 15:2; 28:4–6; 2 Chr 6:5–6; 29:11). This was more for the sake of the people as a whole than in rejection of the people as a whole. The same dynamic underlies the choice of Israel. It belongs in the context of Yahweh's will to be sovereign and savior of the world as a whole and serves that end. There can be no ideological appropriation of belief in election. In terms that will take us into the next section, chosenness belongs with servanthood.

Israel as a King's Servant

As Yahweh's servant (Ps 136:22), Israel is called to obedience and trust as well as worship. A servant has a special relationship with a master or mistress and can rely on his or her care and protection. The servant is also one who is committed to do as the master or mistress directs. This trust and commitment stem from being in covenant relationship with a master whereby the latter promises to look after the servant's future and the servant is committed to obeying the master (cf. Pss 89:39; 119). Israel is, thus, a people covenanted to be Yahweh's people (2 Chr 23:16; 34:29–33). It is the company of the committed (ḥᵃsîdîm; Pss 50:5; 85:8; 97:10). Covenanting with other gods or other peoples is disallowed and disapproved because it indicates reliance on resources other than Yahweh (2 Chr 16:1–12; 25:5–16; 28:16–25; Ezra 8:21–23; cf. Ps 40:4).

The covenanted people is challenged to express its dependence on God and its commitment to God in simple worship and moral uprightness (Ps 50). Israel has known Yahweh releasing its back from its burdens: it is now expected to bow down to Yahweh and no other gods and to walk in Yahweh's ways, and it is invited to look to Yahweh alone for the satisfying of its needs and for deliverance from its pressures (Ps 81). In the Psalms Israel is challenged to trust in Yahweh, delight in Yahweh, commit its way to Yahweh, relax before Yahweh, wait for Yahweh, hide in Yahweh. If it does so and combines that with a commitment to walk in Yahweh's way, it will live long in possession of its country, enjoy security and prosperity there, be upheld and prevented from falling headlong, see the wicked off and be vindicated itself, have its deepest desires fulfilled, and see its posterity (Ps 37; cf. Ps 33:18–22). The narratives in 2 Chronicles 10–36 illustrate the life of Israel lived in trust and obedience— or not. In due course freedom from Yahweh takes Israel into servitude and exile (Lam 1:3), which continues in the Second Temple period in a bondage to Persian overlords (Neh 9:36–37).

Loyal servants "seek" the master and aim to attend on the master with loyalty, commitment, and energy, avoiding anything that conflicts with the master's interests (1 Chr 28:9 and 2 Chr 31:21, where service and seeking are linked; also 1 Chr 22:19; 2 Chr 7:14; 14:3, 6; 15:2–4, 12–15; 17:3–4; 20:3–4; 34:3). They try to draw each other into fuller or renewed commitment to their master's service (2 Chr 17:7–9; 19:4; 29). They seek the master where he may be found (2 Chr 11:16); failure here is one basis for regarding the worship of northern Israel as illicit (2 Chr 13:8–11). Worship itself is one way of serving God (see Ps 102:22 for the verb); service of God is expressed in worship services, and in reforming the temple, Hezekiah restores the service of Yahweh's house (2 Chr 29:35). Such seeking of Yahweh is, thus, the opposite of apostasy or trespass (*ma'al*), a way of worship or life that ignores Yahweh's rights and defers to other gods, by seeking them rather than Yahweh, or by introducing their way of worship into worship of Yahweh, or by associating too closely with their worshipers (1 Chr 10:13–14; 2 Chr 28:22–25; 33:19; 36:13–14; Ezra 9:2; 10:2–3). It involves doing what one likes and ignoring Yahweh's revealed way (2 Chr 12:1–2; 26:16–18; 28:19; 29:19; 36:14).[19]

Psalm 95, the classic psalm of praise already referred to, moves on from enthusiasm and prostration to testing interrogation, not by Israel but of Israel. Israel's voice is silenced by that of another that challenges it to listen to God's voice. When Israel celebrated Tabernacles, it celebrated the giving of the Torah, but the question was whether rejoicing in the Torah was only a matter of heart and lips and not of life. Israel is a community instructed in the Torah and committed in covenant to making the Torah its rule of life (Ezra 7–10; Neh 8–10). There is nothing intrinsically legalistic about Israel's commitment to live by the Torah. Joy in Yahweh and obedience to the Torah happily coexist in Psalm 119, and Nehemiah encourages the people toward this combination when they are inclined to grief upon discovering teaching in the Torah that puts them to shame (Neh 8:9–12).

Israel as a Crushed Remnant

Israel is a vine planted to flourish in ground Yahweh prepared for it, but a vine from time to time unprotected, ravaged, and cut down (Ps 80). Israel as a people is given up to subjection, death, exile, plundering, and shame (Ezra 9:7). It is rejected, abased, defeated, spoiled, slaughtered, scattered, discarded, taunted, shamed, broken, forgotten, cast off, oppressed, resourceless, and powerless, like a bird at the mercy of predators (Pss 44; 74:19, 21). The people of holy ones is subject to oppression and attack by mighty kings (Dan 7:21; 8:24–25). Loyalty to Yahweh seems to stimulate suffering rather than evade it (Dan 11). Jerusalem is like a lonely widow, a serf, let down, disillusioned, weeping, betrayed, homeless, distressed, overwhelmed, desolate, bereft, defeated, dishonored, helpless, mocked, despised, fallen, comfortless, desecrated, hungry, despised, uncared for, trapped, stunned, crushed (Lam 1). In exile Israel weeps and remembers, is taunted and voiceless, reminds and looks for judgment (Ps 137). The people is a mere remnant of what it once was (Ezra 9:13–15). All that remains in Jerusalem or in dispersion is a group of survivors (Ezra 1:4; Neh 1:2–3).

The experience of being turned into a mere remnant can come even when Israel lives in loyalty to the covenant and shapes its life by Yahweh's ways (Ps 44:17–26). But this is not always how things are. Whereas the ideal Israel lives in trust and obedience, the actual Israel does no such thing, and is cut down to size in the way appropriate to a servant who fails. From the beginning Israel forgets, rebels, hustles, craves, tests, envies, forsakes, despises, disbelieves, grumbles, disobeys, abandons, angers, provokes, compromises, nauseates (Ps 106). Jerusalem falls because it has become disobedient, sinful, rebellious, careless, polluted (Lam 1). Israel has failed, gone astray, done wrong, rebelled, trespassed, turned its back on Yahweh's commands, ignored Yahweh's prophets, and refused to turn from its waywardness (Dan 9). Moral and religious failure are a reality of both past and present (Ezra 9). Whereas Israel was designed to be a people where the kingship of God was a reality and, thus, to be a microcosm of what the world was called to be, it had rejected Yahweh's kingship and become a microcosm of what the world also is, and was therefore judged as such.[20]

It is a sign of God's grace that Israel survives at all with a toehold in its country and is able to feel encouraged that it experiences a little reviving even as it has to live under the authority of foreign kings (Ezra 9:8–9). Israel has escaped its enemies like a bird escaping a trap; if Yahweh had not been on Israel's side, its enemies would have quite devoured it (Ps 124). The history of rebellion never ends in Israel's annihilation, because saving them reveals Yahweh's power, because leaders such as Moses and Phinehas intervened on their behalf, standing between them and Yahweh's wrath, because Yahweh could not but hear their cry and remember the covenant relationship with them, because saving them could lead to testimony and glory (Ps 106). They are a people grieved for and prayed for, confessed for and argued for (Neh 1:4–11). As the preserved remnant they are then challenged to be the responsive remnant (Ezra 10; Neh 9).

Israel as an Exclusive Sect

The Writings contain much of the Hebrew Bible's material reflecting Israel's openness to learn from the world (in Proverbs) and to reflect

Yahweh's purpose for the whole world (in Psalms and Ruth). They also contain much of its material that expresses an inclination to separate oneself from the world and from other groups that worship Yahweh, especially in Ezra-Nehemiah. The later controversies that underlie Daniel 7–12 also reflect the conflict between different groups within the community in Judea, such as the party led by Tobias over against that led by Onias.[21] Something of the theological rationale for exclusivism emerges from the crisis over "marrying out" in the time of Ezra and Nehemiah. The theological issue is expressed as a concern for holiness rather than pollution (Ezra 9:10–14) and for people not to lose the ability to speak Hebrew (Neh 13:24). Ezra requires the annulment of many mixed marriages (Ezra 10), but there were broader senses in which the people were expected to distance themselves from other local people as part of their commitment to observing the Torah, including observance of the Sabbath, a distinguishing mark of a true Yahwist as Nehemiah sees it (Neh 10:29–32; 13:15–22). The Torah set ethnic limits on who could belong to Yahweh's congregation; people needed to be able to prove their genealogical right to membership of Israel, of the tribe of Levi, and of the priestly line (Ezra 2), and many people of foreign descent were expelled from the community (Neh 13:1–3). Even the stories in Daniel that envisage Jews successfully involved in imperial politics stress the need for boundaries that preserve Jewish purity and avoid pollution (Dan 1:8). Israel is called to be the holy people of the holy God (cf. Ezra 9:2).[22]

The narrowness of the Second Temple community should not be exaggerated: anyone who had broken with the pollution of the other nations in the country was welcomed to join in the worship of Yahweh (Ezra 6:21; cf. Neh 9:2). Nevertheless, the attitude of a leader such as Nehemiah makes us feel uneasy. It may yet be that his exclusivism made it possible for Israel to survive. The Second Temple community was beginning a new life, "trapped between a political and religious sense of identity" and encouraged by its political overlords to develop as a religious community, so that it necessarily had to define the nature and the boundaries of its own identity if it was to be able to maintain the distinctive witness to God for which it had been chosen.[23]

Further, as Brueggemann observes, "[t]he recovery of ethnic rootage and the special histories of pain . . . may help us see that an alternative perception of reality is not simply a defensive measure but may be an act of identity, energy, and power."[24] It may challenge the claims of the dominant reality around it. Admittedly, it may fall into the trap of defensively keeping its alternative perception to itself lest this truth be contaminated, rather than openly making it available to the dominant community. We

do not know enough about the communities of the Second Temple period to be able to offer an independent evaluation of Ezra-Nehemiah's
stance in relation to them, but the problem of assimilation to a powerful
surrounding culture arises at both ends of the biblical period. Israel repeatedly experienced its conversation partners "as having a more fully
adequate hermeneutic, rationality, or way of experiencing the world" and
needed to be wary of their beguiling if it was to keep alive its distinctive
memory.[25]

Israel as a Theological School

There is no mention of Israel in Proverbs (except 1:1), Job, Song of
Songs, or Ecclesiastes. Evidently Israel (like God) does not always need
mention in theology; the servant status of Israel reaches its apogee when
it can survive or even affirm its own dispensability. These books nevertheless emerge from the life and experience of Israel. Their theological
concern suggests the image of Israel as a theological school. They bear
the fruit of Israel's reflection both on everyday questions about how to
live in a way that is successful, godly, and moral, and on major theological issues concerning revelation, the nature of God, and the basis of
God's relationship with human beings. This theological school belongs
within the life of the believing community. Solomon is its patron as (with
some irony) the great embodiment of God-given wisdom in the Former
Prophets.

Israel is drawn to a theology that holds together confident affirmation
and bold questioning. Confident affirmation is the dominant feature
of Proverbs and the Song of Songs; limitations and ambiguities are the
dominant features of Job and Ecclesiastes, which focus on the degree
to which the orthodoxies and promises of Proverbs and the Song of
Songs do not work out for people. As David Hubbard marvelously put it
in his Tyndale Lecture on "The wisdom movement and Israel's covenant
faith," "Proverbs seems to say, 'These are the rules for life; try them and
find that they will work.' Job and Ecclesiastes say, 'We did, and they
don't.'"[26] Between them they enable Israel's theological school to avoid
both the Scylla of simplistic triumphalism and the Charbidis of despair-
ing agnosticism.

The wisdom of the Writings often profits from the wisdom of the world.
But their conviction is that Israel's wisdom nevertheless quite outclasses
that of the world. The young Judean youths enrolled in theological school
in Babylon not only maintain their purity but prove wiser than their

teachers in both the everyday life-skills that make survival possible and in the capacity for far-reaching insight that makes it possible to understand the riddles of history (Dan 1–6).

In part they do that by utilizing the insights already expressed in their own scriptures, which provide key seed-thoughts and clues for both stories and visions in Daniel. Israel's own scriptures are a key resource in its theological school. The "sermons" in Chronicles, too, utilize earlier scriptures to suggest how Yahweh's word speaks today (e.g., 2 Chr 16:9; 20:20).[27] In Chronicles, in general Israel does its theological thinking by reflecting in narrative form on questions raised by its current context, in the light of historical, prophetic, and worship traditions. In Ruth and Esther it does this by telling a less complicated story, though here, too, aspects of these traditions make an important contribution to it: there is a markedly intertextual relationship between these stories and those of the Torah.[28]

Implications for Today

The Israel of the Writings is the Israel that the NT presupposes. In its genealogical approach, Matthew follows on from Chronicles. In its opening portrait of the worshiping community in the temple, Luke does the same. In his parables Jesus invites both wise and simple into his theological school, and in their attempts to do theology the NT writers show that they themselves have learned from the Writings as well as from anywhere. In identifying "models for the church," the NT recycles the scriptures' images of Israel that we have considered.[29] We ought hardly to assume that it brought to the surface all there is to mine from this rich resource; further insights from which we may profit have been implicit or explicit in each of the sections above. Nor ought we to assume that the Church has the right to assume that these images now belong exclusively to it. The Jewish people is still the people of Yahweh, and these images continue to provide it with identity and challenge.

NOTES

1. Cf. E. Gerstenberger, *Psalms, Part 1*, FOTL 14 (Grand Rapids: Eerdmans, 1988) 14.

2. See e.g., W. Brueggemann, *The Message of the Psalms* (Minneapolis: Augsburg, 1984).

3. Cf. W. Brueggemann, *Israel's Praise* (Philadelphia: Fortress, 1988) 6–53.

4. Cf. H. G. M. Williamson, *Israel in the Books of Chronicles* (Cambridge/New York: Cambridge University Press, 1977) 89–140.

5. See G. von Rad, *Old Testament Theology*, 2 vols. (Edinburgh: Oliver and Boyd/New York: Harper & Row, 1962) 1:349.

6. H. W. Wolff, *Anthropology of the Old Testament* (Philadelphia: Fortress/London: SCM, 1974) 217; cf. H. Ringgren, *The Faith of the Psalmists* (London: SCM/Philadelphia: Fortress, 1963) 20–26; H.-J. Kraus, *Theology of the Psalms* (Minneapolis: Augsburg/London: SPCK, 1986) 138–41.

7. J. D. Levenson, *Sinai and Zion* (Minneapolis: Winston, 1985) 170, 172.

8. On this idea, see G. von Rad, *The Problem of the Hexateuch and Other Essays* (Edinburgh: Oliver and Boyd/New York: McGraw-Hill, 1966) 94–102, though he is critical of the Chronicler.

9. P. D. Hanson, *The People Called* (San Francisco: Harper & Row, 1986) 122.

10. The rock in Daniel 2:35 is taken to refer to Israel by G. A. F. Knight, *A Christian Theology of the Old Testament* (Richmond: Knox/London: SCM, 1959) 189 = rev. ed. (London: SCM, 1964) 174, but there is no indication of this in the context. On this and on Daniel 7 see J. Goldingay, *Daniel*, WBC 30 (Dallas: Word, 1989/Milton Keynes: Word, 1991). I will always be grateful to David Hubbard and the other editors of the Word Commentary that, when other commitments made me decline their invitation to contribute to the series, they simply ignored me and sent me a contract to write on Daniel.

11. See G. von Rad, *Holy War in Ancient Israel* (Grand Rapids: Eerdmans, 1991) 129–31.

12. See R. E. Prothero, *The Psalms in Human Life* (London/New York: Nelson, 1903) 228–36.

13. Cf. W. Vischer, "The Book of Esther," *EvQ* 11 (1939) 3–21 (the date is significant); B. S. Childs, *Introduction to the Old Testament as Scripture* (Philadelphia: Fortress/London: SCM, 1979) 606.

14. See E. L. Fackenheim, *The Jewish Bible after the Holocaust* (Manchester: Manchester University Press, 1990) 62, 90.

15. See S. A. White, "Esther," in *Gender and Difference*, ed. P. L. Day; (Minneapolis: Fortress, 1989) 166–73.

16. The words are *nahᵃlâ* (used for the country as Israel's personal and inalienable possession) and *sᵉgullâ* (used for "treasure" in Eccl 2:8; 1 Chr 29:3).

17. Cf. R. Martin-Achard, *A Light to the Nations* (Edinburgh: Oliver and Boyd, 1962) 54–60; Levenson, *Sinai and Zion*, 207–8.

18. Von Rad, *Old Testament Theology*, 1:347.

19. On *maᶜal* see J. Milgrom, *Cult and Conscience* (Leiden: Brill, 1976) 16–35.

20. See J. Goldingay, *Theological Diversity and the Authority of the Old Testament* (Grand Rapids: Eerdmans, 1987) 74–75; in that chapter I have studied the people of God in the OT and its implications for today more broadly.

21. Among adventurous attempts to trace the development of the parties in Second Temple Judaism are M. Smith, *Palestinian Parties and Politics that Shaped the Old Testament*, 2nd ed. (New York/London: Columbia University Press, 1971; London: SCM, 1987); P. D. Hanson, *The Dawn of Apocalyptic* (Philadelphia: Fortress, 1975).

22. Cf. D. Bossman, "Ezra's Marriage Reform," *BTB* 9 (1979) 36.

23. See H. G. M. Williamson, *Ezra, Nehemiah*, WBC 16 (Waco: Word, 1985) 159–60.

24. W. Brueggemann, "The Legitimacy of a Sectarian Hermeneutic," *HBT* 7 (1985) 11

= *Interpretation and Obedience* (Minneapolis: Fortress, 1991) 46, though in this paper Breuggemann does not apply his observation to the Second Temple community. For a more critical but still sympathetic evaluation of Ezra and Nehemiah, see also Hanson, *The People Called,* 291–300.

25. Brueggemann, "Sectarian Hermeneutic," 22 = *Interpretation and Obedience,* 54.

26. *TynBul* 17 (1966) 6. Followed by the word "Discuss," I have often used this *bon mot* as an examination question. See also R. Davidson, *The Courage to Doubt* (London: SCM, 1983).

27. See G. von Rad, "The Levitical Sermon in I and II Chronicles," in *The Problem of the Hexateuch and Other Essays,* 267–80.

28. See, e.g., D. Nolan Fewell and D. M. Gunn, "'A Son Is Born to Naomi!'" *JSOT* 40 (1988) 103–7; G. Gerleman, *Esther,* BKAT 21 (Neukirchen: Neukirchener, 1973) 11–23; S. B. Berg, *The Book of Esther* (Missoula, MT: Scholars Press, 1979) 6–8, 123–65, 174–77.

29. See A. Dulles, *Models of the Church,* 2nd ed. (Garden City, NY: Doubleday, 1974/ Dublin: Gill and Macmillan, 1976, 1988); also P. S. Minear, *Images of the Church in the New Testament* (Philadelphia: Westminster, 1960/London: Lutterworth, 1961).

12

IMAGES FOR TODAY: LEARNING FROM OLD TESTAMENT WISDOM

Robert K. Johnston[1]

As America moves toward the twenty-first century, it is ever more apparent that the framework of the Enlightenment that we have inherited is proving inadequate for the world we experience. Although science has accomplished much, the world does not seem to be a better place, at least for many. As Lesslie Newbigin observes, "More and more people among the most powerful nations on earth feel themselves helpless in the grip of irrational forces." Students in Paris during the 1968 uprising summarized the discontent well when they wrote as graffiti: "We reject the alternatives—to die of starvation or to die of boredom."[2]

In his small booklet, *The Other Side of 1984: Questions for the Churches,* Newbigin characterizes the creation of this Enlightenment culture as "a shift in the balance between faith and doubt."[3] Rather than knowledge flowing out of a relationship of trust in a personal reality greater than ourselves, humankind's critical faculty was viewed as alone important for understanding. And there is no denying that the results have been magnificent. In the words of Michael Polanyi:

> The critical movement which seems to be nearing the end of its course today was perhaps the most fruitful effort ever sustained by the human mind. The past four or five centuries, which have gradually destroyed or overshadowed the whole medieval cosmos, have enriched us mentally and morally to an extent unrivalled by any period of similar duration. But its incandescence has fed on the combustion of the Christian heritage in the oxygen of Greek rationalism, and when the fuel was exhausted, the critical framework itself burnt away.[4]

For the modern, critical mind, belief has been reduced to the level of the personal and the subjective. This sterility and false objectivism increasingly are being challenged. We are beginning to realize that the balance between faith and doubt in the knowledge equation needs again to shift. Trust needs to be rediscovered. Renewal will not come from within the framework of the assumptions of the Enlightenment—these are no longer "self-evident." Instead, a new paradigm, a new intellectual and imaginative framework, is called for. An alternate, life-giving way of imaging our world must be conceived. This new thinking will need to be post-critical, post-modern.

It is the thesis of this essay that OT wisdom can help us reconceive our world and our relationships within it. In particular, OT wisdom might help us beyond our present crisis in three areas: (1) in our response to the ecological dilemma we face, (2) in our response to a male bias in our culture that persists stubbornly, and (3) in our response to the pluralism of the global village which we now experience at home as well as abroad. As long as we see the world as a resource to be used; as long as we remain complacent about sexism that is structural as well as personal; and as long as we think of the Western world as the real, if not sole, possessor of truth, the crisis will deepen. Instead, we need a new orientation, new images, new metaphors, new thinking.

Wisdom's Alternate Viewpoint

There is a core of literature in the OT that is acknowledged to be wisdom—Job, Proverbs, and Ecclesiastes (and in the apocrypha, Ecclesiasticus and the Wisdom of Solomon). But there is also a larger portion of Scripture where wisdom's influence is apparent. Scholars have long debated whether Psalms (at least a portion of them) and Song of Songs are also wisdom. Though neither are technically wisdom books, the sapiential character of these edited collections seems evident, even in its imprecision. More recently, a spate of articles has appeared positing wisdom's role in the shaping of a wide variety of other OT texts. Genesis 2–3, the Joseph narrative (Gen 37–50), the Succession Narrative (2 Sam 10–1; 1 Kings 1–2), Deuteronomy, Amos, Isaiah, Esther—all evidence "wisdom's echoes."[5]

Basic to the wisdom viewpoint perceived in these writings (whether in a direct or a more indirect way) is its focus upon creation. Zimmerli's statement (1964) is now considered almost axiomatic: "Wisdom thinks resolutely within the framework of a theology of creation."[6] Solomon, for example, Israel's wise man par excellence, has his wisdom described in 1 Kings 4:29–33 in these words:

> God gave Solomon very great wisdom . . . so that Solomon's wisdom surpassed the wisdom of all the people of the east, and all the wisdom of Egypt . . . . He would speak of trees, from the cedar that is in the Lebanon to the hyssop that grows in the wall; he would speak of animals, and birds, and reptiles, and fish. (NRSV)

Or again, the wisdom writings are filled with themes taken from creation, as the discussion below will indicate. They listen to and make use of much from the world about them. However, Zimmerli's point is neither Solomonic nor textual, but theological. In Genesis 1:28 the Creator said to the woman and the man: "Be fruitful and multiply, and fill the earth and subdue it; and have dominion" (NRSV). Wisdom, argues Zimmerli, is rooted in creation as God's gift and God's command. It is part of the God-given, human agenda.

The other side of wisdom's creational focus is its lack of reference to Israel's saving events. There is no mention of election, exodus, or Sinai until late in wisdom's development in the post-canonical period. Instead, wisdom turned for its sources to its family traditions, on the one hand, and to its neighbors, on the other. The teaching and practice of parents and clan and the "wisdom" teaching of others Israel encountered became for her the twin resources for her reflection on God's gift of life. This material was in all probability first codified and cultivated in the wisdom schools of the royal court, but it did not begin there. Rather, sensitive observers of life itself became her teacher. To suggest that Israel encountered God in other ways than her historical grounding is not in any way to disparage or minimize that sacred history. It is only to recognize that Israel's resources for her theological reflection on life as created and redeemed were wider than is sometimes recognized.

Allied to international wisdom and rooted in the day-to-day interaction between human beings and with their environment, biblical wisdom attempted to help people live in the world. As Roland Murphy has successfully argued with regard to the book of Proverbs, wisdom's "kerygma" was life itself.[7] "For whoever finds me finds life and obtains favor from the LORD" (Prov 8:35, NRSV). This life was viewed concretely in terms of long years, riches, and honor (Prov 3:16). It was symbolized as a fountain and a tree (Prov 10:11; 3:18). Wisdom's offer of life to its readers was in no way secular, nor was it materialistic in a modern sense. Rather, wisdom saw life as a divine gift. As Ben Sira expressed it:

> Good things and bad, life and death,
> poverty and wealth, come from the Lord. (Sir 11:14)

It would have been inconceivable to the wisdom teachers for their knowledge of life to function independently of their faith in Yahweh.[8] In this regard it is not accidental that wisdom's close linkage to the "fear of the Lord" provides "bookends" for the sayings of Proverbs, serving both as a beginning statement and as a concluding refrain (Prov 1:7; 31:30). A commitment to God lies clearly at the heart of wisdom (cf. Prov 2:5; 9:10; Job 28:28; Eccl 8:12; Ps 111:10; Sir 1:14; 19:20; Wis 7:25).

In the discussion below, we will return to wisdom's personification as a woman, but it is important in this context to note that wisdom's invitation of life to her readers is offered personally. Wisdom is not presented as an "it" but a "she":

> At the busiest corner she cries out;
> at the entrance of the city gates she speaks. (Prov 1:21, NRSV)

Or again:

> "Come, eat of my bread
> and drink of the wine I have mixed.
> Lay aside immaturity, and live,
> and walk in the way of insight." (Prov 9:5–6, NRSV)

In the thick of life, Woman Wisdom begs all to hear her message of life and death. Having prepared a feast in a large banquet hall she has built for the occasion, Woman Wisdom invites all to accept her invitation. At the heart of this personified wisdom a threefold relationship is envisioned—she rejoices in the presence of God, rejoices again in the world, and delights in the human race (Prov 8:30–31).

Those who accept Woman Wisdom's invitation are characterized by attentiveness, wonder, trust, and humility. One need only read the opening chapters of Proverbs to observe the importance given to a receptive heart:

> Hear . . . making your ear attentive . . . inclining your heart . . . seek . . . search . . . be attentive . . . . Do not forsake her . . . . Hear . . . . Keep hold . . . guard her . . . be attentive . . . incline your ear . . . . Keep your heart . . . . (Prov 1–4 NRSV).

Writes the sage, "Those who are attentive to a matter will prosper, / and happy are those who trust in the LORD" (Prov 16:20, NRSV). As John Eaton comments, "So valuable is attention that it is thought of as fresh from the Creator's hand:

> A listening ear and a seeing eye,
>> the Lord indeed has made them both (Prov 20:12)."[9]

Such attentiveness spills over into a posture of wonder at times:

> Three things are too wonderful for me;
> four I do not understand:
>> the way of an eagle in the sky,
> the way of a snake on a rock,
>> the way of a ship on the high seas,
> and the way of a man with a girl. (Prov 30:18–19, NRSV)

Amazement based on careful observation lies at the heart of Yahweh's speeches to Job as well. The sea mist, the dawn, the wild ox, the rain and lightning—"To all these the poet-sage gives his attention, and thus he hears them speak to him of the mystery of creation and the Creator."[10]

For the OT sage, the truth about the world and those within it never became theoretical or abstract. It remained in the crucible of trust and necessitated a humility of spirit. As Gerhard von Rad concludes, for Israel "reliable knowledge can be achieved only through a relationship of trust with things." He adds that it was even wiser "to let things retain their constantly puzzling nature, and that means to allow them to become themselves active and, by what they have to say, to set [humankind] to rights."[11] There was a hiddenness, an otherness, a continuing mystery to life that was affirmed and valued. In a fundamental sense, the whole books of Job and Ecclesiastes are attempts to give expression to human limits, and to the necessary posture of trust that must result. When God speaks out of the whirlwind, revealing nature in its depth, Job can only say, "I had heard of you by the hearing of the ear, / but now my eye sees you" (Job 42:5a,

NRSV). Analogously, the writer of Ecclesiastes, after recognizing that wisdom was far from him (Eccl 7:23), simply asserts the need for trust in life as created: "Go, eat your bread with enjoyment, and drink your wine with a merry heart; for God has long ago approved what you do" (Eccl 9:7, NRSV).

Our Ecological Dilemma

One need only say Chernobyl, Bhopal, or the *Exxon Valdez* to make concrete the ecological crisis we face. Whether in communist, third-world, or capitalist lands, an exploitive mentality toward the world is easily observable. But the situation is much more severe than simply the highly publicized "mistakes." The list of perils is sobering: greenhouse gases, ozone depletion, erosion of croplands, the desertification of grazing lands, diminished yields in fishing, water degradation, deforestation, habitat destruction, species extinctions, acid rain, the multiplication of hazardous wastes, global toxification. Life on our planet is being threatened in unprecedented ways by "factors that are largely of human origin . . . . Humanity has been conducting an enormous experiment with the creation, the ultimate consequence of which could be catastrophic."[12]

Much of the crisis has its roots in human greed and exploitation, but not all. Poverty is also implicated. Those with few options often feel forced into actions that are counterproductive in the long run but provide immediate relief. At the root of the crisis, however, is neither greed nor poverty, but a defective world view. The industrial/post-industrial age in which we live has treated nature simply as a "natural resource" to be used for profit. Humanity is understood as having both the right and the ability to dominate nature. Most of science and technology affirms the Enlightenment's assumption that humanity is at the center of the universe. Although this anthropocentric orientation has accomplished much, and although we would be the poorer without the contributions of science and technology, it is also the case that we continue to believe blindly in technological progress as the means beyond our present dilemma. And, thus, the crisis grows and deepens.

The Church has contributed to the assumptions of Western culture in this area by largely removing God from creation. As Lynn White, Jr., argued in his influential article,

> Our science and technology have grown out of Christian attitudes toward [humankind's] relation to nature which are almost universally held not only by Christians and neo-Christians but also by those

who fondly regard themselves as post-Christians. Despite Copernicus, all the cosmos rotates around our little globe. Despite Darwin, we are not, in our hearts, part of the natural process. We are superior to nature, contemptuous of it, willing to use it for our slightest whim.[13]

Some have understood the church's mistake biblically to be our over-emphasis upon the Genesis 1 creation text, which stresses dominion. We have failed to take adequate account of other creation texts (Gen. 2; Ps. 104; Ezek. 37; John 1) that are more theocentric, where the Spirit is present in life and where reciprocity and communion are stressed. The result has been the misinterpretation of "dominion" as "domination." Others have viewed our error to be theological, that is, an overemphasis on God as Creator rather than as Sustainer. In the process, nature has been robbed of its divine mystery, and the immanence of the Creator in creation has been functionally denied. Still others have criticized our belief in the instrumental value of the world. We have failed to recognize its intrinsic value. With each explanation, it is clear that we lack a theology of creation capable of giving compelling motivation to a call to change—to the ecological necessities we face as we enter the twenty-first century.

In this situation, OT wisdom can make an important contribution. For here, nature is revered, creation's intrinsic value is affirmed, and the Creator is not separated from creation. Although wisdom's creational perspective does not address ecological issues directly, it does provide a corrective mind set to our present human assertiveness. To use an ecologically "mixed metaphor," wisdom's outlook can have positive ecological fallout.[14]

According to von Rad, "The most characteristic feature of [Israel's] understanding of reality lay, in the first instance, in the fact that she believed man to stand in a quite specific, highly dynamic, existential relationship with his environment."[15] This relationship meant concretely that humans sought to learn both, from each other and from their environment, lessons concerning life. Creation was listened to and insights were appropriated.[16]

> Iron sharpens iron,
>> and one person sharpens the wits of another. (Prov 27:17, NRSV)

> Go to the ant, you lazybones;
>> consider its ways, and be wise.
> Without having any chief
>> or officer or ruler,
> it prepares its food in summer,
>> and gathers its sustenance in harvest. (Prov 6:6–7, NRSV).

Wisdom looked for interrelations in life. There was no "disinterested" knowledge. At the same time, wisdom's attitude was not instrumental. While we value oil for fuel, animals for food, and nature as a playground for humans, wisdom stressed the intrinsic worth of all creation. The divine speeches in the book of Job make the point strongly that our attitude toward the created order must change for it is too anthropocentric. Where is the ulterior usefulness to human beings of the grass in the desert "which is empty of human life" (Job 38:26–27, NRSV)? The animals in the first speech, similarly, consist mostly of those whose existence is of little benefit to us: the mountain goat, the wild ass, the wild ox, the ostrich, the hawk (Job 39). Their uselessness is even noted: "Is the wild ox willing to serve you? / Will it spend the night at your crib?" (Job 39:9, NRSV). In the second round of dialogue, God lists animals who are not even related to humankind, animals of a different scale—Behemoth and Leviathan. The world does not just, or even primarily, operate according to human standards. Jon Levenson is right when he concludes: "The catalogue of weird animals ought to show Job that there is no reason to think it should."[17] God made the creatures and delights in them for their own sake. Mystery is allowed for; intrinsic value affirmed. We can but wonder.

Not only is nature revered and creation's intrinsic value affirmed by wisdom, but creation is not separated from Creator. God is seen as active in all things. There is no secularism in OT wisdom. Neither is God's transcendence asserted at the expense of divine immanence. Although humankind has been given responsibility to act, God is nevertheless the sustainer of all life. As the psalmist writes:

> You make springs gush forth . . .
>   You cause the grass to grow . . .
> You make darkness, and it is night . . .
>   O Lord, how manifold are your works! (Ps 104:10–24, NRSV)

A particularly powerful example of the presence of God mediated indirectly through creation is found in Job. God answers Job from out of the whirlwind, asking him if he has the power and knowledge of the Creator. Of course he does not, so Job is led to put his trust in the Lord. Although it is our modern culture's assumption, we do not own the creation. As the Lord declares through the psalmist, "the world and all that is in it is mine" (Ps 50:12, NRSV). Von Rad has captured the essence of Wisdom's posture: "The experiences of the world were for [Israel] always divine experiences as well, and the experiences of God were for her experiences of the world."[18]

ought of only as childbearer or as mere chattel. She has her indepen-
nt, and yet complementary, worth. In this Genesis text, as in the Song,

> The rule of man over woman is not accepted as the intended order
> of creation. It belongs to the realm of historical chaos, like murder,
> or the Tower of Babel. It is a manifestation of sinfulness, not of cre-
> ative grace.[25]

Our Global Village

ericans live in a global world. We travel worldwide and much of the
comes to us. There is, for example, hardly a university campus where
tional students do not make up a significant portion of the study. We drive foreign-made automobiles, wear clothes that are sewn
countries, and watch Asian-made television sets. Our stores and
are filled with products from the world economy. One can no
gnore his or her neighbor, even if out of prejudice some may

ristians living in Asia, recognizing our neighbor has meant learn-
with Buddhism, Hinduism, Confucianism, Shintoism, Taoism,
e, for these other religious expressions are simply a part of the
text. But in the United States as well, religious pluralism has
fact of life. Although we remain in many ways a Christian na-
e Bible a best-seller and church attendance markedly higher
ost every other industrialized nation, we are at one and the
emarkable for our religious diversity. In any of our large cit-
e Jewish synagogues, Muslim mosques, Buddhist temples,
ientologists, Mormons, representatives of various Chinese,
Japanese religions, traditional Native American and Afro-
igionists, Moonies, New Agers, Spiritualists, Theosophers,
host of representatives of smaller groups.
duction to *Christ's Lordship & Religious Pluralism*, Donald
es the latter part of the twentieth century as a time when
facing in a new way the continuing and seemingly incur-
pluralism of the world."[26] This is not a temporary phe-
persistent fact. There are millions of people who share
believe that they have answers to the mystery of life and
ire the Christian alternative, particularly as it is identi-
n thought and life more generally. This rejection is the

Our Continuing Male Bias

I am writing this paper in Berkeley, California, where I am presently
on sabbatical. Here the joke is told that Berkeley's city council will be the
last communist administration left on the face of the earth. Berkeley is
known for its liberal/radical spirit. Its university, one of the best in the
world, has a similar reputation. And yet, in the student newspaper, *The
Daily Californian*, there was a lead article this week (October 31, 1991)
entitled "UC report reveals faculty pay inequities." The article reported
on a two-year study, conducted by the office of the Faculty Assistant on
the Status of Women, which found a direct link between gender and salary inequities at UC Berkeley. Overall, white male professors were paid 6
percent more than female faculty. The greatest pay inequity occurred at
the full professor level where women hired in the 1980s received 10 percent less salary than men hired in the same period. In a related finding,
it was revealed that of the UC faculty who received their doctoral degrees
eight to eleven years ago, only 3 percent of the women are now full professors versus 40 percent of the men. The university had conducted a
similar study in 1981 with similar results. "If it happened in 1981 and
now we're seeing it in 1991, clearly there must be some problems sys-
temically," said a woman faculty person who was interviewed.

And systemic problems there are. Despite landmark legislation in some
areas and wide-scale media coverage concerning issues related to gender
discrimination, a persistent male bias continues to exist in American society. As Catherine MacKinnon summarizes the present situation:

> Women are poor, and pay is at least as far from being sex-equal as it
> was before the passage of legislation guaranteeing pay equality by
> law. Women are more and more losing custody of their children, in
> part because of legal reforms feminists helped put in place. The rape
> rate is increasing significantly, while the conviction rate for rape is
> not, in spite of legal changes feminists fought for and won over the
> last decade.[19]

There have been real gains, thinks MacKinnon, in the laws on sexual ha-
rassment and against domestic battery and marital rape. But MacKinnon
was writing in 1987. After Clarence Thomas and Anita Hill, her opinion
might well be different. MacKinnon, a noted feminist and legal scholar,
is claiming that "Feminism has not changed the status of women."[20]

While MacKinnon might be guilty of overstatement (surely my daugh-
ters' approach to and opportunities within the world are different than

and to be preferred to those my mother had), her point is a sobering one. The power of men over women in society remains one of our most persistent and serious social ills. In addition to the unfair advantages of money, speech, education, and respectability, there is a sexual domination that dehumanizes. Commenting on a photograph of Marilyn Monroe, Norman Mailer is quoted as saying, "She is a mirror of the pleasure of those who stare at her."[21] Is it any wonder she killed herself?

It is the thesis of this essay that, as with the ecological crisis we face, OT wisdom might in fact help us move beyond present destructive patterns of thought, envisioning woman in new ways. This will seem at first surprising, for in the biblical tradition, most of the instruction is given within a man's world. Most of the proverbs are addressed to "my son" (although the NRSV tries to mitigate this by changing the name to "my child"; cf. Prov 2:1). With warnings against nagging wives, but with nothing similar regarding "defective" husbands, wisdom would seem an unpromising context for insight that would move us beyond our male centeredness. But by suggesting a pool of female images connected to the divine and by providing an alternate vision, or model, of who a woman is, wisdom can assist in breaking down our systemic male bias, creating a new orientation toward both male and female.

In an era that increasingly struggles with exclusively male misrepresentations of the divine, the wisdom literature provides a welcomed resource of words and images regarding God that are female. Just as a misunderstanding in the biblical narrative of "dominion" as "domination" has contributed to the ecological crisis we face, so a misunderstanding of masculine imagery for God as implying "his" maleness has contributed to the continuing male bias in our culture. And just as an interpretive correction might become easier to visualize when other creational texts, including those of wisdom, are referred to first, so it is with regard to our visualization of the divine. Rather than argue rightly, but abstractly, that Israel did not consider her God as either male or female but simply used male imagery to emphasize God's personalness, might it not be preferable to hold up to the light some of the female language the OT also uses for the divine?

Various texts portray Woman Wisdom poetically (Prov 1, 3, 4, 8, 9; Job 28; Sir 24, 51; Wis 7–9), but the portrayal of this divine personification is neither consistent nor systematic. In Job she is remote and unknowable; in Proverbs she offers the gift of life; for Ben Sira she is identified with the Torah; and in Wisdom she is a reflection of God (an image later picked up in the NT and applied to Christ). Some scholars believe her to be the divine mystery of creation, a cosmological, feminine principle.[22] And at

times she is this (cf. Sir 1). But her connection with the divi texts more integral than that. She is God's revelation, not revelation. Others have thought her to be a personification of the divine, a literary device to speak of God's characte flat and breaks Woman Wisdom's connection with crea posit Woman Wisdom to be a goddess. But clearly this i other direction; it claims too much. For Israel, God tra At times Woman Wisdom is a characteristic of the Lor at times the divine secret resident in creation, at times a with special status, and at times a metaphor of God. T Wisdom is associated with creation. She is an exter human beings, God's creation-centered address to

In Proverbs 31, we find the human equivalent of this acrostic concerning a Capable Wife (v. 10) to b Wisdom (chs. 1–9), thus combining to form fer text. "Happy are those who find wisdom" (Prov 3 called "happy" by her children and husband, to such a structure for the book is intended can nection with personified Wisdom seems reaso tation of the wife in this text is exceptional an dent in Israel's social life. The activity of this We are given a "down-to-earth and yet ideal dent, and diligent woman who effortlessly family affairs."[23] This woman who fears th band can rely on her abilities and reput based on hers. Here is the human expre

Such a portrayal of woman in her ind confirmation in other biblical texts th portrayal of the couple in the Song of every way the equal of the man. She tion. In fact, she is more often the ini more imaginative and significant th chal bias here; full equality in the the Song harkens back to the nar dom characteristics as well. The help in man's loneliness. Far from ment, the crowning of creation. full equality, the natural, expec scription: it is now the woman w might be sexually initiated (G ther and mother to cling to

Am world interna dent b in othe homes longer i want to.

For Ch ing to liv and the li Asian con become a tion with t than in alr same time ies, there a groups of S Indian, and American re Baha'is, and In his intro Dawe describ "Christians ar able religious nomenon but life with us wh who do not de fied with Wester case despite the modern missionary movement and despite efforts at cross-cultural evangelism within the United States. Moreover, millions more are increasingly secular, dismissing any and all institutionalized religion with its dogma and authority. How are we as Christians to respond?

In a series of lectures given at the Graduate Theological Union in Berkeley and later published as *Wisdom for a Changing World*, Ronald Clements argues that such a situation finds its biblical analogue in the post-exilic period when Jews became scattered throughout the diaspora and fundamental patterns of conduct and piety had to be recast in less nationalistic terms. Grounded in creation rather than in election and covenant, wisdom provided the Jews who were scattered throughout the empire such a theology. Having as its source no single revelatory act, but based in a "non-national and cosmic interpretation of creation and human society," wisdom could be adapted in the postexilic period for a people who lived at least metaphorically "in an unclean land." For such a situation, the "fear of the Lord" became "a more universalistic grounding for morality than the ancient concept of holiness offered." The benefits of long life and blessing that Deuteronomy linked to holiness, to obedience to the Law, wisdom posited as its reward. Although the initial origins of wisdom literature were pre-exilic, "it was the urgency of the situation created by the destruction of the temple as the cultic center of Israel life in 587 B.C.E which raised such a shift of intellectual focus to a matter of major significance."[27] It was the inherited tradition of wisdom that provided the post-exilic Jewish community the theological resources necessary for its survival.

Clements' thesis is provocative. Because the cult was tied territorially to the temple in Jerusalem, its benefits were viewed as limited for a people in a strange land. But rather than abandon its traditional piety in favor of an alien faith, post-exilic Judaism looked, instead, to an alternate tradition within its theology, pursuing wisdom based in the "fear of the Lord." As we have noted above, this tradition had earlier found Sinai too narrow a perspective in which to live in the world. There were everyday experiences to be learned, and both family tradition and international dialogue proved useful resources.

It is significant that Job and his friends are presented as non-Israelites, as are Agur and Lemuel (Prov 30–31). Proverbs 22:17–24:22 is too close to the words of Amenemope for it to be accidental. Its "thirty sayings" find their source in this earlier Egyptian wisdom instruction. Deliberately bracketing their salvation history, Israel's sages understood God's revelation also to be mediated through creation. It was the same Lord who had revealed himself savingly in Israel's history who was also understood to have revealed

himself in the lives and thought of Israel's neighbors. Just as the Lord offered life as a reward for obedience to the Law (Deut 30:15–20), the Lord
promised life to all who found wisdom (Prov 8:32–36). Robert Davidson
rightly cautions:

> In Israel we should view the attitude of the wise, not as non-theological
> over against a religious tradition dominated by a view of a God who
> revealed himself in historical events, but rather as an alternative and
> equally valid way of doing theology. The Old Testament as a whole,
> within the framework of belief in Yahweh's presence, purposes and
> activity in the world, invites us to share in a theological pluralism.[28]

There is no secularism or humanitarianism here. Neither is there any
syncretism or relativism. The one leads to theological bankruptcy, the
other to theological confusion. Rather, there is found in wisdom an appreciation for truth wherever it may be found. While affirming the uniqueness of Yahweh to which they continued to bear witness, Israel's wise recognized God's creative work in the religious expressions of people of other
faiths around them. Here is a model for our interaction with peoples of
other faiths today. Rather than dismiss their wisdom as a priori mistaken,
or rather than simply proclaim the gospel in monologue, Christians can
enter into authentic dialogue with their neighbors, seeking to learn from
them God's truth as revealed in his created world, even while sharing
God's truth as they know it.

At the World Council of Churches Assembly in Vancouver in 1983, such
a suggestion was hotly debated and finally tabled to committee. They
asked, Was not the recognition of God's creative work in the religious
experience of other faiths a denial of the uniqueness of Jesus Christ? The
Central Committee was directed to take up the question after the assembly ended, and they eventually concluded that God's creative work was
present only in "the seeking for religious truth among people of other
faiths."[29] But is this not to deny that one can learn of the Lord through
experience and through creation? The openness of Israelite wisdom to
the wisdom of Israel's neighbors, the international tenor of the wisdom
movement, the actual borrowing from non-Israelite wisdom, the focus
upon creation—here is a biblical basis for positing that the non-Chris-
tian today can respond in faith to the same Creator who has revealed
himself to us also as Redeemer.[30]

Questions obviously remain. Is this faith saving faith? For the Christian
there is no salvation outside Christ (John 14:6). How does wisdom's offer of
life fit here? Some may want to build on this insight from wisdom in arguing

that those who are faithful to the light that they have will be given the opportunity to respond to Christ's invitation, even after death.[31] Others will want to encourage a dialogue between OT wisdom and such NT texts as Romans 1. But bracketing the questions of how the exclusive claims of Christ work themselves out in a world in which many never encounter him, we can say in confidence that the presence of God in wisdom is seen biblically to be in continuity with God's presence in Christ.[32] We can hear God speak to us through his creatures and creation, including their religious expressions. Wisdom would invite an openness of perspective and real dialogue, even while celebrating God's full revelation in Jesus Christ (1 Cor 1:24).

Conclusion

Too often the Bible is used to justify theological positions arrived at on independent grounds. We have seen that danger in the above discussion, where male imagery for God is used to elevate the status of man, or where the divine mandate to have dominion is thought justification for human domination of the world and its resources. Although we read the Bible necessarily as the modern readers we are, this does not give us license to assign the text meaning at will. Bernhard Anderson's caution bears repeating:

> This sober realization of our "location" does not, in my estimation, mire us in interpretive relativism, as though the Scriptures and other literary works are "like a picnic to which the author brings the words and the reader the meaning," to invoke the celebrated words of Northrop Frye. To be sure, we come to the Scriptures in our social location and hopefully, with some creative imagination; but the words of Scripture, spoken or written in their own context, may criticize where we stand, limit our use of them, and challenge us with their strange social setting and theological horizon.[33]

OT wisdom does indeed challenge us with its theological vantage points. It believes humankind to live in a dynamic, reciprocal relationship with its environment. Wisdom deals with the relation of women and men in God's good creation, assuming an equality that harkens back to images before the fall. And again, wisdom listens for God's revealing word in creation, not simply in redemption, even hearing her call in the religious wisdom of those of differing faiths.

The goal of such wisdom is not the elimination of mystery, but a more faithful response to God's gift of life. As we close this millennium and look for new life-giving ways to understand our world, wisdom's personal address invites us to adopt a new way of knowing. And yet this way is not new; it is spoken by those sensitive to her call in every generation. Saint Anselm, who lived at the start of this millennium, expressed wisdom's insight in this prayer:

> Lord, I am not trying to make my way to your height, for my understanding is in no way equal to that, but I do desire to understand a little of your truth which my heart already believes and loves. I do not seek to understand so that I can believe, but I believe so that I may understand; and what is more, I believe that unless I do believe, I shall not understand.

NOTES

1. This greeting honors David Allan Hubbard. David has been both a mentor and a personal friend. I am deeply in his debt. Among his other influences on me was his introduction to me of the potential relevance of OT wisdom for our contemporary age as I sat in his seminary classroom. The following essay attempts to extend the dialogue that he has already begun.
2. L. Newbigin, *The Other Side of 1984* (Geneva: World Council of Churches, 1983) 17.
3. Newbigin, ibid., 20.
4. Quoted in Newbigin, ibid., 21.
5. R. Murphy, *The Tree of Life*, ABRL (New York: Doubleday, 1990) 97. David Hubbard has, himself, contributed to this corpus with his Tyndale Old Testament Lecture for 1965, "The Wisdom Movement and Israel's Covenant Faith," *TynBul* 17 (1966) 3–33.
6. W. Zimmerli, "The Place and the Limit of the Wisdom in the Framework of the Old Testament Theology," *SJT* 17 (1964) 146–58.
7. R. Murphy, "The Kerygma of the Book of Proverbs," *Int* 20 (1966) 3–14.
8. Cf. G. von Rad, *Wisdom in Israel* (Nashville: Abingdon, 1972) 64.
9. J. Eaton, *The Contemplative Face of Old Testament Wisdom* (Philadelphia: Trinity, 1989) 40.
10. Eaton, ibid., 42.
11. Von Rad, *Wisdom in Israel*, 318.
12. *Between the Flood and the Rainbow*, second draft document for the World Convocation in Justice, Peace and the Integrity of Creation, Seoul, Korea, March 5–13, 1990, World Council of Churches, Geneva, 12.
13. L. White, Jr., "The Historical Roots of Our Ecological Crisis," *Science* 155 (March 10, 1967) 1203–7; reprinted in W. Granberg-Michaelson, *Ecology and Life* (Waco: Word, 1988) 135.

14. Murphy, *Tree of Life*, 121.
15. Von Rad, *Wisdom in Israel*, 301.
16. Cf. R. Murphy, "Israel's Wisdom: A Biblical Model of Salvation," *Studia Missionalia* 30 (1981) 18–21.
17. J. D. Levenson, *The Book of Job in Its Time and in the Twentieth Century* (Cambridge: Harvard University Press, 1972) 27.
18. Von Rad, *Wisdom*, 62, quoted in Murphy, *Tree of Life*, 114.
19. C. A. MacKinnon, *Feminism Unmodified: Discourses on Life and Law* (Cambridge: Harvard University Press, 1987) 1.
20. MacKinnon, ibid., 2.
21. Quoted in MacKinnon, ibid., 16.
22. Cf. S. Terrien, "Toward a Biblical Theology of Womanhood," in *Male and Female: Christian Approaches to Sexuality*, ed. R. T. Barnhouse & U. T. Holmes, III (New York: Seabury, 1976) 22; von Rad, *Wisdom*, 144–76.
23. K. A. Farmer, *Who Knows What is Good?: A Commentary on the Books of Proverbs and Ecclesiastes*, ITC (Grand Rapids: Eerdmans, 1991) 126.
24. S. Terrien, *Till the Heart Sings* (Philadelphia: Fortress, 1985) 12–14; cf. A. Brenner, *The Song of Songs*, OTG (Sheffield: JSOT, 1989) 83.
25. Terrien, "Toward a Biblical Theology of Womanhood," 20.
26. D. Dawe, "Introduction," in *Christ's Lordship & Religious Pluralism*, ed. G. H. Anderson & T. F. Stransky (Maryknoll, NY: Orbis, 1981) 3.
27. R. E. Clements, *Wisdom for a Changing World* (Berkeley: BIBAL, 1990) 18–32.
28. R. Davidson, *Wisdom and Worship* (Philadelphia: Trinity, 1990) 14.
29. J. S. Ukpong, "Pluralism and the Problem of the Discernment of Spirits," in *To the Wind of God's Spirit*, ed. E. Castro (Geneva: WCC Publications, 1990) 84.
30. This argument is a paraphrase of Roland Murphy's conclusion ("Israel's Wisdom," 42–43), but without making Murphy's final step, which would equate the non-Israelite religious response to the Creator with saving faith. Murphy's thesis is that wisdom provides a biblical model of salvation that can support the possibility of salvation for non-Christians. Murphy maintains the centrality of redemption through Christ, but this does not destroy the basis of faith that God establishes with his creatures.
31. Clark Pinnock and Donald Bloesch have both posited that some will find conversion after death, as has W. Pannenberg.
32. Murphy, "Israel's Wisdom," 43.
33. B. W. Anderson, "Creation and Ecology," in *Creation in the Old Testament*, ed. B. W. Anderson (Philadelphia: Fortress, 1984) 154.

III

THE OLD
TESTAMENT
AND THE WORLD

13

ISRAEL AND THE CHURCH IN
THE WORLD

Richard J. Mouw

During the 1970s a group of Mennonite and Calvinist theologians in the Netherlands met to discuss their long-standing theological and ethical differences. One key item on their agenda was the relationship between the Christian Church and Old Testament Israel. The Anabaptists expressed their long-standing objection to the way Reformed Christians like to speak of the Church as "the people of God." This OT manner of designating the character of Christian discipleship is misleading, the Anabaptists argued. In the OT, the believing community was identical with a political-economic society, but the New Testament Church does not possess this kind of peoplehood.

On the other hand, the Anabaptists were not prepared to argue that there is no continuity whatsoever between the life and mission of the NT Church and that of OT Israel. They were willing to agree with their Reformed dialogue partners that the Church, like Israel, "is elected and called by God to proclaim, as a community of faith, His name in the midst of all nations and to demonstrate how people can live together on earth according to God's purpose."[1]

This exchange is a case in point illustrating an important dynamic at work in the Christian community. Christians operate with different understandings of the relationship between the Church and Israel. And these disagreements play a role in arguments between various Christian groups about the proper patterns of the Church's life and mission in the world. But this discussion between the Anabaptists and the Reformed also reveals another aspect of the dynamic in question: the argument is seldom really about the question of continuity as such. The Dutch Anabaptists agreed with the Dutch Reformed that the Church's life and mission are in an important sense continuations of the life and mission of OT Israel. Their residual differences had to do with how to spell out some key details of this pattern of continuity.

In this essay I will discuss how the life and witness of Israel can serve as resources for the Christian community's pursuit of its calling in the world. As an exercise in what David Hubbard has called "evangelical ecumenism," I will attempt to avoid a narrow theological partisanship in my formulations. This is a topic on which it is important to arrive at consensus formulations wherever possible, so that the whole Church might be renewed for the work of obedient discipleship.

Continuity and Discontinuity

There is a danger, of course, that in working for a consensus we will run roughshod over real and important differences among Christians. This often happens when doctrinal disagreements are viewed as mere impediments to the "real," social-economic-ethical tasks of the community of faith. This is not the mood that informs my probings here. Careful theological reflection is itself a necessary dimension of the life of obedient discipleship. The psalmist pleaded for a prayerful testing of his thoughts so that he could find "the way everlasting" (Ps 139:23–24, NSRV). The Church will falter in its attempts to pursue its complex mission if it does not think carefully about the contours and details of that mission. It will be good to begin, then, by looking at some seemingly irreconcilable theological accounts of the relationship between the life and mission of Israel and the Church's calling of discipleship in the world.

No one who is familiar with evangelical thought will be confused about where to look for formulations that posit a radical discontinuity between the callings of Israel and the Church. Dispensationalist views on this subject have been an important reference point for twentieth-century evangelical discussions of the relationship between Israel and the Church. Here is Lewis Sperry Chafer's classic formulation of the dispensationalist account of this relationship:

> The all-too-common practice of imposing Christianity back upon Judaism or Judaism forward upon Christianity is the cause of dire confusion which appears in some theological literature. The Word of God distinguishes between earth and heaven, even after they are created new. Similarly and as clearly it distinguishes between God's consistent and eternal earthly purposes, which is the substance of Judaism; and His consistent and eternal heavenly purpose which is the substance of Christianity, and it is as illogical and fanciful to contend that Judaism and Christianity ever merge as it would be to contend that heaven and earth cease to exist as separate spheres. Dispensationalism has its foundation in and is understood in the distinction between Judaism and Christianity.[2]

This is a perspective, then, that posits a clear distinction between the callings of Israel and the Church. God has assigned to Israel—in its ancient as well as its contemporary existence—an "earthly" calling; the political-economic patterns of OT life are inextricably linked to this unique calling. The Gentile Church, however, has been given a very different assignment. The Christian community has a "heavenly" destiny, which it must pursue by means of a purely "spiritual" mission. To confuse or mix these two very different assignments can only lead to a violation of God's intentions in calling these two distinct communal entities into existence.

It is not difficult, on the other hand, to find formulations that, in effect, simply negate dispensationalist dualism. For example, Yale Theologian George Lindbeck has insisted that the "Marcionite" desire "to spiritualize and privatize Christianity and neglect the OT" must be countered by a Christian ecclesiology that draws heavily on "Israel-ology."[3] And the late Dutch Reformed theologian A. A. van Ruler regularly insisted on the fundamental continuity between the Church's calling and the political economic program of the OT. Both the OT and the NT, van Ruler argued, focus on "the organization of human society in accordance with the fundamental marks of justice and love"; anyone who refuses to interpret the gospel in a thoroughly "Israelitish manner," van Ruler insisted, "is, in my judgment, compelled to understand it gnostically. *Tertium non datur*: there is no third way."[4]

This strong emphasis on programmatic continuity would be endorsed by many Christian activists today. For all of their political differences, for example, both Calvinist theonomists and Catholic liberation theologians insist that God wants the contemporary Christian community to carry out the political-economic mission of OT Israel.

We have, then, two formulations that set forth stark alternatives: a rigid Israel-Church dualism versus an insistence on a rather strict continuity between Israel and the Church. And again, insofar as these theological theses lead to very different understandings of the Church's life and mission, they must be taken seriously. I, for one, have never been inclined to dismiss the dispensationalist perspective as mere theological confusion. As Frank Gaebelein has observed, one can reject the central theological claims of dispensationalism while still employing it as "a method of interpretation helpful in grasping the progress of revelation in the Bible . . . ."[5] And I would add that as a "crisis" theory of social change, dispensationalism provides an intriguing alternative to the organic "progress" theories of both liberal Protestant and Roman Catholic thought. Similarly, the strong "Israelological" claims of those who posit a strict continuity also deserve to be carefully examined for theological coherency; at the very least they provide a helpful reference point for testing less radical formulations regarding the continuity between Israel and the Church.

It is helpful, then, to be very conscious of these exclusive formulations in thinking about the redemptive economies of the OT and the NT. But it is also important not to worry too much about our inability to settle the differences between these two extreme viewpoints, since it is not at all clear that either of these positions actually holds up as a consistent programmatic emphasis in understanding the relationship between the missions of Israel and the Church. This can be seen in the fact—and I think its factuality can be demonstrated empirically—that the very people who explicitly endorse one or the other of the polar opposite positions actually operate with a functional perspective that falls short of the extreme end of the spectrum.

No Christian, for example, really thinks that the Church's life and witness is *purely* "Israelitish." The continuities are affirmed in such a way that they are always selective. Theonomists and liberationists and Seventh-Day Adventists may all insist on a strict continuity between the OT and the NT. But it is clear that each group is choosing to be Israelitish in a different way; their divergent sociologies instantiate alternative ways of selecting and appropriating OT motifs.

On the other hand, the people who posit a strict Israel-Church dualism seldom act as if the calling of OT Israel is totally irrelevant to the life and witness of the Christian community. The rhetoric employed by Lindbeck and van Ruler notwithstanding, most Christians who fail to embrace a thoroughgoing Christian "Israel-ology" do not thereby slip into "Marcionite" or "gnostic" habits. Dispensationalist preachers, for example, do not consistently avoid OT texts. To be sure, their homiletical treatments of Israelitish materials may be marked by the use of allegorical methods, "prefiguring" motifs, and spiritualizing strategies, but even these habits can be interpreted as evidence of a deep desire to find some linkage between the life of the Christian community and the calling of OT Israel.

Neither the dualists nor the strict-continuity defenders seem to be able in practice, then, to operate with as extreme a position as their respective formulations might indicate. But this is not, I think, only a problem of practical implementation. The difficulties stem from a confusion that is often embedded in the formulations themselves. Dispensationalist dualists, for example, want to operate with a clear distinction between Israel's "earthly" mission and the "heavenly" orientation of the Church. This is the kind of dichotomy that presupposes a corresponding distinction between a "private faith" and a "public faith," or between the "this-worldly" versus the "spiritual." Thus, the insistence that Israel's mission is tied to the political-economic patterns of earthly life, while the Church's life and witness have a predominantly strong spiritual character.

Some continuity defenders employ a similar dichotomy. They, too, insist on a clear distinction between a this-worldly religion and a purely spiritual one. But they argue that the spiritualized version of the religious life has no place in the context of either the Old or New Covenants. When Christians adopt a spiritualized understanding of their faith they become—to use the labels favored by Lindbeck and van Ruler—"gnostics" or "Marcionites." It is significant, though, that neither of these ways of endorsing the dichotomy between a politicized faith and a spiritualized one actually sets forth very clear criteria for distinguishing between the "this-worldly" and the "spiritual." Nor is it easy to spell out in exact terms what these criteria might be.

I once heard a Christian ethicist deliver a lecture in which he attempted to offer an account of the differences between evangelical and liberal Protestant understandings of sin. The evangelicals, he argued, are concerned about such personal moral issues as the use of alcohol, gambling, and sexual immorality; the liberals, on the other hand, focus on more corporate phenomena, such as sexism, racism, and militarism. In spite of the fact that such delineations are very common, it is rather difficult to make good sense of them. Why are condemnations of state lotteries any

less "public" than are condemnations of defense budgets? In what sense
is adultery a "private" sin while the viewing of women as mere sex objects
is a "public" sin? Why is racism any less a manifestation of the pride of
the human heart than is a lifestyle given to drunkenness and promiscu-
ity? What makes the use of obscene words a "personal" sin and the use of
exclusive gender language a "corporate" one?

The problems in employing a sharp distinction here apply directly to
the Israel-Church relationship. Defenders of the continuity thesis mean
to be insisting that the Christian community has a clear obligation to pro-
mote peace and justice. Strict dualists, on the other hand, often set forth
their case with the intention of denying the very obligation that is central
to the continuity perspective.

It is not easy, however, to make a clear case for either side in biblical-
theological terms. Suppose, for example, that for the sake of the argument we grant the dispensationalist case regarding the differences between Israel and the Church—i.e., that Israel has an earthly and political
calling and the Church has a heavenly and spiritual one. Why would this
understanding of the relationship in any way prohibit dispensationalists
in a totalitarian society from speaking out against the political persecution of religious groups? Or why would it keep them from condemning
laws and practices that discriminate against people on the basis of race or
gender? Or why would it keep the Church from showing a deep concern
for the plight of the poor and the downtrodden? Or why would it even
keep dispensationalists from condemning Israeli troops who shoot at
unarmed Palestinian children? Are not such issues relevant to the life
and witness of a people who are called to manifest the very "spiritual"
traits listed in Galatians 5:22–23 (NRSV): "love, joy, peace, patience, kindness, generosity, faithfulness, gentleness, and self-control"?

But we must also turn the argument against the "Israelologists" who
want to eliminate "spiritualizing" from the Christian life. It is difficult to
avoid the impression that many of the prohibitions found in the Book of
Leviticus deal directly with issues of a "personal morality." Nor is it easy
to read the Psalms without concluding that they are highly "spiritual" in
nature. And is that not appropriate? Can we really pursue a ministry of
justice and peace without caring about how individual people relate to
God? Is it not important that civil rights leaders and feminist spokesper-
sons experience divine forgiveness and acceptance in a personal way? Have
the poor and the oppressed really heard "good news" if they have not
learned that the power of the gospel can cleanse them from all
unrighteousness, including the unrighteousness of individual hearts that
are oppressed by superstition and pride?

H. H. Rowley has aptly observed that "in no period of the life of Israel do we find extreme collectivism or extreme individualism, but a combination of both." At specific times, he explains, stress is placed on "the one side of this dual nature of man more than the other, but both sides belong to the wholeness of biblical thought in all periods."[6] Rowley's comment can also be extended to cover the other dichotomies—i.e., "personal/corporate," "this worldly/spiritual"—that are relevant to comparing Israel's mission to that of the Church. God issues complex mandates to each of these communities of faith. Neither a simple dichotomy nor a simple continuity will suffice to capture the relationship between them.

We are looking for a consensus perspective on the ways in which the Christian community can learn from the life and mission of Israel in its own efforts at discipleship. And I have been arguing that the existence of two polar-opposite formulations regarding the Israel-Church relationship is not a real barrier to finding a consensus perspective, since the two formulations are not as coherent and exclusive as they seem to be at first glance. For all practical purposes, most Christians—including many Christians who officially subscribe to the more extreme formulations—act as if the relationship between Israel and the Church is a mixture of continuities and discontinuities.

Not that there is any clear agreement among Christians as to what the proper mix of continuities and discontinuities *is*. Views about the relationship between Israel and the Church fall on a spectrum, and a rather lengthy one at that. In my probings here, I will respect the diversity of viewpoints on this spectrum. But I also think that there are some aspects of the relationship between Israel's mission in the world and the Church's discipleship mandate about which all, or at least most, Christians can reach agreement. I will briefly examine three of these aspects here, noting elements of both continuity and discontinuity in each case: the call to peoplehood, the theocratic structure of the community of faith, and the proper patterns of practical obedience to the will of God.

Peoplehood

The Dutch Mennonites whom we mentioned at the beginning of this essay are worried about the idea of peoplehood. They are convinced that the Church is not a "people" in the OT sense. It is not difficult to fill in some of the details of the Mennonites' worries about this notion. Not only has the Anabaptist community had long-standing misgivings about the Constantinian impulse to equate Christian discipleship with a specific manifestation of national citizenship; these misgivings have been greatly intensified in twentieth-century Europe by the unspeakably perverse uses to which the idea of peoplehood, of a *Volk* identity, have been put.

This topic deserves much attention. No contemporary discussion of the relationship between Israel and the Church can ignore the ways in which understandings of this relationship have taken actual historical shape. And unfortunately, Christians are not always consciously aware of the ways they appropriate and distort the biblical notion of peoplehood. This has been especially true of the ways Christians have incorporated the "chosen people" motif into the ways they have thought about the nations of which they are citizens.

"American civil religion" has been subject to careful critique in recent decades from a variety of perspectives, including the theological.[7] Civil religion is not a uniquely American phenomenon, however. It also plays a significant role in South Africa, Scotland, South Korea, and many other national settings. In each case the historical experience of a national or ethnic group is interpreted in categories that are drawn from the OT narratives. The group in question is viewed as having a special covenant with God, which brings with it a special sense of "manifest destiny"; for example, in both the North American and Afrikaner versions, direct parallels are drawn to Israel's wilderness ordeal and promised-land legacy.[8]

The persistence of the civil religion phenomenon is an indication of a strong propensity for appropriating "chosen nation" themes. This is done even when there is no sound theological basis for doing so—and even when, as in the case of those dispensationalists who embrace American civil religion, their theology stipulates that the state of Israel is the only present-day "chosen nation." This attempted connection directly violates the stated theological convictions of the Christians involved. To counter this tendency, at least two corrective strategies are necessary, beyond mere negative critique. We must develop a carefully formulated theological alternative understanding of biblical peoplehood. And we must translate this healthier understanding into a pastorally sensitive communal spirituality that will speak effectively to the deep need for belonging and corporate identity that leads so many Christians to draw on the resources of a civil religion.

In his study of Afrikaner civil religion, T. Dunbar Moodie argues that the post-biblical application of the "chosen nation" concept is given explicit endorsement by John Calvin who, Moodie, observes, "insisted on a distinction between the individual's 'special call' to salvation and the 'intermediate election' of an ethnic group called by God to fulfill His special purposes."[9] Moodie is correct in noting that Calvin made such a distinction,[10] but he is wrong in suggesting that Calvin thought that the "intermediate election" of a specific ethnic or national entity is a repeatable phenomenon.

It is clear from the context of the passages cited by Moodie that Calvin is referring only to the election of OT Israel—by way of explaining the sense in which Israel as a corporate people could be elected even though not every individual citizen of Israel was elected in the soteriological sense. To be sure, Calvin intended that a parallel distinction could be applied to the NT Church: the visible Church as a whole is an elect community, even though not every member of the Church is necessarily elected in the individual sense. But there is nothing in any of this to indicate that Calvin thought that post-biblical national or ethnic entities could be beneficiaries of a corporate election.

On biblical grounds, there are only two collective entities in the contemporary world who could conceivably qualify for chosen-people candidacy: the Jewish people and the Church. We need not debate here the question of the present-day status of the Jewish community in the divine economy. A viable consensus perspective will surely have to leave that question open for continuing debate. But the question raised by the Dutch Mennonites does need to be treated with care: Is it appropriate to refer to the Church today as "the people of God"?

There seem to be strong considerations in favor of an affirmative answer to this question. For one thing, the NT seems clearly to give permission for doing so. Peter's First Epistle is an obvious case in point here. It begins by addressing the Church as "the exiles of the Dispersion" (1:1, NRSV); then the apostle applies, in the second chapter, a series of key "Israelitish" designators to the Christian community, including the peoplehood concept:

> But you are a chosen race, a royal priesthood, a holy nation, God's own people, in order that you may proclaim the mighty acts of him who called you out of darkness into his marvelous light.
> Once you were not a people,
>   but now you are God's people;
> once you had not received mercy,
>   but now you have received mercy. (1 Pet 2:9–10, NRSV)

Furthermore, there do seem to be some ecclesiological benefits to be gained from making use of the peoplehood motif. In his masterful study, *Models of the Church*, Father Avery Dulles has detailed the positive changes that were brought about in Roman Catholicism when the Vatican II documents replaced some of the older images of the Church, such as the mystical body concept, with a strong emphasis on the Church as the people of God.[11] And on Dulles's telling of the story, the peoplehood concept served, if anything, to move Catholicism away from many of the Constantinian emphases and practices that the Mennonites associate with a contemporary appropriation of the people of God motif.[12]

This is not to dismiss, however, the Mennonite concern. The peoplehood image may sometimes have reinforced a healthy self-understanding in the Christian community. But it has also served to do much damage, both when the image is superimposed onto the civil religion of a specific ethnic or national entity and when a sense of peoplehood has contributed to a prideful, exclusivist "chosen people" spirit within the ecclesial community.

A consensus perspective on NT peoplehood, then, must recognize both the strengths and the dangers of a reliance on the people of God motif. Where the concept contributes to a healthy sense of Christian community and to a mission of shared servanthood, it plays a positive role. Where it evokes and reinforces ethnocentric and nationalistic communal self-definitions, it must be subjected to careful biblical critique.

There can be no argument that under the conditions that prevailed in the OT, God chose to bestow special covenantal blessings upon an elect people who were bound together by ties of ethnic nationhood. But neither can there be any doubt that such ties are no longer central features in the body of Jesus Christ. In this redeemed community the ancient promise has begun to be fulfilled: "a feast of rich food" has been prepared for all nations, and "the shroud that is cast over all peoples" has been destroyed on the mountain of the Lord (Isa 25:6–7, NRSV). The question of ethnicity was settled decisively at the Jerusalem Council (Acts 15), and the eschatological hymn now proclaims the inclusive purposes of the work of the Lamb, by whom men and women are formed into a royal priesthood drawn "from every tribe and language and people and nation" (Rev 5:9, NRSV).

Theocracy

The story of evangelical non-involvement in the social arena for many decades of this century is by now an oft-told tale. The impression is sometimes given, however, that the primary cause of this non-involvement was simply inattention on the part of evangelicals to questions of social justice. This is not completely accurate. Many evangelicals who avoided political activity in the past did so out of a sincere conviction that such involvement could not be justified on biblical grounds. They were convinced that there was very little in the Bible that could be cited in support of Christian social action.

The key term in the previous sentence is, of course, the adjective "Christian." No one denies that the book of Amos is in the Bible. But many evangelicals have insisted that Amos's prophetic message is not meant as normative guidance for the Church. One common rationale for this partitioning of the political-economic message of the OT is this: the book of Amos was written for a *theocratic* setting, whereas the Church is meant to function in a very different sort of context.

There are at least two possible strategies for undermining this claim. One possibility is to argue that the kinds of political-economic judgments that we find, say, in the writings of the Minor Prophets are not inextricably linked to a theocratic setting. Another strategy is to insist that Christians are not exempt from a theocratic understanding of social reality.

Each of these lines of argument has much plausibility. Suppose, for example, that we grant that Amos lived in a kind of theocratic society that is no longer appropriate in a Christian age. It is difficult to see how this assumption justifies our ignoring the substance of his prophetic message. In his excellent study of OT ethics, Walter Kaiser has rightly observed that the basic tenets of OT morality have an abiding quality, because they are expressions of the unchanging character of God—an emphasis that has been repeated in Bruce Birch's more recent study of OT justice.[13]

It is difficult to imagine that God could care deeply about the oppression of widows and orphans in one historical setting and abandon this concern in another context. Indeed, Amos himself makes it clear that his message is an expression of God's will, not just for citizens of an explicit theocracy, but for all of humankind: Amos mentions the political sins of Israel's neighbors as well as those of Israel itself (cf. Amos 1–2).

But there is a deeper issue at stake—one that requires attention to the second strategy. The claim that we, unlike the Jews of the OT, do not live in a theocracy seems to presuppose a rather superficial understanding of theocratic patterns. Theocracy means literally "God-rule." Theocratic government is often treated as one among many forms of government: democracy is the rule of the people; meritocracy is the rule of those who have demonstrated a certain kind of excellence; aristocracy is the rule of the elites; technocracy is the rule of those who have mastered certain technical skills; and theocracy is the rule of God.

The problem is, of course, that theocracy does not fit very neatly into a list of this sort. To be sure, it is possible to think of a theocratic society that would exhibit a unique alternative to the decision-making patterns of these other forms of government. In such a society, when a law or policy is to be decided, the citizens would consult, not an elite human ruler, or a scientific expert or a majority vote of the people, but the will of God. God would tell them what to do—and the law or policy would thereby be established.

But this is not how things typically went in the OT—except, perhaps, in the Garden of Eden where we may have the clearest example of a pure theocratic pattern of policy formation. What is much more common in the history of Israel is that the rule of God would be administered through some other pattern of decision-making. When John Calvin argued, for example, that the best form of government is a mixture of aristocracy and democracy, he appealed to the OT where, he says, the Lord "ordained among the Israelites" a form of government that featured "aristocracy bordering on democracy."[14] We need not argue here about whether Calvin has correctly characterized Israel's politics (although I think he has). The point is that when Calvin talks about the "form" of Israel's government he does not think in terms of theocracy. But this does not mean that he denies that Israel was in a profound sense ruled by God.

The question of whether a given society is theocratic or not has to do, we might say, with where the fundamental authority resides in that society. In that sense, Israel did not think of itself as either aristocratic or democratic—the OT community knew that God was their true sovereign. But that did not mean that God exercised the rule in a direct sort of way. To be sure, sometimes the kings or the elders of the people went directly to God for advice. On other occasions, though, they decided policy questions by exercising their own discerning judgment as to what would be a God-pleasing way to act. The fact that conformity to the will of God was the ultimate court of appeal meant that the society was fundamentally a theocratic one. The fact that, say, the *elders* were the ones who were responsible for determining what would in fact please God meant that the government was structured along aristocratic lines.

What made Israel a theocracy, then, was not that God made all of the decisions in a direct way. The theocratic character of Israel's political life had to do with these two facts: first, that God claimed the ultimate authority over the life of the nation and, second, that the nation acknowledged this fact, so that all human leaders and processes were viewed as instruments and strategies for implementing the divine rule in the nation's life.

Strictly speaking, only the first of these conditions needs to prevail in order for a theocracy to be maintained. When God effectively exercises sovereign authority over a social order, we have what we might label an *actual theocracy.* If the second condition also exists—if the divine authority is consciously acknowledged by God's human subjects—then we have an *acknowledged theocracy.*

This pair of terms can help us in analyzing our contemporary situation. Do we have any theocracies in the world today? It seems clear that we do. Indeed, the whole world is a vast actual theocracy. The great proclamation of Psalm 24:1 is no less true than when it was first uttered: "The earth is the LORD's and all that is in it, / the world, and those who live in it" (NRSV).

Do we have any acknowledged theocracies in our contemporary context? It seems unlikely that any present-day nation qualifies as an acknowledged theocracy in the sense that Israel was one. No existing societal system even comes close to approximating ancient Israel's patterns of obedience to the revealed will of God. Nor, some of us will be quick to add, should any contemporary nation attempt to be this sort of theocracy. And even those—e.g., present-day theonomists—who do insist that the legislative details of Israel's national life are normative for contemporary political life, even those Christians do not believe that literally all of the details of Israel's political-economic existence are to be replicated in today's world. Some of the legislation in ancient Israel had to do with cultic practices and specific offices that are no longer applicable, even on a strict theonomic reading of the situation. To point this out is not to quibble: it illustrates that arguments among Christians on this topic are nearly always disputes over the degree of replication, and not about all-or-nothing implementation questions.

However our arguments about these issues turn out, there should be no question about the appropriateness of characterizing one present-day corporate entity as a theocracy: the Church of Jesus Christ. The Christian community is a gathering of people who acknowledge the sovereign rule of God over all of life. To repeat the formulation upon which the Dutch Anabaptist and Reformed dialogue partners agreed: the Church of Jesus Christ "is elected and called by God to proclaim, as a community of faith, His name in the midst of all nations and to demonstrate how people can live together on earth according to God's purpose."

As a unique kind of "holy nation," the Church inherits, at least in broad terms, some key features of the mission of OT Israel. Indeed, the Church's political character is most like that of Israel during the time of its exile in Babylon, when the people of God were no longer a distinct political-economic unit. But their exiled situation did not cancel the need to live in obedience to the will of God in the manner appropriate to a community that is living in the midst of a pagan environment. The apostle Peter seemed to have this very situation in mind when he instructed the Christian community in the way of obedience: "as aliens and exiles . . . conduct yourselves honorably among the Gentiles, so that, though they malign you as evildoers, they may see your honorable deeds and glorify God when he comes to judge" (1 Pet 2:11–12, NRSV).

Practical Obedience

The question of how we can make proper use of the social-ethical materials of the OT is a large and complicated one. I will not attempt to answer the question here; but I do want to offer some brief observations about the *scope* of the resources that are available to Christians as we attempt to make use of the example of Israel in our present-day efforts at discipleship.

In thinking about how the Church ought to behave in the world, Christians have made use of at least three strands of ethical material in the life and mission of Israel. First, many Christians have drawn heavily on the *narrative* literature of the OT. On a deep level, of course, all Christians make use of the narratives, since every Christian group seems to identify, to one degree or another, with some aspect of Israel's historical experience. Reformed communities often think of themselves as "Zion." Post-Vatican II Catholicism has made much use of the "pilgrim people" image. Anabaptists have employed "wandering in the wilderness" and "exile" themes. And so on.

But for some groups, OT narratives serve as their primary ethical material. This seems to be true, for example, of much of the African-American Christian community, for whom "story" has often been a central genre. African-Americans have drawn special comfort and inspiration from the comparison of their plight to that of Israel in Egypt; their quest for freedom has often made much use of "promised land" imagery; the biblical heroes of slavery and exile—especially Moses and Daniel—have had a prominent place in black hymnody. These narrative themes have been central to spiritual and ethical formation in the African-American Church. More recently, liberation theology has also espoused a narrative emphasis, by insisting that the exodus story is in an important sense "constitutive" of God's redemptive dealings as such.

Second, the *legal* materials of the OT have played a prominent role in some communities. An obvious case in point here is the Reformed community, where divine law has had a privileged position in liturgical and instructional contexts. And third, the *prophetic* literature has loomed large in some segments of the Church. For example, both the "evangelical left" and the proponents of the older "social Gospel" have focused in a special way on the Hebrew prophets' call for a social order that is characterized by justice and peace.

Each of these is an important category of OT ethical material. And each has been given extensive treatment in both scholarly and popular writings about Christian praxis. What has not been given adequate attention is the relevance of the *wisdom* writings of the OT for Christian social-political thought and action. Bruce Birch has observed that until very recently in the modern period scholars looked with suspicion on the wisdom literature as much "too secular, highly pragmatic and individualistic, elitist in tone and intent, and out of step with the prevailing interest in Israel's salvation history." Birch is convinced that this assessment does not do justice to the important contribution that the wisdom writings can make to contemporary Christian thought, and he welcomes the new appreciation for this genre of biblical literature that is developing more recent scholarship.[15]

Not that the ethical contribution of the wisdom literature can stand on its own. But then, neither can any of the other ethical strands in the OT materials stand alone. How the contributions of Israel's teachers of wisdom fit into the larger OT framework is nicely characterized by David Hubbard:

> Israel's sages did not have a religion different from that of the prophets and the psalmists. Everything we know about them suggests that they worshiped Yahweh in the temple, prayed to God regularly, held the law in devout esteem, and sought to practice justice and righteousness in the community. Yet they had tasks distinct from those of other religious leaders. They left it to others to interpret law, recite Israel's history and receive oracles that shed light on national crises. Their role was to call the best of Israel's youth and the more seasoned statesmen and administrators to apply their covenant faith in all its ramifications to everyday life. They focused the lamp of creation on the day-to-day decisions and transactions and thus reinforced and complemented the ethical commands of law and prophecy. So doing, they put heart, feet, hands, and tongue to the conviction that Yahweh, the Creator-Redeemer-Lawgiver-King, was indeed Lord of everyone and everything.[16]

Here Hubbard is commending the very features that others have criticized in the wisdom tradition. What many have seen as (using the terms of Birch's account) its "secular, highly pragmatic, . . . individualistic, elitist" approach,

Hubbard celebrates as an appropriately contextual, this-worldly, leader-ship-oriented address to the complex challenges of a life devoted to the service of God.

Hubbard's portrayal of the value of the biblical wisdom materials corre-sponds to some important emphases in recent social-ethical theory. Recent ethicists—and this is especially (but not exclusively) true of Christian think-ers—have given new attention, after a long period of philosophical and theological neglect, to the need for an ethics of *virtue*. As Robert Bellah and his associates argue in *The Good Society*:

> A just social system is impossible without people being just. Justice is first and foremost a virtue, and it inheres in individuals and institu-tions that carry out God's commandment to care for one another.[17]

When we recognize this, thereby adopting a perspective where, as Gil-bert Meilaender has put it, "*being* not *doing* takes center stage,"[18] a much greater emphasis will be placed upon the cultivation of the kind of prac-tical/situational reasoning associated with the Aristotelian virtue *phronesis*: the capacity for wisely adjudicating specific cases.[19]

The biblical wisdom writings provide the believing community with instructions in a God-honoring phronesis. This is an important resource for the contemporary Church for at least two reasons. First, the wisdom teachings are present in the biblical canon, encoded in a unique body of biblical literature. They are obviously intended to complement the other biblical materials, which is an important reason for taking them seriously. Second, they focus on the particularities of living in complex and un-clear situations. The Proverbs collection, as David Hubbard points out, was meant to be utilized in the training of persons being groomed for the day-to-day work of government administration,[20] while Ecclesiastes was written during a later period of much social-religious confusion.[21] In each context, practical wisdom was a much-needed commodity. There is at least a cultural parallel between our own times, then, and the periods in which biblical wisdom materials originated. Contemporary Christians desper-ately need guidance for the exercise of a new kind of leadership in a bro-ken and complex cultural context.

But there is, I suspect, a third reason that the contemporary Church needs to place a strong emphasis on the kind of godly phronesis set forth in the wisdom literature. Not only does our situation *happen* to parallel the crisis times in the experience of Israel; it may be that there is a kind of *theological* necessity to this parallel. The fact that Peter salutes the Church in his First Epistle as a community of "aliens and exiles" is, I suspect, no incidental feature of his understanding of the Church's cultural role. This characterization points to an essential feature of the Church's mode of cultural self-understanding prior to the Lord's return. It is God's intention that we think of ourselves as most like Israel during the time of her exile. We must, to be sure, draw on the legal and prophetic writings—but with a clear recognition that it is not appropriate for us to think that we can implement these norms in a "landed" theocracy type of setting. We are called to live out our patterns of theocratic obedience in a very different cultural context. "Let us then go to him outside the camp and bear the abuse he endured. For here we have no lasting city, but we are looking for the city that is to come" (Heb 13:13–14, NRSV).

Admittedly, it would be difficult to gain complete consensus on this theological observation. We have already pointed to several strains of ethical thought that presuppose the real possibility of implementing "Zion" types of laws and practices in a contemporary setting. But perhaps even here some sort of minimal working consensus would be possible if we explored the matter seriously enough together. It is an observable fact of life that we have a long way to go before our contemporary society is ready for a "holy commonwealth" kind of political and economic order. Whatever the variations on millennial or amillennial thought that shape our expectations as we prepare for the City that is to come, we desperately need to encourage each other in the practical wisdom that is necessary for cultivating obedience in the midst of a generation that boasts of its "post-modern" consciousness.

Diversity as a Blessing

To emphasize the need for consensus is not to call for uniformity. Indeed, this is a topic on which a continuing diversity is a blessing. North American evangelicalism seems especially blessed in this regard, since evangelical viewpoints on the Israel-Church relationship are more diverse than in other Christian movements; nothing like the dispensationalist option, for example, shows up in Catholicism, Orthodoxy, or liberal Protestantism, nor do these other groups work with the nuances that characterize evangelical debates about pre-, post-, and a-millennialism.

Consensus can be reached on some items, I have been arguing, in spite of this diversity. All Christians should make deliberate but discerning use of the peoplehood motif. The Church, like Israel, is a theocracy, a community of people living under the rule of God in order to show forth the divine glory to the ends of the earth. And each of the diverse strains of ethical material in the OT is profitable for Christian living as we seek to cultivate a God-honoring phronesis amid the complexities and confusions of contemporary life.

But various groups will implement this consensus in different ways. Plymouth Brethren will behave differently from Anglicans, Mennonites from Calvinists, Wesleyans from Lutherans. This is a good thing. The Roman Catholic tradition learned long ago that encouraging diverse "orders" to pursue their own way of living out Catholic ideals is no real threat to consensus on the basics of Catholic identity. Evangelicalism, too, has its diverse orders. And one way to view this diversity is that different groups are experimenting with different ways of being the New Israel. Such experimentation is appropriate—it is perhaps not an incidental fact of OT life that the Lord structured Israel herself as a federation of twelve tribes. The important thing is that we hold each other accountable for the diverse ways in which we seek to be a people who are acting wisely in the world over which God rules.

NOTES

1. H. G. vom Berg et al., eds., *Mennonites and Reformed in Dialogue*, Studies from the World Alliance of Reformed Churches 7 (Geneva: World Alliance of Reformed Churches, 1986) 66.

2. L. S. Chafer, *Dispensationalism* (Dallas: Dallas Seminary, 1936) 41.

3. G. Lindbeck, "Confession and Community: An Israel-like View of the Church," in *How My Mind Has Changed*, ed. J. Wall & D. Heim (Grand Rapids: Eerdmans, 1991) 34–35.

4. A. A. van Ruler, "Christ Taking Form in the World," in *Calvinist Trinitarianism and Theocentric Politics: Essays toward a Public Theology*, ed. A. A. van Ruler, Toronto Studies in Theology 38 (Lewiston, NY: Mellen, 1989) 116–17.

5. F. E. Gaebelein, Foreword to C. C. Ryrie, *Dispensationalism Today* (Chicago: Moody, 1965) 8.

6. H. H. Rowley, *The Faith of Israel: Aspects of Old Testament Thought* (London: SCM, 1956) 100.

7. For a good overview and sampling of this critique, see R. E. Richey and D. G. Jones, eds., *American Civil Religion* (San Francisco: Harper & Row, 1974).

8. A helpful comparison of American and South African civil religion is provided by W. A. DeKlerk, *The Puritans in Africa: A Story of Afrikandom* (London: R. Collings, 1975).

9. T. D. Moodie, *The Rise of Afrikanerdom: Power, Apartheid, and the Afrikaner Civil Religion* (Berkeley: University of California Press, 1975) 26.

10. See John Calvin, *Institutes of the Christian Religion*, 2 vols., ed. J. T. McNeill, Library of Christian Classics 20–21 (Philadelphia: Westminster, 1960) III. XXI. 5–7.

11. A. Dulles, *Models of the Church* (Garden City, NY: Doubleday, 1978) 27–28.

12. Dulles, ibid., 35–36.

13. W. C. Kaiser, Jr., *Toward Old Testament Ethics* (Grand Rapids: Zondervan, 1983) 29–30, 37–38; B. C. Birch, *Let Justice Roll Down: The Old Testament, Ethics, and Christian Life* (Louisville: Westminster/John Knox, 1991) 37–40.

14. Calvin, *Institutes*, IV. XX. 8.

15. Birch, *Let Justice Roll*, 323.

16. D. A. Hubbard, *The Communicator's Commentary: Proverbs* (Dallas: Word, 1989) 29.

17. R. Bellah et al., *The Good Society* (New York: Knopf, 1991) 282.

18. G. C. Meilaender, *The Theory and Practice of Virtue* (Notre Dame: University of Notre Dame Press, 1984) 5.

19. For an influential recent treatment of the significance of *phronesis* for the moral life, see A. MacIntyre, *After Virtue: A Study in Moral Theory* (Notre Dame: University of Notre Dame Press, 1981) ch. 12.

20. Hubbard, *Proverbs*, 26.

21. D. A. Hubbard, *The Communicator's Commentary: Ecclesiastes, Song of Solomon* (Dallas: Word, 1991) 23–26.

14

ENVIRONMENTAL
ETHICS AND
THE CONVENANT
OF HOSEA 2

William A. Dyrness

David Hubbard has nurtured a lifelong interest both in the book of Hosea and in a theology of creation. In his Th.M. thesis on the "Knowledge of God in Hosea" he argued that Israel's fundamental sin was harlotry, their insistence on running after false gods.[1] Moreover, as he goes on to point out in his recent commentary, this sin has important cosmic dimensions. Israel, he notes, has "credited the Baals with what can only be gifts of Yahweh"—the goods of the earth.[2]

This writer also remembers President Hubbard speaking in Fuller chapel in the late 1960s on the need for Christians to develop a theology of creation—an idea that was certainly new to many listening to him at that time. Now more than twenty years later the question of how we are to manage the gifts of the earth is a matter of growing concern. If Hubbard is right, the book of Hosea may have important light to shed on the relation between our care for the earth and our worship of whatever God (or gods) we choose to serve. To put the matter in other terms, Hosea may draw an important link between theology and environmental ethics.

While there are many in this technically oriented age who insist that religion and its private worship have no relevance to our stewardship of the earth, their voices are being increasingly drowned out by those who argue that religion is at the center of the environmental question. This was the fundamental point of Lynn White's now classic indictment of Christianity. Because of their uniquely anthropocentric view of creation, White alleged, Christians have been guilty of carelessly exploiting the earth. "In antiquity," White argued, "every tree, every spring, every stream, every hill had its own *genius loci*, its guardian spirit . . . . Before one cut a tree, mined a mountain, or dammed a brook, it was important to placate the spirit in charge of that particular situation, and to keep it placated. By destroying pagan animism, Christianity made it possible to exploit nature in a mood of indifference to the feelings of natural objects."[3]

While White did not himself endorse a return to these pre-Christian views, there has been a growing body of thinkers who believe that our salvation as a race depends on a recovery of more integrative patterns of life and thought. Reiterating White's thesis, Starhawk, a leading goddess theologian, believes the very idea of a God outside of nature leads inevitably to our attempts to "conquer" nature as we try to conquer our sin. By contrast "the model of the Goddess, who is immanent in nature, fosters respect for the sacredness of all living things . . . . Its goal is harmony with nature, so that life may not just survive but thrive."[4]

The most sophisticated expression of this holistic thinking is probably that of James Lovelock, who was a respected NASA scientist when he developed his "Gaia Hypothesis." According to this view, all that exists functions as part of a single living organism. As a result, Lovelock believes "we may find ourselves and all other living things to be partners of a vast being who in her entirety has the power to maintain our planet as a fit and comfortable habitat for life."[5] Lovelock presented his thesis cautiously—he did not intend necessarily to see Gaia as a sentient being, nor was he sure one ought to take up a religious attitude toward her. Yet Lovelock's followers were quick to see this framework as suggesting a religious perspective that was far more environmentally sensitive than the exploitive version of Christianity they saw around them. Many adherents of the green movement were convinced that some Gaia-like faith was necessary to harmonious living with the earth. But the deeper question is rarely asked: does substitution of faith in an immanent power for belief in a transcendent God necessarily translate into a higher and more convincing environmental sensitivity? Does it really provide, as Lovelock says, "A new look at life on earth"?

In this article we will argue that these religious notions and the environmental ethic they support constitute a reiteration of the major themes of Canaanite religion against which Hosea was speaking. We will note that Hosea spoke against them as a misreading of the theological realities, and consequently as leading to a false understanding of how humanity is related to the earth. Learning from Hosea may help us see that our practices toward the earth must reflect God's new creative intervention, what is called in Hosea the new covenant. Our presence in creation then must reflect not merely our interconnection with all things but our responsibility to reflect a new order.

Hosea 2 and the Covenant between Israel and Yahweh

Writing in the middle of the eighth century, Hosea is the purest representative of northern (or Israelite) sensitivities of any of the prophets.[6] There the memory of the wilderness wanderings and God's gracious provision of their needs during that time was kept alive. But there, too, was the challenge most keenly felt from the neighboring Canaanite Baal cult. The encounter between these spiritualities is poignantly symbolized in Hosea's marriage to Gomer in ch. 1, and in the parallel drawn between this and Israel's unfaithfulness described in ch. 2. These false loves are not merely religious errors but threaten the creation itself.

Hosea receives instructions from the Lord in ch. 1 to marry Gomer. It seems clear that the harlotry of Gomer commences after her marriage to Hosea, much as Israel's own harlotry comes within the context of her covenant relationship with Yahweh.[7] Chapter 2 makes specific the parallel between the unfaithfulness of Gomer and that of Israel. Verses 2–15 (Heb. 4–17) are set off as a "kerygmatic unit,"[8] introduced by the personal appeal of the Lord and followed by the promise of a renewed covenant. The passage contrasts two very different covenant relations and two corresponding spiritualities.

As we examine this passage, we note that the relationship between Israel and Yahweh is not a "natural" relationship. That is, there was a time when Israel was "born" (v. 3, she will be stripped naked [lit.] "as the day she was born"). When she was born she was naked and the land in that day displayed a similar nakedness—it was wilderness, parched (v. 3b). Clearly, the passage refers to the time in the wilderness when Israel was brought out of Egypt and formed as a nation. Notice that the original relationship with the land was not viewed as one of harmony and plenty. Israel was in bondage when God found them: "Yet it was I who taught Ephraim to walk, / I took them up in my arms; / but they did not know that I healed them" (Hos 11:3, NRSV). Already it is clear that the peace and goodness of creation were not in evidence when God intervened. Further, it is clear that the peace and goodness of creation were not to be taken for granted but resulted from God's activity.

The other side of God's deliverance from bondage and wilderness is that Israel was brought into the place that is called in Deuteronomy the "Good Land." In the OT generally, blessing and peace are tied to fertility and the goodness of the earth, and this comes to be supremely symbolized in the land God gives to Israel. As Johannes Pedersen pointed out long ago, there is a consistent link between the fruitful earth and peace. "In the vine tree there is 'peace' in that it yields its fruit, while at the same time the earth yields its crops and the sky its dew."[9] Yet, the peace was constantly threatened by the unfaithfulness of God's people. Pedersen puts it this way: "If sin and curse got such a hold of man that the blessing was reduced to nothing, then the wilderness would be there at once."[10] For this reason the land for Israel becomes both the location of God's blessing and the special place of testing the unique arena of Israel's obedience.[11]

This relationship between blessing and obedience is articulated in the ancient creed of Deuteronomy 26:5–11, which must have featured prominently in the tradition Hosea used: "[the LORD] brought us into this place and gave us this land, a land flowing with milk and honey. So, now I bring the first of the fruit of the ground, that you, O LORD, have given me" (vv. 9, 10, NRSV). It is very important to observe that blessing becomes the context and not the consequence of Israel's obedience. Notice how the cult, for Israel, is meant to celebrate and remember the previous acts of God's goodness and deliverance—the first fruit is brought in recognition that all the blessing of the earth comes from God. We will see how stark is the contrast between this and the Canaanite cult, which is meant to ensure the continuing fertility of the earth.[12]

Notice what this is meant to imply for Israel's attitudes toward the earth. The blessing and fertility were gifts that they were to receive with gratitude toward the creator and giver of them. These gifts could be nurtured and enjoyed, or, as we will note, human disobedience and ignorance could threaten them. But there is no sense that Israel's religious worship earned or guaranteed their abundance.

When Israel entered the land—when the nomadic wanderers became an agrarian society—she tended to overlook God's role in her success. In spite of the deliverance of God and the gift of the land, when Israel was exposed to the cult practices of the Canaanites, she could not resist "play[ing] the whore" (2:5). Just as Gomer went after other lovers who paid her with bread, wool, flax, and oil, so Israel went after other gods who were believed to provide them with the goods of creation. These gods were the Baals of Canaanite religion (see 2:8, 13).[13]

The Baals (or Baalim) as they were known collectively were the gods of fertility of Canaanite religion. Though they were sometimes thought of as a localized god of a particular land or soil, their precise relation to the earth is a matter of some discussion.[14] To attempt to gain a clearer picture of their role in the natural order, and thus of the environmental ethic this implied, we need to turn to the ancient epic myths that described their activity. In mythic perspective how did their activity affect natural processes? What role did the cult play in all this?

In the collection of Canaanite myths edited by G. R. Driver there are some sixteen references to the relation between the gods and the processes and fertility of the earth. In two of them El, the supreme father god, is spoken of as the "source of the rivers" and "owner of the mountains."[15] In several others Baal, a lesser and localized deity,[16] seems to direct the activities of nature. He "appoints a time for his rain" (60) and he "sets his thunder bolt" (51, 61). Especially interesting is a group of references in which Baal is in the forces themselves, hardly distinguished from them, and certainly not always in control of them. In the myth of Baal and Mot (god of death), Baal struggles and is afraid. If Baal dies as a result of their cosmic struggle, so do the rains and winds, mists and showers (72). But "[i]f Baal is alive and if the prince Lord of earth exists, then . . . the heavens should rain oil, the ravines run with honey" (77). In a further reference, the rain of Baal is a source of blessing to the earth (98).

The worshiper is called upon to "put an offering of loaves [in the earth], pour a peace offering in the heart of the earth, honey from a pot in the heart of the fields" (49 ff.). Such offerings are urgently called for. This is the message of mightiest Baal, one instruction reads, the mightiest of warriors: "Let your feet run towards me, let your legs hasten toward me. For I have a tale that I would tell you . . . that mankind does not know" (49).

One is struck with two elements that are inseparable in the Baal cult. On the one hand, there is the constant struggle of powers. Baal struggles first with Yam, the god of the sea, and then with Mot, the god of death.

Baal is a mighty warrior, but his control of natural processes fluctuates in accord with whether he is victorious or defeated.[17] On the other hand, while religious practices are intended to secure the victory of Baal over the forces of chaos, these forces appear to be inherently capricious, so one can never be sure that the cult has done its work. While the cult practices are demanded for maintenance of creation, there is no clear relation between these practices and fertility.

In spite of this uncertainty, the people of Israel were attracted to the Canaanite faith. Their motive is hinted at in v. 5b: "I will go after my lovers, those who give my bread" (author's trans.). Perhaps the Baalim would produce the material benefits they so urgently wanted. Of course, from the beginning of the OT there was the temptation to seek religion out of the desire for material goods alone (cf. Gen 28:20, 21, NSRV, where Jacob says: "If God will . . . give me bread to eat . . . then the LORD shall be my God"). And the particular claim of Canaanite religion was that a manipulation of the forces of nature was possible. It turned out to be an uncertain claim, of course, but the promise seemed to tie physical well-being to the strict adherence to the cult. The general process is what is called sympathetic magic. That is, through the performance of analogous activity, such as cult prostitution, a more general and widespread fertility could be assured.[18]

The appeal to the imagination, especially when linked to erotic elements, proved irresistible. Of course, the great period of prosperity under Jeroboam II merely reinforced the mistaken notion that Baal was responsible for the blessings they were enjoying. So they began following the Canaanite cultic practices and celebrating their feasts (cf. 2:11) in the belief that these practices assured their prosperity.

The response of God as recorded in the prophecy of Hosea was dramatic and unmistakable. Notice first that God's intervention is based on a prior and controlling relationship with Israel, which reflected God's role as creator. God's concern over Israel's unfaithfulness springs from the prior reality of his covenant love for them (see 11:4; 14:4). That is, God had cared for Israel, because God loved her, not because she had performed certain rituals. And just as the blessings of creation followed God's loving care, so the judgment that is pronounced necessarily threatened those blessings. In our passage God first promises judgment on Israel because of her unfaithfulness, then promises a renewed creation. In both cases the earth and its processes are intimately involved.

God must pronounce judgment on Israel. V. 9 indicates that the error of Israel was twofold. First, she did not realize the true source of these gifts of the earth. Yahweh was the true "God of fertility," who lavished gifts on his people, and not because of their cultic faithfulness. He gave his gifts simply because they were his to give—notice the emphatic "my grain," "my wine," etc.—and because Israel was God's people. But not only did Israel refuse to acknowledge the true source of these blessings, she went to the extent of using these very gifts to serve Baal. God had given the "gold that they used for Baal" (v. 8, NRSV). In fact, elsewhere it seems that there is a relation between these two realities. The more God blessed Israel, the more she turned away from God. Compare 10:1: "The more his fruit increased, the more altars he built" (RSV).

Since the goods of the earth were misused, they would be taken away when God came to judge his people. In fact, the exact gifts that Israel believed in v. 5b were coming from her lover, God promises in v. 9 to take back.[19] But God will not simply take back these special gifts. Her creator will take away her mirth (v. 11), and lay waste her vines and make her a forest where beasts will devour them (v. 12). Finally, God says, "I will . . . bring her into the wilderness" (v. 14) back to the time of her youth when "She came out of the land of Egypt" (v. 15, NRSV).

Through this series of graphic images, God reverses the symbolism of the land that we noted above. As the land and the vine are signs of blessing and God's presence, so their absence are the inevitable results of God's judgment. The menacing powers of chaos that in Canaanite myths surround the people, in Israel's case lie in the past, before God began his delivering work. But their destructive power can again threaten if God's judgment comes on his people. To put this in the strongest possible language, ch. 2 suggests that Israel's unfaithfulness can cause the very redemptive work of God to be undone.

That this is a possible interpretation can be seen from a comparison with the promised judgment in ch. 4. There God has a controversy with inhabitants of the land because there is no faithfulness or knowledge of God (v. 1). "Therefore the land mourns" (v. 3, NRSV). In his study of this passage, Michael Deroche points out that the order of the judgment pronounced on creation is very significant. Because Israel has broken the covenant stipulations (v. 2), the "land mourns, and all who live in it languish," and the beasts, birds, and fish are taken away (v. 3, NRSV). Deroche points out that here (and in Zeph 1:2, 3) the order is exactly the reverse of the creation account, forming a chiasm with the list of that narrative. As Israel's unfaithfulness can undo what God has done in redemption, so it can undo creation itself. Deroche concludes: "If Israel breaks the covenant by following the idolatrous practices of the nations, God's creation will be uncreated."[20]

What recourse is there for such calamity? According to 2:16–20 the answer is to be found solely in the new covenant that God proposes to

make with the created order. Notice that this focuses on a new relationship with God in which he is no longer to be called "my baal" (here the
general meaning of *ba'al* as lord is probably intended, though the over-
tone of Israel's syncretism cannot be excluded[21]). Building on the dramatic imagery of Hosea's own marriage, a new and more intimate relationship with God is envisioned at the heart of the new covenant—here
mentioned for the first time in its relation to the end time.[22] The erotic
element so prominent in the Canaanite cult has been replaced by love
between God and his people—here also featured in a new and deeper
way than any previous place in the OT. This new name for God, and the
new relationship it entails, is so exclusive and so demanding that it sup-
plants even mention of the name "Baal."[23]

Growing out of the new relationship with God, and dependent on it,
will be a new relationship with the created order (v. 18). On the one hand,
this covenant involves a new relationship between Israel and the rest of
creation. No threat either to the human order or to the crops is to be
feared from the wild animals (which had been made a part of the promised judgment in v. 12), and neither will their security be any longer threatened by war—the instruments of war will be broken (NRSV "abolished")
so that Israel can lie down in safety. This situation is described as a betrothal to God in "righteousness and in justice, in steadfast love and in
mercy . . . in faithfulness" (vv. 19, 20, NRSV), all of which describes the very
character of God, who stands behind this promise.[24]

Attached to this description of the new covenant is an oracle assur-
ing Israel of God's favorable response "in that day"—the special
eschatological formula for the last days (vv. 21–23). Indeed, it is God
himself that will "answer" the heavens who will "answer" the earth with
grain, wine, and oil.[25] God's power over the created order is here stated
in such a categorical manner that it is clearly meant to stand in contrast
to the uncertainty of Baal's lordship. In the epic of Baal's battle with
Mot, it is said:

> And if [the mightiest Baal] is alive,
>> and if the prince lord [of the earth] exists,
> (then) in a dream of Latipan kindly god,
>> in a vision of the creator of creatures,
> the heavens should rain oil,
>> the ravines should run with honey,
> that I may know that mightiest Baal is alive,
>> that the prince lord of earth exists.[26]

Clearly, Hosea's vision of the future was meant to become a controlling reality for God's people—it suggested a confidence that Canaanite faith knew nothing about. David Hubbard often says to his classes, "The eschatological vision must dictate the interim ethic." As we will argue, it did this precisely in suggesting an alternate way of seeing the creation, and of our human place in it. There can be no question but that the reality of God—in both Canaanite and biblical religion—is tied in the closest possible way to the fruitfulness of the earth. Its fertility is quite literally an "answer" to God's promise. But so far from their religious practices being necessary to maintain this fertility—as the rituals of Canaanite religion were meant to "maintain" the cycles of nature—this answer itself must be made and guaranteed by God. In a play on words, the heavens will answer Jezreel (or "God sows," used here for Israel[27]), and God says: "I will sow him for myself in the land" (v. 23a, RSV). That is, God will himself re-establish Israel in the land, which, we have seen, is the condition for her of any fertility and blessing.[28]

Contemporary Environmental Ethics

In contemporary discussions of human responsibility toward the earth, the concept of "homeostasis" has come to play a major role. Though there are many different variations of this position, one leading exponent, Holmes Ralston, puts the matter in these terms: our duty as human creatures is to "stabilize the ecosystem through mutually imposed self-limited growth." This imperative is based on the premise that "we ought mutually to preserve human life."[29]

In certain respects this fundamental assumption has been pioneered by James Lovelock, one of the most nuanced and influential of these writers, whom we quoted above. In the important book we cited earlier, he developed his "Gaia Hypothesis," which understands the earth as a single, large, internally related, and living organism. This led him to propose that the final goal of all life was one of homeostasis, or, as he defined it, "[t]he maintenance of constant conditions by active control."[30] Since he implied that natural pollution was much worse than anything humanity could do and insisted that human activity was not in any sense privileged, it was not clear what ethical imperatives might be derived from his hypothesis.[31] Does "Gaia" maintain the conditions necessary to life on her own, or is human effort called for? A further question relates to whether a religious attitude toward "Gaia" is appropriate. Is it fitting to call her a "goddess"?

Lovelock has recently sought to answer these questions in an elaboration of his famous hypothesis. As to the first question, Lovelock seems now to be saying that the mechanisms regulating life are maintained by Gaia "naturally." He writes: "The Gaia hypothesis said that the temperature, oxidation state, acidity, and certain aspects of the rocks and waters are at any time kept constant, and that this homeostasis is maintained by active feedback processes operated automatically and unconsciously by the biota."[32]

What then is the appropriate human response to this reality postulated by Lovelock? Here Lovelock answers the objection that his hypothesis seems to excuse any human mischief toward the earth, since Gaia will always take care of us. The truth, he notes, is exactly the opposite. Gaia is neither a tolerant mother that overlooks our misdemeanors nor a fragile damsel threatened by our ignorance and greed. "She is stern and tough, always keeping the world warm and comfortable for those who obey the rules, but ruthless in her destruction of those who transgress."[33]

So it appears in the end that we are responsible for the pollution and, as a result, even for the pain of poverty and filth that our relentless urbanization has caused. We must recognize and celebrate our connectedness with the living reality around us, but we must also adjust our lives to its heartbeat if we are to survive and prosper. Still, a further question arises: while we may be driven to wonder at the complexity of all things, do we take up a religious attitude toward it? Lovelock as a scientist was clearly taken off guard by this question, which came to him from every religious direction as soon as his hypothesis was formulated. And he is apparently still puzzled. The most he can say is that he is positively agnostic. "That Gaia can be both spiritual and scientific is, for me, deeply satisfying," he concludes.[34]

Between the ancient Canaanite religions and the contemporary spirituality associated with the Gaia hypothesis there are significant differences. The one represents a fundamental polytheism that sees divine powers in the natural processes; the other reflects a scientific world view that understands much more about natural processes. The first felt deeply the mysterious depths and our human vulnerability before their processes; the second, from the perspective of people who take for granted the comforts of civilization, is able to take a more detached and fundamentally positive view of the order of nature.

But in their basic orientation toward the earth and its processes they are in fundamental agreement: the order of things is a given that must be managed and kept in good working order. In the Canaanite world view this management involved a more specific invocation of the gods through ritual processes; for the other, management is achieved through understanding and mastery of the "natural" order of things, though even these in many cases have their rituals of earthkeeping.[35] But the environmental ethic that is implied in both is essentially a maintenance of the status quo. While in both cases there is hope that processes of decay or of drought can be overturned, the powers necessary for change are all immanent. The earth and its processes are ultimately a closed system. The gods can be victorious over the powers of death and destruction; Gaia can renew herself. But no power can intervene from outside the created order.[36]

While there is some insistence that our modern perspective on these things is advanced and enlightened—who can deny that "homeostasis" involves complex scientific insight?—in the end we are left with the same nagging uncertainty that must have plagued the thoughtful Canaanite believer. Can the forces that seem to lead to darkness and death finally be overturned? Granted that I am called to work toward the stability represented by the order of things, will my work (or my ritual acts) finally make any difference? Or are the forces that control my destiny finally capricious?

Conclusion: Toward a Christian Environmental Ethic

There has been much discussion about the uniqueness of Christian views of creation and history, and the results have not been conclusive.[37] But our brief discussion has put us in a position to make some preliminary comments on this general theme. This may allow us to suggest a direction in which a genuinely biblical environmental ethic may be sought.

We are arguing that the failure of both the Canaanite and modern homeostatic views lies along similar lines. Both not only suppose that the powers necessary to renew things are immanent, but both fail, for this reason, to realize the depths of the abnormality and distress of the created order. While both have a sense that the problem is a religious one— either the gods or the order of Gaia must be appeased—neither understands how completely ecological disaster focuses on human rebellion against the creator. This is the reason Hosea's second chapter begins with that haunting appeal to Israel: "Plead with your mother, plead— / for she is not my wife, / and I am not her husband / —that she put away whoring from her face" (2:2, NRSV).

It is clear that the New Covenant, which God here promises, and which is picked up and developed by Jeremiah (see 31:31–34), is God's provision for Israel's rebellion. It provides a new opportunity for Israel—and eventually through the coming of Christ the Messiah, for all people—to become the wife of God. But what is often overlooked is that this covenant also provides a new opportunity for the created order as well. The heavens and earth are those that will "answer." Because of this new covenant, initiated and realized by the creator God, the order of things, deeply distorted as it is, will be renewed.

When we ask what our human responsibility toward the ecological crisis might be, we are immediately faced with a fundamental question: can we imagine another order of things than the one we encounter day by day? Here is where the uniqueness of the biblical view emerges with great clarity. For the answers that the Baal cult and the Gaia hypothesis give are finally the same: there is no other order than the one we know. But Scriptures insist that because God is above the world and has created it in the first place, he can intervene in a new creative work to bring about fundamental restoration. God is the true fertility God. And precisely as our human hopes fade in this order of things, "as hopes pinned on human rulers are falsified, the vision of a world of abundance and peace becomes part of a hope set on God alone."[38]

But this last point becomes in the end the crucial issue. For the problems we face with our environment are not ultimately between the human creation and the rest of the natural order—debates limited to this horizon are far too restrictive. Our problem relates to our fundamental estrangement from our creator. The listing of these problems—air and water quality, desiccation and loss of soil fertility, etc.—only serves to remind us, as David Hubbard puts it, how fundamental God's provision is and how basic is our error "in not acknowledging [our] full dependence on him."[39]

Our responsibility toward the earth then begins with the announcement of the reality of the New Covenant. We can imagine another world and another way of relating to both the human and the non-human reality. One of the ironies of Christian history is that "evangelism" or the act of announcing the good news of the New Covenant has been sometimes seen as a retreat from the problems posed by the environment. It should be clear from what we have said that nothing could be further from the truth. Our environmental responsibilities not only *include* evangelism, they *begin* there. For the announcement of the new covenant realized in Jesus Christ is not a retreat from the problems of the environment but is the only context in which they can be meaningfully addressed.

Because we can imagine another way of living in the world, we have the imaginative and moral leverage to intervene in the natural order in genuinely new ways. In matters of ecology this means that stewardship can be not only a matter of conservation, but the introduction of new and diverse ways of relating to the created order. We need not think of ourselves as mired in abusive patterns of consumption and exploitation; we are not after merely a sustainable order, though that may be preferable to what we see around us. Based on God's own introduction of a new covenant with the earth, we can envision and act on a new view of the world.[40]

Though we cannot elaborate this perspective here, we argue that this alone provides a firm foundation for proper environmental stewardship. In providing another "imaginative vision," Scripture gives the basis for not only a new ethical practice but a new ecological practice as well. Anthropologists in turning their attention to the OT have helped us see how the ritual practices of Israel became expressive and efficacious of God's redemptive activity. Since they could imagine, and indeed had experienced, another reality, Israel's rituals could celebrate and "represent" this. As Mary Douglas said in her pioneering study of these things, "livestock, like the inhabited land, received the blessing of God. Both land and livestock were fertile by the blessing, both were drawn into the divine order. The farmer's duty was to preserve the blessing."[41] As the farmer then needed to follow the best wisdom he knew, so we too must use all the tools of wisdom and knowledge that we have available. But now as then, our practice goes with the grain of a new order that we have experienced in our own lives and families.

Our rituals may differ from those of the biblical farmer. But they are no less profound. Today we face a situation of serious and long-term environmental degradation. Our rituals will reflect a transcendent reality in which greed and exploitation have been decisively addressed—the new covenant of which Hosea spoke and which has been initiated by the death and resurrection of Jesus and the pouring out of the Holy Spirit. This means that a truly low-impact lifestyle and a peace in human relationships becomes a real possibility in this order of things. Even if we begin with things as simple as recycling and conservation efforts, they reflect something far greater than the ecology movement alone can give us. Our rituals will reflect and re-present a whole new reality, what we might call a simple and peaceful lifestyle; they have been "drawn into the divine order" and so can become echoes of something greater than homeostasis. Indeed, they become images of redemption itself.

NOTES

1. See "The Knowledge of God in Hosea: The Meaning of the Concept and Its Relevance to Biblical Theology" (Th.M. thesis, Fuller Theological Seminary, Pasadena, CA, 1954) 45.

2. D. A. Hubbard, *Hosea: An Introduction and Commentary*, TOTC (Downers Grove: InterVarsity, 1989) 75.

3. L. White, "The Historical Roots of Our Ecologic Crisis," *Science* 155 (1967) 1203–7 = *Western Man and Environmental Ethics*, ed. I. G. Barbour (Reading, MA: Addison-Wesley, 1973) 25. White does argue that there is a tradition of Christianity, viz. Franciscan, that preserves this holistic understanding, but in any case the roots of the problem—and of the solution—are religious.

4. Starhawk, *The Spiral Dance: A Rebirth of the Ancient Religion of the Great Goddess* (San Francisco: Harper & Row, 1975) 10.

5. J. E. Lovelock, *Gaia: A New Look at Life on Earth* (Oxford: Oxford University Press, 1979) 1.

6. H. W. Wolff *(Hosea: A Commentary on the Book of Hosea* [Philadelphia: Fortress Press, 1974] 33, 48) believes that since the disturbances in foreign relations are not reflected, a date early in Hosea's ministry best suits 2:2–15 (i.e., the last years of Jeroboam II or around 750 B.C.), though he dates vv. 16–20 to around 733; cf. F. I. Andersen and D. N. Freedman, *Hosea: A New Translation with Introduction and Commentary* (Garden City, NY: Doubleday, 1980) 33. As to the northern provenance of the book, cf. G. Emerson, *Hosea: An Israelite Prophet in Judean Perspective*, JSOTSup 28 (Sheffield: JSOT, 1984) 1: "Few scholars have dissented from the generally accepted view that the northern kingdom was not only the sphere of Hosea's ministry but probably also his homeland and the environment which had shaped his thought." However, Emerson's study seeks to refine that view through the examination of Judean elements in Hosea.

7. Cf. Andersen and Freedman, *Hosea*, 116; Hubbard *Hosea*, 54.

8. The term is from Wolff, *Hosea*, 31. Andersen and Freedman *Hosea*, (pp. 217, 218) refer to it as a "sustained discourse," whose movement is neither linear nor haphazard. Cf. G. A. Yee, *Composition and Tradition in the Book of Hosea: A Redaction Critical Investigation* (Atlanta: Scholars Press, 1987) 71: "Hosea 2:2–3 is the final redactor's prologue to the story of Yahweh and his wife, Israel. 2:25 is his epilogue."

9. J. Pedersen, *Israel: Its Life and Culture*, I-II (Oxford: Oxford University Press, 1926) 316.

10. Pedersen, ibid., 457.

11. See especially W. Brueggemann, *The Land* (Philadelphia: Fortress, 1977); and in relation to Hosea, see W. Zimmerli, "The 'Land' in Pre-exilic and Early Post-exilic Prophecy," in *Understanding the Word: Essays in Honor of B. W. Anderson*, ed. J. T. Butler et al. JSOTSup 27 (Sheffield: JSOT, 1985) 247, 262.

12. M. Goldberg ("The Story of the Moral: Gifts or Bribes in Deuteronomy," *Int* 38 [1984] 15–25) makes this point well. He illuminates especially the reference to boiling a kid in its mother's milk, noting that God is beyond any such cultic coercion. OT sacrifices are not intended to gain favor but to celebrate the favor Israel already enjoyed.

13. Cf. Wolff, *Hosea*, 38, 39.
14. See K. G. Jung, "Baal," *ISBE* 1:377–8; P. Craigie, *Ugarit and the Old Testament* (Grand Rapids: Eerdmans, 1983) 61–6.
15. J. C. L. Gibson and G. R. Driver, *Canaanite Myths and Legends*, 2d ed. (Edinburgh: T & T Clark, 1978) 37, 121 (other page numbers in the text). I want to thank Rob and Tara Cahill for research assistance on these myths.
16. For a discussion of the relationship between El's kingship and the Baal's rule, see W. Schmidt, *Königtum Gottes in Ugarit und Israel,* BZAW 80 (Berlin: Töpelmann, 1961) 52–54; Wolff, *Hosea*, 39.
17. See Jung, *ISBE* 1:378; cf. Craigie, *Ugarit*, 64: "The orderly rains and seasons make provision for human life and survival, but the chaotic oceans and summer droughts, if they triumph over the orderly world, threaten to end human life."
18. Cf. Andersen and Freedman, *Hosea* 130 and 231.
19. Cf. Andersen and Freedman ibid. 241 who point out the sequence in the two verses, which makes up a chiastic structure that unifies them.
20. M. Deroche, "The Reversal of Creation in Hosea," *VT* 31 (1981) 400-409 (esp.407).
21. See Wolff, *Hosea*, 49. He notes that *ba 'al* also designates the legal position of lord as owner.
22. So Wolff, ibid.,(p. 51) observes.
23. "This memorializing of the Baals by their names suggests the liturgical recitation of the names of Baal in formal worship" (Andersen and Freedman, *Hosea*, 279).
24. According to Wolff (*Hosea* 52), the construction here indicates that these five nouns denote the bride price that Yahweh "pays" for Israel.
25. Hubbard (*Hosea*, 90) notes that "answer" plays a key role in this verse as it relates back to v. 15 where Israel's faith as a child was recalled: "she shall answer as in the days of her youth." Now it is God himself who will answer for them. "We can picture the cries rising upward—Jezreel (Israel) to the crops, the crops to the soil, the soil to the heavens, heavens to Yahweh—and the response being signalled downward."
26. Gibson and Driver, *Canaanite Myths*, 77 ("Baal and Mot," 6.iii, ll. 2–9). Echoes of this are found not only here in Hosea but also in Joel 3:18.
27. So Hubbard, *Hosea*, 90.
28. The imagery here and the reference to Hosea's children (v. 23) tie together at the end of the chapter Hosea's marriage and the marriage between Yahweh and Israel. Both will be a sowing based on love that will issue in fertility. See Andersen and Freedman, *Hosea*, 288, who point out that the parallel between a fertile wife and a cultivated field is an old one.
29. H. Ralston III, *Philosophy Gone Wild* (New York: Prometheus, 1989) 1–3. He quotes the famous naturalist Aldo Leopold: "A thing is right when it tends to preserve the integrity, stability and beauty of the biotic community. It is wrong when it tends otherwise." For a radical expression of this point of view see C. Manes, *Green Rage* (Boston: Little, Brown and Company, 1990). A historical survey of these views is found in R. R. Nash, *The Rights of Nature* (Madison: The University of Wisconsin Press, 1990).
30. Lovelock, *Gaia*, 11.
31. Lovelock, ibid.,120, esp. 145: "Ecologists know that so far there is no evidence that any of man's activities have diminished the total productivity of the biosphere."
32. J. E. Lovelock, *The Ages of Gaia: A Biography of our Living Earth* (New York: Bantam Books, 1988/1990) 19. Lovelock says elsewhere (33) that it seems obvious to him

that the earth is alive in the sense that it is a "self-organizing and self-regulating system."

33. Ibid., 212. He goes on to say: "Her unconscious goal is a planet fit for life."

34. Ibid., 217, though he goes on to applaud all those religious traditions that celebrate the earth and its fertility.

35. Cf. Starhawk, *The Spiral Dance*, 185: "The women climb Twin Peaks, which rise like uplifted breasts above San Francisco Bay. They form circles. Their voices ride the wind. On the summit, they leave gifts for the Goddess: a feather, a shell, a bird's nest. They are reclaiming the heights."

36. Cf. L. Osborn, *Stewards of Creation: Environmentalism in the Light of Biblical Teaching* (Oxford: Latimer House, 1990) 17: "Clearly the principle of interconnectedness has important theological implications. It introduces a strongly monistic tendency into Green thought. Amongst Christian Greens (i.e., ecologists) that tendency may be reflected in an overemphasis on divine immanence at the expense of transcendence. Without the counterweight of Christian tradition, the monistic tendency gives rise to a divinization of the world."

37. It had become a commonplace of the old biblical theology movement, represented by people like G. E. Wright (*The God Who Acts* [London: SCM, 1952]), that the biblical view of history was unique: only in the OT is God viewed as active in history to bring about his purposes. But this view has been qualified because of the influential work of B. Albrektson (*History and the Gods* [Lund: Gleerup, 1967], esp. 23), who showed that the idea of God working in nature and history was common to all peoples of the ancient Near East. A more balanced view, especially with reference to ecological issues, is to be found in J. A. Baker, "Biblical Attitudes to Nature," in *Man and Nature* ed. H. Montefiore (London: Collins, 1975).

38. Baker, "Biblical Attitudes," 93. Cf. Brueggemann who points out (105) that the covenant provides a new way for Israel to imagine her relationship to the land.

39. Hubbard, *Hosea*, 76. Hosea, of course, is speaking within the context of the particular history of God and Israel. But the many allusions to creation and to God's power as creator indicate that this particular history has universal relevance for the new covenant realized and announced in the NT, though Christians for their part have not always been quick to see the covenant sealed by Christ's death as impacting the whole of creation. On this see C. B. DeWitt, ed., *The Environment and the Christian: What Can We Learn from the New Testament* (Grand Rapids: Baker, 1991), esp. ch. 3.

40. Cf. Osborn, *Stewards of Creation*, 49. This, Osborn notes, is the positive point of departure of Christians from secular environmentalists: "Contrary to many voices in the Green movement, stewardship of creation recognizes a positive place for science and technology. Nature is our responsibility: we are called to manage it."

41. M. Douglas, *Purity and Danger* (New York: Praeger, 1966) 50 (esp. 54). Cf. V. Turner, "Body, Brain and Culture," *Cross-Currents* 36 (1986) 156–78, who has spoken of rituals as "transforming performance," and sees in them the generating source of culture.

SELECT BIBLIOGRAPHY OF
DAVID ALLAN HUBBARD

1954

"The Knowledge of God in Hosea: The Meaning of the Concept and Its Relevance to Biblical Theology." Th.M. Thesis, Fuller Theological Seminary, 1954. Pp. vii, 149.

1957

"The Literary Sources of the Kebra Nagast." Ph.D. Dissertation, University of St. Andrews, 1957. Pp. x, 464.

1962

"Amminadib," "Candace," "Elihu," "Ethiopia," "Ethiopian Eunuch," "Fool," "Ithiel," "Jeroboam," "Lemuel," "Lion of Judah," "Massa," "Pentateuch," "Priests and Levites," "Proverb," "Proverbs, Book of," "Seveneh," "Sheba," "Sheba, Queen of," "Shulamite," "Shunem/Shunammite," "Solomon," "Song of Solomon," and "Wisdom Literature," in *New Bible Dictionary*, ed. J. D. Douglas et al. Grand Rapids: Eerdmans, 1962.

"I Thessalonians," and "II Thessalonians," in The *Wycliffe Bible Commentary*, ed. C. F. Pfeiffer & E. F. Harrison. Chicago: Moody Press, 1962.

1967

Old Testament Writings. Pasadena: Fuller Theological Seminary, [1967]. Pp. [125].
"The New Morality and Biblical Morality," *Theology, News, and Notes* 13/3 (September 1967) [8a–10a].
"Our Strategy in the Conflict," *Theology, News, and Notes* 13/4 (December 1967) [5a–7a].

1968

With Bands of Love: Lessons from the Book of Hosea. Grand Rapids: Eerdmans, 1968. Pp. 114.

"No Gimmick," *His* 28/7 (May 1968) 5–7.
"The Old Testament and Worship Today," *Theology, News, and Notes* 14/3 (May 1968) 11–13.

1969

Is Life Really Worth Living? Answers to Ten of Life's Toughest Questions. Glendale, CA: G/L Regal Books, 1969. Pp. 103.

1970

What's God Been Doing All This Time? Glendale, CA: G/L Regal Books, 1970. Pp. 116.
What's New? Thoughts on the New Things Happening to God's People. Waco: Word Books, 1970. Pp. 80.
"How Do I Learn To Love?" *Eternity* 21/9 (September 1970) 18–20.
"How We Got Our New Testament," *Eternity* 22/2 (February 1971) 14–15f.
"Man Who Makes Us Human. Pt. 2," *His* 32/2 (November 1971) 28–31.
"Paul van Imschoot: *Theology of the Old Testament*," in *Contemporary Old Testament Theologians*, ed. R. B. Laurin. Valley Forge, PA: Judson Press, 1970. Pp. 191–215.
"When Man Was Human. Pt. 1," *His* 32/1 (October 1971) 1–3f.

1971

Does the Bible Really Work? [addresses from "The Joyful Sound" (Radio Program)]. Waco: Word Books, 1971. Pp. 75.
Is the Family Here to Stay? Waco: Word Books, 1971. Pp. 97.
Psalms for All Seasons [addresses from "The Joyful Sound" (Radio Program)]. Grand Rapids: Eerdmans, 1971. Pp. 96.
"What Every Marriage Needs," *Theology, News, and Notes* 17/1 (April 1971) 13–15.

1972

How to Face Your Fears. Philadelphia: A. J. Holman, 1972. Pp. 140.
"Fear of an Unknown Future," *Theology, News, and Notes* 18/1 (March 1972) 19–20.
"Symbol of Living Hope," in *The Splendor of Easter*, ed. Floyd W. Thatcher. Waco: Word Books, 1972. Pp. 11–16.
"The Theology of Section Two [WCC Stance on Missions]," in *Eye of the Storm: The Great Debate in Mission*, ed. D. McGavran. Waco: Word Books, 1972. Pp. 269–272.

1973

The Holy Spirit in Today's World. Waco: Word Books, 1973. Pp. 121.
"Postscript on Discipleship," *His* 33/5 (February 1973) 1ff.

"Should Evolution Be Taught as Fact or Theory?" *Eternity* 24/5 (May 1973) 23–25f.

"Some Musings on the Preacher's Task," *Theology, News, and Notes* 19/2 (June 1973) 13–16.

1974

Church: Who Needs It? Glendale, CA: G/L Regal Books, 1974. Pp. 145.

They Met Jesus [addresses from "The Joyful Sound" (Radio Program)]. Philadelphia: A. J. Holman, 1974. Pp. 120.

"Ethiopic Versions of the Bible" and "Old Testament," in *The New International Dictionary of the Christian Church*, ed. J. D. Douglas. Grand Rapids: Eerdmans; Exeter: The Paternoster Press, 1974.

"Leon Lamb Morris: An Appreciation," in *Reconciliation and Hope* (*Festschrift* for Leon L. Morris), ed. R. Banks. Grand Rapids: Eerdmans, 1974. Pp. 11–14.

"The Song of Hannah (1 Samuel 2.1–10) A Bible Study," *Theology, News, and Notes* 20/2 (June 1974) 12–14.

1975

An Honest Search for a Righteous Life [addresses from "The Joyful Sound" (Radio Program)]. Wheaton: Tyndale House Publishers, 1975. Pp. 128.

More Psalms for All Seasons. Grand Rapids: Eerdmans, 1975. Pp. 96.

1976

Beyond Futility: Messages of Hope from the Book of Ecclesiastes [addresses from "The Joyful Sound" (Radio Program)]. Grand Rapids: Eerdmans, 1976. Pp. 128. Chinese ed., 1981.

Colossians Speaks to the Sickness of Our Times [addresses from "The Joyful Sound" (Radio Program)]. Waco: Word Books, 1976. Pp. 96.

Happiness: You Can Find the Secret [addresses from "The Joyful Sound" (Radio Program)]. Wheaton: Tyndale House Publishers, 1976. Pp. 96.

"Lessons from the Book of Ecclesiastes," *Theology, News, and Notes* 23/4 (December 1976) 5–9.

"Marginal Notes on the 'Strange Case of Fuller Theological Seminary,'" *Theology, News, and Notes Special Issue* (1976) 7–10, 23–28.

"Seminary Management from the President's Perspective: A Bicentennial Overview," *Theological Education* 13 (Autumn 1976) 44–52.

"What We Believe and Teach," *Theology, News, and Notes Special Issue* (1976) 3–4.

1977

Galatians: Gospel of Freedom. Waco: Word Books, 1977. Pp. 118.

Strange Heroes. Philadelphia: A. J. Holman, 1977. Pp. 208.
Thessalonians: Life That's Radically Christian. Waco: Word Books, 1977. Pp. 99.
Themes From the Minor Prophets. Glendale, CA: Regal Books, 1977. Pp. 143. Prev. published as *Will We Ever Catch Up With the Bible?* Glendale, CA: Regal Books, 1977. Pp. 143.
"Current Tensions: Is There a Way Out?" in *Biblical Authority,* ed. J. Rogers. Waco: Word Books, 1977. Pp. 149–181.
"See You in Church," *His* 37/8 (May 1977) 16–19.
"The Theology of Section Two," in *The Conciliar-Evangelical Debate: The Crucial Documents, 1964–1976,* ed. D. McGavran. South Pasadena, CA: William Carey Library, 1977. Pp. 269–72.

1978

Why Do I Have to Die? Glendale, CA: G/L Regal Books, 1978. Pp. 79.
"ATS in the 80's: Visionary Realism," *Theological Education* 15 (Autumn 1978) 7–17.
"Biographical Sketch and Appreciation," in *Unity and Diversity in New Testament Theology* (*Festschrift* for George E. Ladd), ed. R. A. Guelich. Grand Rapids: Eerdmans, 1978. Pp. xi–xv.
"Congruence in Ministry," *Theology, News, and Notes* 25/4 (December 1978) 5–6.
"Door Interview: David Hubbard," *Wittenburg Door* 46 (December 1978) 10–13f.
"Everett Falconer Harrison: A Tribute," in *Scripture, Tradition, and Interpretation* (*Festschrift* for Everett F. Harrison), ed. W. W. Gasque & W. S. LaSor. Grand Rapids: Eerdmans, 1978. Pp. 1–5.
"William Sanford LaSor: A Personal Tribute," in *Biblical and Near Eastern Studies* (*Festschrift* for William S. LaSor), ed. G. A. Tuttle. Grand Rapids: Eerdmans, 1978. Pp. 1–4.

1979

Destined to Boldness: A Biography of an Evangelical Institution (Ezra Squier Tipple Lectures, Drew University). Madison, NJ: Drew University, 1979. Pp. 27, 32.
What We Evangelicals Believe: Expositions of Christian Doctrine Based on 'The Statement of Faith' of Fuller Theological Seminary. Pasadena, CA: Fuller Theological Seminary, 1979. Pp. 168.
"Ethics: OT Ethics," "Proverb," "Proverbs, Book of," and "Queen of Sheba," in *The International Standard Bible Encyclopedia.* 4 vols. Rev. ed., ed. G. W. Bromiley et al. Grand Rapids: Eerdmans, 1979–1988.

1980

The Book of James: Wisdom That Works. Waco: Word Books, 1980. Pp. 137.
"Candace," "Jeroboam," "Lemuel," "Lion of Judah," "Massa," "Priests and

Levites," "Proverb," " Proverbs, Book of," "Seveneh," "Sheba," "Sheba, Queen of," "Shulammite," "Shunem/Shunammite," "Solomon," "Song of Solomon," "Wisdom," and "Wisdom Literature," in *The Illustrated Bible Dictionary*. 3 vols., ed. J. D. Douglas et al. Leicester: InterVarsity Press; Wheaton: Tyndale House, 1980.

"Evangelical Churches," with Clinton W. McLemore, in *Ministry in America: A Report and Analysis*, ed. D. S. Schuller. San Francisco: Harper & Row, 1980. Pp. 351–94.

"Fuller Today: Epilogue," *Theology, News, and Notes* 27/1 (March 1980) 26–28.

"An Interpretation," in ch. 2, "The Discovery and Nurture of the Spirit" in *The Recovery of Spirit in Higher Education: Christian and Jewish Ministries in Campus Life*, ed. R. Rankin. New York: Seabury Press, 1980. Pp. 25–41.

1981

Parables Jesus Told: Pictures of the New Kingdom. Downers Grove, IL: InterVarsity Press, 1981. Pp. 94.

Right Living in a World Gone Wrong. Downers Grove, IL: InterVarsity Press, 1981. Pp. 112. German ed., 1984.

"Parachurch Fallout: Seminary Students," *Christianity Today* 25/19 (Nov. 6, 1981) 36.

Review of R. B. Coote, *Amos Among the Prophets* (1981), *TSF Bulletin* 5/1 (Sept.-Oct. 1981) 25.

1982

Old Testament Survey: The Message, Form, and Background of the Old Testament, with W. S. LaSor and F. W. Bush. Grand Rapids: Eerdmans, 1982. Pp. xiii, 696.

Word Biblical Commentary [general editor, with G. W. Barker, J. D. W. Watts, R. P. Martin]. Projected 44 volumes. Waco/Dallas: Word Books, 1982–

"Hazarding the Risks," *Christian Life* 44 (October 1982) 36–38.

"Scholarship and the Body of Christ," *Reformed Review* 35/3 (Spring 1982) 127–31.

"Wisdom of the Old Testament," *Occasional Papers* (Messiah College) no. 3 (August 1982). Pp. 47.

Review of D. F. Morgan, *Wisdom in the Old Testament Traditions* (1982), *TSF Bulletin* 7/1 (Sept.-Oct. 1983) 34.

1983

The Practice of Prayer. Downers Grove, IL: InterVarsity Press, 1983. Pp. 95. Prev. published as *The Problem with Prayer Is.* . . . Wheaton: Tyndale House Publishers, 1972. Pp. 91. Spanish ed. 1972; Chinese ed., 1979.

"Hope in the Old Testament," *TynBul* 34 (1983) 33–59.

"Implementing a Shared Vision," *Theology, News, and Notes* 30/3 (October 1983) 27–28.

1984

The Second Coming: What Will Happen When Jesus Returns? Downers Grove, IL: InterVarsity Press, 1984. Pp. 121.
"Antichrist," "Hypocrisy," "Last Judgment, The," "Monophysitism," in *Evangelical Dictionary of Theology*, ed. W. A. Elwell. Grand Rapids: Baker Book House, 1984.
"How Your Faith Really Affects Your Family," *Family Life Today* 10 (February 1984) 36–37.
"An Open Letter to Congress [Declaration of Independence, Creation, and Providence]," *Reformed Journal* 34/8 (August 1984) 9–12.
"Perspectives on Peace," in *Perspectives on Peacemaking*, ed. J. Bernbaum. Ventura, CA: Regal Books, 1984. Pp. 27–38.

1985

Pentecost 1, Series B (Proclamation 3: Aids for Interpreting the Lessons of the Church Year). Philadelphia: Fortress Press, 1985. Pp. 63.
Unwrapping Your Spiritual Gifts. Waco: Word Books, 1985. Pp. 132.

1986

The Holy Spirit in Today's World. Rev. ed. Waco: Word Books, 1986. Pp. 130.
"Response [to F. Arinze, "Globalization of Theological Education]," *Theological Education* 23/1 (Autumn 1986) 32–36.

1987

Word Biblical Themes [general editor, with J. D. W. Watts, R. P. Martin]. Dallas: Word Books, 1987–
"Geoffrey W. Bromiley: An Appreciation," in *Church, Word, and Spirit* (*Festschrift* for Geoffrey W. Bromiley), ed. J. E. Bradley & R. A. Muller. Grand Rapids: Eerdmans, 1987. Pp. xi–xiii.
"[Influences on the life of] David A. Hubbard," *Theology, News, and Notes* 34/3 (November 1987) 16–17.

1989

Hosea: An Introduction and Commentary. Tyndale Old Testament Commentaries. Leicester; Downers Grove, IL: InterVarsity Press, 1989. Pp. 234.
Joel, Amos: An Introduction and Commentary. Tyndale Old Testament Commentar-

ies. Leicester; Downers Grove, IL: InterVarsity Press, 1989. Pp. 245.

Proverbs. Communicator's Commentary. Dallas: Word Books, 1989. Pp. 486.

"Foreword: An Appreciation," in *Incarnational Ministry: The Presence of Christ in Church, Society, and Family (Festschrift for Ray S. Anderson)*, eds. C. D. Kettler & T. H. Speidel. Colorado Springs: Helmers & Howard, 1990. Pp. ix–xi.

"John 19:17–30," *Int* 43/4 (October 1989) 397–401.

Review of R. T. Handy, *A History of Union Theological Seminary in New York* (n.d.), *Journal of Religion* 69 (July 1989) 414–415.

1991

Ecclesiastes, Song of Solomon. Communicator's Commentary. Dallas: Word Books, 1991.

Forthcoming
Song of Solomon-Lamentations. Word Biblical Commentary. Dallas: Word Books.

Additional contributions in *The Bible Expositor* (1960), *The Higley Commentary* (1967), *KJV Holman Family Reference Bible*, and *God, Man and Church Growth* (1973).

Additional articles in *Christian Life, Christian Herald, The Covenant Companion, Eternity, Family Life Today, His, Insight, Mennonite Brethren Herald, Renewal News* (Presbyterian and Reformed Church), *Together, World Vision.*

LIST OF EDITORS AND CONTRIBUTORS

Elizabeth Achtemeier, Ph.D.
Adjunct Professor of Bible and Homiletics
Union Theological Seminary, Richmond, Virginia

Leslie Allen, Ph.D.
Professor of Old Testament
Fuller Theological Seminary, Pasadena, California

Carl E. Armerding, Ph.D.
Director Schloss Mittersill Study Centre–Austria
(on leave as Professor of Old Testament)
Regent College, Vancouver, British Columbia, Canada

Frederic W. Bush, Ph.D.
Associate Professor of Old Testament
Fuller Theological Seminary, Pasadena, California

David J.A. Clines, Ph.D.
Professor of Biblical Studies
University of Sheffield, Sheffield, England

Max DePree
Chairman, Board of Directors
Herman Miller, Inc., Zeeland, Michigan
Member, Board of Trustees
Fuller Theological Seminary, Pasadena, California

William A. Dyrness, D. Theol.
Dean and Professor of Theology and Culture, School of Theology
Fuller Theological Seminary, Pasadena, California

Daniel P. Fuller, D. Theol.
Professor of Hermeneutics
Fuller Theological Seminary, Pasadena, California

John Goldingay, Ph.D.
Principal
St. John's College, Nottingham, England

Vernon C. Grounds, Ph.D.
President and Professor of Counseling and Ethics Emeritus
Denver Seminary, Denver, Colorado

Robert L. Hubbard, Jr., Ph.D.
Professor of Old Testament
Denver Seminary, Denver, Colorado

Robert K. Johnston, Ph.D.
Provost, Dean of the Seminary and Professor of Theology and Culture
North Park College and Theological Seminary, Chicago, Illinois

Walter C. Kaiser, Jr., Ph.D.
Senior Vice President of Education and Academic Dean
Trinity Evangelical Divinity School, Deerfield, Illinois

Robert P. Meye, D. Theol.
Associate Provost for Church Relations and Christian Community, and Professor of New Testament Interpretation
Fuller Theological Seminary, Pasadena, California

Richard Mouw, Ph.D.
Provost and Professor of Christian Philosophy and Ethics
Fuller Theological Seminary, Pasadena, California

Roland Murphy, O. Carm., S.T.D.
George Washington Ivey Emeritus Professor of Biblical Studies of
Duke University
Whitefriars Hall, Washington D.C.

Leon Pacala, Ph.D.
Executive Director, 1980-1991
Association of Theological Schools in the United States and Canada,
Pittsburgh, Pennsylvania

John D. W. Watts, Ph.D.
Senior Professor of Old Testament
Southern Baptist Theological Seminary, Louisville, Kentucky

Timothy P. Weber, Ph.D.
Professor of Church History
Denver Seminary, Denver, Colorado

INDEX OF AUTHORS

INDEX OF FOREIGN WORDS

LATIN WORDS

INDEX OF BIBLICAL TEXTS

INDEX OF SUBJECTS